D1327216

Out of the Fire

Out of the Fire

by Ernst Papanek
with Edward Linn

WILLIAM MORROW & COMPANY, INC.
NEW YORK   1975

PRINTED IN THE UNITED STATES OF AMERICA.

1   2   3   4   5   79   78   77   76   75

Library of Congress Cataloging in Publication Data

Papanek, Ernst
    Out of the fire.

    1. World War, 1939–1945—Jews—Rescue—France.
2. Jewish children.   3. Inion O.S.E.   4. Refugees,
Jewish.   5. Papanek, Ernst.   I. Linn, Edward, joint
author. II. Title.
D810.J4P28   940.53'15'03924   74–26674
ISBN 0-688-00337-0

BOOK DESIGN: HELEN ROBERTS

As long as a man's name is remembered with love anywhere in the world, that man is not dead.

And even if, as the generations pass through, his name is forgotten, but the life he led illuminates one life anywhere in the world, that man is not dead.

By the tokens in which mankind measures out its time, Ernst Papanek will live for a long time.

Contents

viii   CONTENTS

INTRODUCTION

I am Ernst Papanek's second son. My older brother Gus and I lived with the other children of Montmorency. One day a gang of us seven- and eight-year-olds stole some string from the kitchen, cut some saplings (beech is very good) and made ourselves some bows and arrows. We chose up sides and went at each other. When this warlike behavior was reported to my father, he hurried out to deliver a stirring speech in opposition to war and in favor of brotherhood. I immediately stepped up alongside him to urge my friends to demonstrate the error of our ways by throwing our weapons into a pile and ceremoniously burning them. My father beamed. Clearly, the apple had not fallen far from the tree. But as my comrades were dutifully, if somewhat sheepishly, complying, I whispered to them to hold onto the string. I had realized halfway through his talk that the string was all that mattered. We could pick up new branches anywhere. Five minutes after my father had left we were happily playing cowboys and Indians again. Of course he found out about it. As he confronted me, all of him was laughing.

He hit me twice in my life, both times because he had lost his temper at my unkindness to someone else. Normally, misbehavior was met with a serious talk, an appeal to reason and judgment. Once, at Montmorency, it came to me in the middle of such a talk that I had nothing to be afraid of. I arranged my face into the semblance of contrition and resolved to wait him out. Suddenly he began to grin. "I'll bet I know what you're thinking!" he said.

"What am I thinking, Ernst?"

"You're thinking, 'I'll just let the old dope talk himself out, and then I'll go on about my business.'"

"You're wrong. I didn't think, 'Old dope.'"

Ernst Papanek died on August 5, 1973. Most of the family was together in Vermont on the day before he became acutely ill for the first time. It was a sunny day. My children gathered wildflowers, and we made them into a garland for him. He and I took a stroll. He knew he was going to die and he talked to me about this book. His anger still flared at those American Jews who he felt had unwittingly participated in the murder of many children he had loved. Yet he did not want to wound anyone still alive. I know he wanted this book to be a record and not an indictment.

For several years before he became ill he worked on this book with Ed Linn. After his death those of us in the family who had been in Europe with Ernst went over Ed's final reworking of the material. As we loved Ernst Papanek, so all of us have worked toward the closest accuracy to his thoughts that we could find. If errors remain, blame them on us.

Àbientôt, Papa.

GEORGE PAPANEK

BOOK I

The Children
of Montmorency

1. One Came Alone—Emil Geisler

With his bright red hair and his sunburned, freckle-splattered face, Emil Geisler would undoubtedly have been described in America as "a typical Huck Finn." But that was not quite the way I thought of him when I found him in front of our gate in the summer of 1939, an undersized, skinny boy of thirteen holding onto the hand of a little blond girl.

On the previous day, I had been summoned to the office of the prefect of police in Versailles to be confronted with a German Embassy complaint that we were harboring children who had been smuggled across the border. Since I had not the slightest doubt that the prefect of police knew that the German Embassy was right, I admitted quite readily that we had some children who might not have papers. "But," I said solemnly, "it is a very small group. For humanitarian reasons we could hardly turn them away."

We were playing a scene, you understand, and one of the rules was that we had to play it straight. There was no smile on either of our faces, no flicker of mutual understanding. He was the stern, conscientious chief of police doing his job—an unpleasant job perhaps but still his job. His secretary, our only audience, was frowning over a sheaf of papers, totally immersed as far as anyone could see in his work. My own role was to be surprised and concerned but, of course, helpful.

And so when the prefect asked me, in the line of his duty, how many of our children were in the country illegally, I answered that I could not give him a precise figure offhand. "But," I told him, "I would be happy to get the figures to you tomorrow if you would like."

"Yes, give me the figures," he said. "And I will want a list of all the names, too."

He rose abruptly and came around the desk to shake hands before I left, an inevitable ritual in France and a very useful one for officials who want to indicate that an interview is over.

He would receive no names, he knew. Not the next day, the next week or ever. I would never hear from him again, I knew, unless the pressure came from his own government, and we both knew that France was not going to turn any children over to the Nazis. The prefect would dictate a memo of our conversation, drop it into a file folder and hope to God he would never have to open it again.

The Homes for refugee children were being run by the OSE (Organisation pour la Santé et l'Education, a private Jewish organization), and I went immediately to the Paris offices to report that we had nothing to worry about. Since I was still living in Paris with my family myself at the time, it was not until about 7:00 the following morning that I returned to the Villa Helvetia.

The villa was completely surrounded by a high wrought-iron fence built upon a low cement footing. Atop the cement was a kind of gilt metallic lining rising high enough inside the fence to prevent anyone from looking in. My route to the villa every morning took me along a side road running the full length of the grounds, but since I could not see through the fence, it was only after I had turned past the broadly curved column that guarded the far side of the gate that I saw Emil and the girl.

My immediate impression was that they were children of ours who had somehow managed to slip out of the house. Still, I did not recognize either of them and I had been quite certain that if I did not yet know all the names, I could at least recognize all the faces.

"What in the world are you doing out here this time of the morning?" I asked the boy in French. When the boy and girl exchanged bewildered glances I repeated the question in German, quite sure now that they were recent arrivals who had not learned any French.

"We do not belong to this Home," the boy answered in German. "We have come here from Saarbrücken."

And standing there, holding onto the girl's hand, Emil told me how he had come to our gate.

Saarbrücken is the largest of the German border towns that had been ritually passed back and forth between France and Germany as prizes of war. In 1935, when Hitler occupied the Saar, it fell under Nazi rule.

On one of the stormtroopers' random assaults upon the Jewish population, they burst into Emil's home and dragged his father off to a concentration camp. A few months later, they returned to hand his mother an urn. Inside were the ashes of his father. Mrs. Geisler let out a wail and hurled herself upon them, screaming that they were murderers. And so, the stormtroopers carried her off to a concentration camp too.

The door closed behind Emil and he was alone. From that moment on, he would always be alone in the world.

Within the day, the rabbi of Saarbrücken came to the house to warn Emil to get out of Germany before the stormtroopers came back for him, also. The rabbi wrote out the words *Maison d'Enfants, Villa Helvetia, Montmorency près Paris* on a slip of paper and assured him that if he could get to us he would be taken care of.

While Emil was waiting for darkness to fall, the woman next door—a Gentile—came to the house, begging him to take her six-year-old daughter to Montmorency with him. Her husband, a Social Democrat, had gone into hiding months earlier to escape arrest. The Underground was prepared to get them across the Alps into Italy, she told Emil, but they were afraid the little girl couldn't survive the terrible rigors of a flight across the mountains.

At night, Emil and the girl slipped across the carefully guarded border. So close to a customs post, he told me, that it hardly seemed possible the customs officer hadn't seen them. Walking on through the rest of the night and into the early hours of daylight they finally came upon a group of farmers working in the fields.

Emil approached the nearest one, showed him the slip of paper and asked for directions to Montmorency. "Montmorency?" the farmer laughed. "That's almost three hundred miles from here. Don't tell me you're going to walk?"

Emil had been under the impression that he had only to cross the border to get to the Home. Faced with the prospect of having to walk another three hundred miles or so, he asked only if he were on the right road.

The farmer stared at the two children. "Wait right here," he said. Gathering the others around him, he collected enough money to buy two train tickets to Paris. Then he put the children on his wagon and drove them to the station. "When you get to Paris," he said, "just do the same thing you did with me. Show your slip of paper to somebody and they will tell you how to get to Montmorency."

Arriving in Paris at five o'clock the following morning, Emil dutifully showed the paper to the first person he came across. Again, tickets were immediately bought; again, the children were placed on the proper bus. They had been standing where I had found them for perhaps half an hour, waiting for someone to open the gate.

This was a very moving story, to be sure. Yet as he was telling it, in his soft, halting way, a strong misgiving about these children began to grow in me. Yesterday, I had been called to Versailles to answer complaints that we were taking in children without valid passports or visas. Today, waiting for me upon my return, were two such children. Could it, I had to ask myself, be merely a coincidence? If the German Embassy were trying to bait a trap for us, would they not have chosen just such children and just such a story? A Jew and a Gentile, a religious refugee and a political refugee. A boy barely old enough to take care of himself and yet taking on the added burden of a helpless little girl. The girl's father, like myself, a Social Democrat.

Since rules and regulations are the last refuge of all bureaucrats I asked the boy if he had any papers. All he could offer me was the slip of paper on which his rabbi had written out the name of our Home.

"I am sorry," I said. "But that is not the kind of identification I had in mind. You cannot just come to the door and expect us to let you in. We will have to take you to Paris for processing."

The little girl, who had not uttered a word through his entire story, now began to weep, her hands hanging limply at her side, the tears rolling down her cheeks.

Up to this point, Emil had put on a facade of vitality, something I had carefully noted. All our children tried very hard to look energetic and useful and worthwhile when they first came to us. Having been so well instructed in their own inferiority, they automatically assumed that we too were judging them on their right to be alive.

When the girl began to cry, Emil's bones just seemed to collapse. And then he began to cry too.

"All right," I said, hastily. "We will see. You can come in and have breakfast anyway and then we will decide what to do."

"If it's a trap," I told Margot Cohn, the directress of Helvetia, "so all right, we've been trapped. Better to take the risk than to turn them away and find out later that their story is true."

Still, we agreed it would be wise to keep an eye on them just to make sure that no attempt was made to contact anybody on the outside. Instead of having them eat with the other children in the big dining room, we had them sit with us at a small private table. After they had eaten and showered and had their hair searched for nits, the little girl, who was practically asleep on her feet, was put to bed. Emil was something else again. Refreshed by the food and the shower, he was eager to prowl the area and examine his new home. It was absolutely impossible, I discovered, to keep track of him. I had only to turn my back for a moment and he would vanish into thin air. A half hour later, just as I was having visions of furious activity around the German Embassy telephone, I would turn around and find him hovering at my elbow again. It was not, as you may well imagine, the most relaxed morning I have ever spent in my life.

He was no German plant, of course. He was a wanderer. He was a loner. He was, it soon developed, a complete outsider. Even with the little girl. Once he had fulfilled his obligation to bring her to our door, he took nothing that could be called a brotherly interest in her. When her parents showed up in Paris about six months later to claim her, they insisted naturally enough on letting Emil know how grateful they were. He enjoyed that. He ate up their praise. He was proud that he had succeeded in doing the job.

That was Emil exactly. He could get the job done. It was not at all difficult to see, once I got to know him, why a desperate mother would entrust her daughter to him with some real expectation that he would be able to bring her to us.

And still, when I say he was an outsider I do not mean it in the usual sense of the cynical observer. I mean, on the contrary, that he did not feel that he measured up. For one thing, he was much smaller than most of the other boys his age. For another, he could barely read or write. As a Jew, he had been excluded from the schools of Saarbrücken for three years and, as it became abundantly clear, he had been driven by no great scholarly passions before that. To him, the brilliant intellectuals from the *St. Louis,* the ship that had wandered the Atlantic after the Cuban government had refused to allow it to land, might as well have been people from another planet. The politically aware and scholarly sons and daughters of the political refugees even more so. He was uncomfortable among them; he was edgy.

Horst Meyer, a brooding, sensitive boy, was not only one of our really outstanding students but he was an extremely talented musician with the kind of ascetic features that sends artists racing to their canvases. A tall boy with thick black hair, small tapering fingers, narrow face and dark burning eyes. In diverse and indirect ways, Emil made it obvious that he could not stomach him—which did no great harm since Horst scarcely knew he was alive.

Another boy from the *St. Louis,* Guenther Heilbron, was a handsome, well-built athlete, beloved by everybody because of his good humor and his sweet nature. Guenther's artistic ability was limited to his harmonica; he would sooner have gone without his pants than without his harmonica. Like Emil, he was a terrible student, and so Emil felt safe in poking a little fun at him. "This is all he can do," he would say. "Did you ever see him help in the kitchen or did you ever see him make anything decent in the carpenter shop? Never. The only thing he can do, he can play his harmonica. If Guenther does not learn, nobody complains. But if I do not learn, they hold special meetings."

The unfortunate part of it was that this disquiet about himself was wholly unnecessary. In his own way, Emil was very smart. With his hands, he could do anything. Our school system was set up so that everybody, girls as well as boys, was given vocational as well as academic training. Emil was made an apprentice shoemaker, perhaps the most important of our trades. We did all of our own repair work, and with four hundred children the repair work was considerable. In no time at all he was the best we had, although you would hardly have thought so to listen to his complaints. What he really wanted to be, he insisted, was a carpenter. He wanted to be a carpenter, that is, until we gave him the run of the carpentry shop, and then he wanted to be a bricklayer.

His real ambition was to learn the tricks of every trade. He had a curiosity about workmanship that yielded not a thing to the intellectual curiosity of those he took to be his superiors. He had only to watch any kind of craftsman at work once to be able to do the job himself, step by step, down to the smallest detail.

As our need for water grew, we had to hire a crew to put in a new sewer. Emil, quite naturally, wandered down to the diggings to see how it was done. At the end of the first day, he came to me and said: "All right, Ernst, you can let them go now. I can organize it all from here."

"Now, Emil," I said. "These men have to earn a living. You only want to stay out of school."

We were both right. He *could* have organized the rest of the job and he *did* want to get out of his schoolwork.

When a window was broken in an upper story of one of the buildings—and large groups of children are always accompanied by broken windows—we would ask that someone go up and take out the remaining shards of glass before one of the younger children cut himself. Emil was always the first to volunteer. "While I'm up there," he would say hopefully, "I might as well replace the pane, too." Having watched the glazier at work, he could, of course, install a windowpane with the best of them. At times we would let him do it; at other times, we would send him—not quite kicking and screaming—back to his classroom.

Actually, he was the only pupil we "allowed" to cut his classes, mostly because we came to realize that it was impossible to track him down every time he felt like disappearing. The only thing we insisted upon was that he learn to read and write in both German and French. For the rest of it ... well, he was so helpful in so many ways that the other children called him the Deputy Executive Director. Which made it seem like rank ingratitude to keep badgering him about studies we all knew he would never use.

For his own part, Emil was always shrewd enough to know exactly how far he could push us. Was it important to us, for incalculable adult reasons, that he learn to read and write? All right, he would learn to read and write. His strongest characteristic, his main weapon for survival, I believe, was this animal instinct for sniffing out the paramount interests of the important people in his environment.

As a practical craftsman, for instance, he could not have been less interested in our ongoing policy of beautifying the grounds, and yet he would frequently return from his journeys into the surrounding woods with plants or flowers for the beds around the houses. One day I found him staring reflectively at an empty spot on the lawn, directly across from my office window. "You know," he said, with that appraising frown all craftsmen seem to be issued along with their toolboxes, "I passed a very nice tree about five kilometers from here. I think I'll dig it out and plant it right here. It will improve the whole view for you."

I had to remind him that since our land hardly extended out anything like five kilometers, the tree undoubtedly belonged to somebody else. Apparently, I did not make my point clearly enough. A day or two later, I found a beautiful little decorative tree planted across from my window. As he had promised, it improved the view considerably. As he had anticipated, I weighed the absurdity of forcing him to return the tree against the visual pleasure it afforded and ... well, reached the only sensible conclusion.

Being useful was part of Emil's survival kit. He was as familiar with every nook and cranny of the villa itself as he was with the forests outside. If a key were missing from the clothes closet, someone would immediately say, "Emil, do you know where it might be?" And he would say, "Well, now, I believe I did see such a key on the second shelf in the workshop." And, sure enough, he would bustle off to the workshop, reach up to the second shelf and there it would be. If some of the children suspected that he sometimes misplaced things accidentally-on-purpose in order to polish up his reputation as a very useful boy to have around, no one ever came right out and said it to his face.

Because that's what Emil Geisler was. The Jew as a Survivor. He had survived to come, unannounced, to our Home in Montmorency. He would continue to survive, through the war and after, in ways that defied all logic or calculation or even chance.

2. Children in Wartime

At noon on September 2, 1939, I received a telephone call from the prefecture in Paris alerting me that the German army had marched into Poland, making war with France inevitable. Air attacks were expected at any moment. Our four Homes for refugee children were spotted within a three-mile area in Montmorency, which is about ten miles north of Paris, and that placed us well within the danger area.

The children ranged in age from three-year-old babies to fifteen-year-old young men and varied widely in background. Some were sons and daughters of political refugees who were living in Paris, some of Jewish refugees who were being held in the French internment camp at Le Mans. And, of course, some were children who had been smuggled out of Nazi-occupied countries by the OSE, an organization of Russian and Polish doctors—if you can imagine a more unlikely group for that kind of work—which had been transplanted to France. In eight months we had taken in 250 children, and the rescue operation was just beginning to pick up steam. A fifth castle had already been bought in the south of France, and a sixth had been selected. The plans were to keep buying them as fast as they could be filled.

The goal of the OSE was, quite simply, to save as many children as possible. Their client, if they had been forced to put it into words, was the seed and culture of Middle European Jewry. My goal, as executive director, while perhaps less grandiose was

13

also more arrogant. My goal was to see to it that these children who had been brutalized in so many ways not only survived but survived whole. My clients, as I saw it, were their parents. Alive or dead. If they were alive, we owed them the comfort of knowing that their children—their last and dearest possessions—were in good hands. To that end, we had a strict policy of letter writing. At least once a week by either the child or his counselor whether any answers came back or not. If the parents were dead, my duty was still to "send back" the kind of healthy, unbroken child they would have wanted. Because, don't you see, making the parents my client was a device that enabled me to best serve the interests of the child. By keeping the children in touch with their parents, I was keeping them in touch with themselves.

Upon being informed of the German attack, I immediately phoned the directors of each of the Homes and instructed them to assemble their children and staff. A terrible, foreboding silence came over each group when I told them, "You must not, at least for the present, expect mail from your dear ones." A terrible, stony silence, which I shall never forget.

In dealing with children, though, it is necessary to be completely truthful. They were entitled to know exactly what was happening and exactly what to expect. "I have grave news for you," I began at each Home. And then I told them everything I knew. England had already declared war and "we" would be at war within the hour. Not France; we. Children who had been so completely uprooted, so recently, could be expected to view an attack on France as the arm of Hitler reaching out for them again. I wanted them to understand that as necessary as it would be for us to set up our own protective measures, we would be acting not as a small band of displaced Jews huddling together in fear but as part of a vast national effort.

Still and all, the initial reaction at every Home was one of almost total gloom and hopelessness. Few of the children thought that Hitler could be stopped. I was expecting, quite frankly, that Hitler's bombers would attack Paris immediately and London soon afterward, and as I began to describe the measures we would be taking to protect ourselves, Horst, a sensitive, brooding fourteen-year-old boy, stood up and shouted, "No, this is the end. There is nothing that can be done anymore. It is best that we just commit suicide."

There was always something that could be done, I reminded him. He and I were there only because something had been done. "The French will resist. The British will resist. We too will resist. We will not give in to it."

At each Home, I expressed every confidence that by following the protective measures being put into effect we would be reducing the danger to ourselves considerably. There is always relief in the simple knowledge that you do not have to stand by helplessly and wait for your fate to overtake you, that it is possible to do something about it. And, I knew, an even deeper relief that comes with the physical act of doing it.

Immediately, we went to work on our defenses. The school bells clanged out their signals for air raid drills every hour. On one signal everybody marched down to the cellar. On another, they evacuated the house completely. In either event, the children would be following very familiar routes no matter how dark it might be when the real thing came.

Shoes and coats were laid out alongside their beds so that no time would be lost in groping for them. Volunteers from each room were to remain behind until everybody else was out. To make sure nothing happened to the volunteer, he or she was given a counselor to report to. As a further precaution, every child was placed within a subsidiary five-man group down in the cellar, with each group assigned a specific place to assemble and a leader to report to.

Down in the cellar, we laid in a large enough supply of flashlights, water and chocolate to see us through a prolonged stay, plus enough picks and shovels to dig ourselves out if we had to.

In between the air raid drills, there was plenty of work to keep everybody occupied. The coal and wood had to be cleared out of some of the cellars, not only to make room for a shelter but because they constituted a fire hazard. In all of the Homes, the boys were put to work filling sandbags with earth and piling them in front of the cellar windows. Since we didn't have any gas masks—and since I had every reason to believe that the Nazis would not hesitate to drop gas bombs—the girls were given the job of sewing elastic bands onto washcloths in such a way that the washcloth could be fixed tightly over the nose and mouth. Our doctor (who also happened to be my wife Lene), prepared a sodium bicarbonate solution into which the washcloths could be dipped. As further protection against gas fumes, heavy covers were hung over the windows and sprayed with bleach water. Beyond *that,* we practiced walking against the wind so that we would be prepared to get out of the gas zone as quickly as possible.

There was hardly enough time to get everything done in one afternoon and evening, of course, but we all worked so hard to do as much as humanly possible that by midnight everybody had dropped off to sleep. Toward two o'clock in the morning the sirens sounded, and a minute later our school bell was clanging. The description of what followed comes from a school report written a few years later by one of our volunteer room-leaders, a boy of thirteen:

> What's the matter, can't they keep quiet. Making a lot of noise during the night. Leave me alone, will you. Suddenly, I heard something that made me wide awake. *"Alerte"* somebody yelled into my ear. In the next moment I was feverishly dressing myself. I was excited, afraid and somehow I had to give this feeling expression. I began to yell: "Hurry up, get going, faster. *Alerte, alerte!* Wake up, wake up." But everybody else had done the same thing and all of us were yelling. Above the noise we were making we clearly heard the booo-uuuhuu of the air-raid sirens and the shrill Ding-Ding of our own clock-bell. I was dressed in a hurry, and the next moment I was looking around my room to see if everybody had left. Gerhart who had been even harder to wake than myself was still there but everybody else had left. I almost hated him that moment for keeping me from going into the *abri* [shelter] but my duty was my duty. He left, a last glance with my electric torch over the beds, then I was running with all my might after the last of the others onto the great lawn that stretched before our house. As soon as I arrived there we all were ordered to go into the cellar. A really wonderful discipline was preserved

considering that we all were afraid, as we thought that the Nazi planes would come in thousands to try to undermine the resistance of the people. Not one of us ran, everybody walked calmly into the *abri* although we were shaking inside. As soon as we were in the cellar the attendance was taken, and everybody was present. Only the names of the leaders [of each 5-man group] had to be called thus making the roll call less complicated.

All things considered, the children followed their instructions remarkably well. Except for one thing. Many of them either forgot to put on the shoes and coats which had been so carefully laid out ahead of time or bolted out of the room without bothering to. But that was all right. Each Home had elected two representatives to the Children's Parliament, and these student leaders were responsible for going from room to room with two of the teachers to collect the clothing that had been left behind. Most instructional. It was cold in those cellars in the early fall mornings. While the offenders were shivering in their pajamas, they could also shiver at the thought that they were placing the people they most admired in unnecessary danger. After that first night, no child ever forgot his clothing again.

While we were getting settled in, we were all tremendously impressed by the calmness and confidence—the composure really—of the children. Everybody followed instructions faultlessly. The makeshift gas masks were soaked in the solution, distributed and set into place. That done, we sat back and waited. One lone flashlight shone weirdly in the cellar.

And with the waiting came the first signs of nervousness. And so I told them stories about the battling between the Austrian Socialists and Fascists, partly because they made the kind of exciting adventure stories that were sure to hold a child's attention, partly to let them understand that in resisting tyranny they were part of a long and honored tradition and partly, I suppose, because they were the stories I knew best. And then we sang together. First the "Marseillaise," which is not only the French national anthem but is also the most rousing call to freedom ever written. I defy anyone to sing the "Marseillaise" with his comrades during a time of danger without experiencing a thrill of defiance, a stiffening of the will and a renewed commitment to not only survive but conquer. Having roused and uplifted ourselves so thoroughly the first time around we went back, by popular acclaim, and sang it again. And then on, in a similar mood of defiance and triumph, to "La Victoire en Chantant."

When the all-clear sounded, we were as much astonished as we were relieved. No bomb had fallen, no gun had fired. Had it only been a drill or had the French air force driven the Luftwaffe off? Our kids—becoming kids again—were sure that a historic battle had taken place somewhere out of earshot between two great airborne armadas. Gleefully, they estimated the number of Nazi planes that had been downed. Ten? No, fifty. What? Are you joking? A hundred planes anyway. A thousand. *Thousands!*

Floating in such fantasies, swept along on a great wave of relief, they marched back to their rooms and their beds.

But not for long. Our usual rising time was 7 A.M., and at seven sharp we had everybody up again. Routine carries its own structure, and in times of personal or social disorder as much structure as possible has to be preserved to keep things from falling apart. I wasn't thinking primarily as an administrator, though. I had told them we weren't going to give in to it, hadn't I? All right, we still had plenty to do, so let's get up and get doing. Sleep? Sleep was for babies. A sense of urgency was imparted. Not only did it have to be done, we were the ones who had to do it. And, as they could see, I had every confidence that we—and they—could.

This was the part we had been given to play, I explained, in the national effort. By taking the responsibility for our defense upon ourselves, we were relieving the fighting men of that burden. By following our normal routine, we could be sure we were doing nothing that might distract them.

And so to work again. The windows had to be painted black to complete the blackout. Strips of paper were pasted in a crisscross design on the inside of the windows to prevent them from being shattered during an attack. The more talented mechanics among the boys went to work in the shop to construct the extra fire extinguishers we needed—fire extinguishers which, however primitive, tested out marvelously well.

One other defect in our well-laid plans had become evident during the long night in the shelter. The children had been sitting on piles of rags, and after an hour or two, the rags had provided very poor protection against the hard, cold floor. From now on, everyone was going to carry his own chair with him and this, of course, called for another round of dry runs.

The big boys were back on the sandbag detail, filling the burlap bags with dirt and piling them higher and higher in front of the cellar windows. "We really were a ghastly-looking lot," wrote one boy with a nice dramatic flair. "Our faces were black from the coal dust. Our noses were filled with it, as well as our ears. When we gnashed our teeth, the particles could be heard crackling between our teeth. We worked until it was too dark to continue. Then we crawled home."

> Before going to bed we greeted each other with: "See you in the air-raid shelter" or with "Good air-raid." We all expected the bombers to come this night, and although everyone was dead tired, we could not sleep for fear that we might sleep soundly and miss our chance of getting to the shelter fast enough. But finally everyone was sound asleep and only the clothes and the flashlights at our sides showed that we were ready for anything. Suddenly the air carried a far-off noise to us. Here and there someone's head would be seen above the pillow. Listening. Then hell burst loose. The sirens wailed in the neighboring communities, our own bell rang furiously and everywhere figures jumped out of their beds. Shielded flashlights flared up and in their beam everyone could be seen dressing as fast as possible. Figures began walking rapidly toward the shelter, silhouetted against the searchlights on the surrounding hills. We made it in two minutes flat, two minutes from the first sound of the air-raid warning to the arrival of the last person in the shelter.

As I hurried from house to house, checking up on the procedure, I spotted a light mist along the ground. In normal times, I would have taken it for no more than the usual morning mist but ... *the swine!* I broke into a quick trot, nostrils flaring furiously, and—sure enough—picked up a sharp, stinging chemical odor which became stronger and more sickening as I neared the cellar door. "The swine!" I muttered, clenching my fists. "The filthy swine, they're gassing children now!"

It was essential, of course, not to show any fear. Outwardly calm, inwardly seething, I instructed Lene to complete the preparation and distribution of the gas masks as quickly as possible. Then I summoned the teachers and student leaders into a huddle to prepare for a swift but orderly departure off to the east, away from the wind. I was outside the door again, ready to lead the way when I suddenly realized where the smell was coming from. Our antigas brigade had thrown the covers over the windows and, in their zeal, had all but saturated them with the bleach water. Hence, the foul odor which, added to the morning mist, the dim light and the prevailing war psychosis, had been instantly translated into the gas attack I had been so afraid of.

As why shouldn't I have? I had seen civil war in both Austria and Spain, and that's the kind of experience that makes you more apprehensive, not less. Age, all by itself, is an experience. The older children had read enough books and seen enough movies to be able to picture the bombs falling and imagine the death and destruction that would follow. They—even more than the adults—were convinced that every action of the enemy was aimed directly at us. Oh, intellectually, they were perfectly aware that Hitler's grand design for the conquest of France was not really dependent upon the destruction of a handful of children's institutions, even if 80 to 90 percent of the children were Jews. What can the mind tell you, though, when the feeling in your bones tells you otherwise? When they read about gas bombs they were sure we would be the first targets. When they read about bacteriological warfare they were sure our water would be the first to be poisoned.

The least frightened at all times were the preschoolers and kindergarten children of the Petite Colonie. At that age, children are feeling creatures rather than thinking ones. Neither a blackout nor the wail of the sirens holds any terror for them unless they have been personally injured in an air raid or have seen someone injured close by. They fear blackouts only if they are already afraid of the dark. They fear the sounds of bombs and guns only if at some previous time they have been made to fear noise.

The protective measures, the air raid drills, were just another game to the little ones. The only concession we had to make to their age was to have teachers from the other Homes sleep at the Petite Colonie at night so that they could carry the babies down to the cellar. With those who were old enough to walk the only problems were that they would sometimes be cranky about leaving their bed in the early morning hours or were just so tired that they would sit down on the stairs along the way and drop right off to sleep. Once they were in the cellar, though, it was no more than a matter of tucking them in. Children of that age perceive the threat to them only by the reactions of the trusted people around them, their parents and teachers, their older sisters and brothers, and their comrades. Since we were careful not to alarm them, they literally slept through every alert.

The most vulnerable children were those between the ages of eight and twelve, because that is the age of intellectual transition. They were old enough to understand the dangerous situation they were in and young enough to be only too conscious of their own limitations. But this was one instance, fortunately, where the cure could be found in the malady. Their fear and confusion arose out of their developing intellect, and we were able to help them to overcome both the fear and the confusion by intellectual persuasion. With them, even more than with the others, it was necessary to explain things completely and never to underestimate their ability to understand what we were saying—even, if you follow me, when they did not seem to understand. They'll understand when they're ready. They may want a little time to think about it, that's all.

The expanding intellect combined with their all too recognizable weakness can also bring on a childish bravado. "I can do that," the ten-year-old boy will say after each new demonstration of strength and skill at the circus. To understand how something is done at that age becomes the same as being able to do it . . . or will be, anyway, as soon as he grows up. It isn't his fault he's still so small and weak, is it?

If you can make the wish as good as the deed you possess a magical power which can be turned at will into a magic cloak or a magic carpet. Or both. Once while I was sitting through a particularly long air raid with a group of eight-to-ten-year-olds, we sang the "Marseillaise" over and over. Finally, I was ready to call it quits. They insisted on singing it one more time. "When our fliers hear us they will be inspired to do their best. When the Nazis hear us they will know that we are not afraid and they will fly back and worry."

They not only saw themselves as the main object of the attack, they saw themselves as participants in the battle.

For just so long as the adults were able to conceal their fear, the children of all ages behaved with courage and spirit. My friend, General Theodor Koerner, the much-decorated war hero who became the second President of the Austrian Republic, often told me: "Bravery is not showing that you are afraid." And so, we were all heroes.

One night, it did happen that a woman teacher in the Girls' Home became hysterical and in no time at all the whole place was in an uproar. By the time I arrived, there wasn't a girl who wasn't crying. Many of them were clinging to each other, trembling and shaking. Others were standing by themselves, screaming at the top of their lungs. The directress of the Home, Margot Cohn (who was, as we shall see later, a woman of incredible courage), hadn't been able to get through to them, and it became clear to me soon enough that I wasn't going to be able to either until the hysterical teacher was brought under control. I shouted at her cruelly, and when that didn't work ordered her, even more cruelly, to leave. Once the hysterical adult was removed from their sight, I was finally able to get the children's attention. By degrees. It wasn't until I gave the big girls the responsibility of looking after the smaller ones that the panic very slowly began to subside. And vanished completely when we began to sing together.

After the all-clear had sounded, a few of the girls came to me and confided that they were still in fear of the next air raid. What were they afraid of? Well, they didn't really know. No, it wasn't the fear of dying. They couldn't even begin to imagine anything as concrete as their own death. They were afraid of "it." Just "it." A free-floating fear they could give no name or shape to. I was so lucky, they said, because I was so brave.

Many of the other girls had gathered around by then, and I raised my voice to include them all. They were very, very mistaken, I declared, if they believed that I wasn't afraid. I wasn't afraid of "it," though. I was afraid of the airplanes and of the bombs they carried. I could picture very vividly the devastation those bombs could bring—and my reaction was to determine in the most concrete and realistic terms how we could best protect ourselves. And that, I told them, was what I wanted them to do, too. Because once we were all committed to contributing our best efforts toward the common defense—each and every one of us—there would be no time left to worry about "it."

They left, full of resolve and commitment, vastly relieved. And yet . . . if panic had broken out in one place it could break out in others. To overcome fear, rather than to just repress it, the children had to understand not simply what the situation was and what could be done about it but also why we believed it had to be accepted. The next morning we assembled the children in each Home. I began by reviewing the likelihood of our coming under attack and the damage that might be reasonably anticipated. As someone who had been through bombing attacks in Spain I could tell them that the danger for any particular individual during an average air raid was not very great. Which, I took care to add, in no way minimized that danger or the greater danger that existed to the institution as a whole.

And so to a discussion on fear. With so much real danger around us, I said, we had no time for imaginary dangers. We fear war, yes; we hate it. But we fear more the dangers and destruction and the loss of freedom with which our enemies threaten us. We discussed how bombs work. We described the antiaircraft. Fear wasn't going to enable us to escape any of those dangers.

Fear had never been known to alter the course of a single bomb or drive off a single enemy plane. At best, fear accomplished nothing; at worst, it prevented you from acting constructively to protect yourself.

An open discussion followed on the measures France was taking to protect itself, and therefore us. Yes, France had its own air force and its strategically placed batteries of antiaircraft guns to drive the Luftwaffe off. If some of the bombers did get through, there were civilian defense units and fire departments ready to swing into action. All right. With us, too, positive action could be taken. Every child who did not have a specific air raid duty now was given one, even if it was only to put out the lights in his room when the air raid siren went off. Even if it was only to open a window or keep the water canteens filled or turn on the radio so that we could listen to the news reports. Even if it was only to clean up the paint that was spattered around after a fresh coat of black was applied to the windows.

Children are optimists; that's why the race survives. Their every little attempt to do something gives them hope of full success. When I was a child of, oh, maybe nine years, I read in the paper that the melting snow had flooded an alpine village and taken many lives. The pictures in the paper impressed me deeply. On that very day, the snow began to melt in the streets of Vienna and so I went out into the street armed with a child's shovel. I stood in the gutter and hacked away at every piece of snow that got stuck long enough to hold up the flow. I was much relieved by my activity, for I was sure that I was preventing the whole sewage system from being stopped up. I had no doubt that I was saving the whole city from being flooded.

Never be afraid to ask children to make a contribution. They long to serve a cause; they ache to be used. On the second night, as an example, there were two air raid alarms with no more than half an hour between the first all-clear and the second alert. To add to the general confusion, a new group of girls had arrived, making it necessary for us to convert the wooden house at the far corner of the grounds into a dormitory. Seven of the most responsible boys were detached from the work on their own

Home to clear out the cellar for them and build up the sandbag defense. Wrote one of them:

We worked like madmen. Faster and faster all the time, until we were running with the wheelbarrows, dumping our bagsful of dirt and running back to fill the next one as fast as we could. We took more and more bags at a time until we thought we could stand the strain no longer. Although we wore as few clothes as we could, sweat was pouring down our bodies and formed little rivulets on our faces. The mountains of bags grew before the windows, but we were not satisfied. Nothing short of perfect could satisfy us. And so we worked more and still more. We ran mechanically, we saw no more, our eyes were dimmed by the sweat. Lunchtime finally arrived and we sank down on our seats, content to be able to rest.

After lunch there was no time for rest, we had to go on, the shelter had to be finished before the evening. For the whole afternoon we went on with our work. Wooden boards were nailed on the inside of the window, chairs were put into the shelter, safety precautions against gas attacks had to be taken and the sandbags were covered with sod. This is not a very hard kind of work, but we made it so by doing everything as fast as we could. Chairs were not handed from one to another, they were thrown, the sod was brought in running and the hammers flew and drove the nails into the boards with lightning speed. When evening came all the rough work had been done. With a last, "Hope you enjoy your new shelter," we started to run home. We ran as fast as we could, so as not to be surprised by an alarm while on the way from one home to the other.

When we came home we could see immediately that everything had not been going as well with us. Deprived of seven pairs of strong arms the work on our shelter was not finished by a long run. Especially as our shelter was bigger than the girls'. So after a quick supper we went to work again. The evening came but we could not stop. Flashlights were fastened to the trees and work went on. At about eleven in the evening the work was finished. A sense of security came over us as we looked over our handiwork. We knew it was our own work, we knew its strength and its safety, and we felt secure.

We knew it was our own work, we knew its strength and its

safety, and we felt secure. The sense of common labor in the midst of common danger, the feeling of security that comes from contributing to a common cause, is the single most important factor in overriding fear. "Two men are heroes; one man is a coward," was another of General Koerner's favorite sayings. Once during an air raid we had to leave a grippe-ridden little boy in the sickroom because Lene felt it would be far more dangerous to expose everybody else to the grippe than to expose him to the much smaller risk of a direct hit by a bomb. One of the counselors, a young woman with a reputation for coolness, was almost automatically assigned to stay with him. When I came upstairs to look in on them during the attack, I found the child holding the counselor's hand, listening quite happily to the story she was telling him. But the counselor . . . The counselor smiled weakly at me through tear-filled eyes, tears of fright at having been left alone with a sick child. And this was a woman who had always been a tower of strength when she was with the whole group in the shelter.

Many of the children who were not a bit frightened when they were with the group were afraid to go to the bathroom during an attack, even though the bathroom was right there in the cellar. They would go only after we had given them permission to leave the door open a crack so they could have a reassuring glimpse of the other children.

The risk we ran was that the common emotion would become a common psychosis. One day the rumor spread that the Nazis had dropped poisoned candy and booby-trapped fountain pens. Instantly, every piece of candy, every fountain pen became suspect. We pointed out that we bought our candy from a long-established and perfectly reputable store in Paris. We reminded them that they had been using their pens for months with perfect safety. Nothing could convince them. The more hysterical were positive that their pens had been switched during the night by the Nazis. Hitler's spies were suddenly everywhere. I would take a pen from a child, send him across to the other side of the room and write with it. See? It hadn't exploded, had it? They still weren't convinced. There may be ways to treat a mass psychosis but history tells us that the application of sheer logic isn't one of them.

How these rumors start no one ever knows. How they spread so quickly is a phenomenon which has defied the best minds of the ages. Within twenty-four hours, this one spread through all the schools of France, including our Homes in southern France. Thousands of fountain pens were destroyed. (Immersion in water seemed to be the most acceptable method.) Tons of candy were thrown away.

> We collected fragments of shells on the way to school. Once we found a pack of cigarettes, not French, which we thought was poisoned and turned it over to the police. Once we thought we saw parachutists coming down beyond the trees and scouted the whole area, chasing down innocent Frenchmen.
>   —One of the older boys

We had one little girl, Judith, who came to us labeled deaf and mute and retarded. She, of course, had no fear at all. She was a sweet little girl, and she had a peculiar little dance which she might break into at any time. It consisted, in its entirety, of holding up her hands and making faces. Today, she would probably be called autistic. At any rate, Judith was in the toilet at the Girls' Annex one evening when the sirens sounded. The other girls pounded frantically on the door, shouting for her to come out until it suddenly dawned on them that she wasn't going to hear a word no matter how loud they yelled, whereupon they all looked at each other and burst out laughing.

Lene worked very hard with her and eventually had her pronouncing a few words that sounded vaguely like *bonjour, au revoir, merci,* etc.

> After the war, Ruth Heilbron and I checked for survivors at the OSE office and saw but one familiar name, namely Judith's, the retarded one. To see that she alone was alive seemed a crowning irony and twisted the knife.
>   —Ilse Shellen, who came to us from
>   the *St. Louis*

Through it all, night after night, the alerts went on. As we became accustomed to spending our nights in the shelter, some of the children began to read by flashlight. Others took to playing bridge, which was a novelty. Upstairs, we had no bridge players; upstairs, we had chess players and Monopoly players. It was somehow understood that bridge was to be played only in the shelter. The children thought of it as a special game to be played only under combat conditions. The truth was that they knew that they were really using it as a tranquilizer, and so upstairs where they pursued an entirely different kind of life they wanted no part of it.

The all-clear never failed to bring a relaxation of tension, signaling as it did not only one more fortunate escape but a favorable omen for the future. In their elation, the children would make jokes which were not very funny to the adults around them. "What kind of an alert was that? Not a single bomb!" Or, "No dead again? Not even a little casualty?" It was difficult, impossible really, to rebuke them on the spot. Better low humor, after all, than low spirits. And, of course, we adults shared their relief. The next morning in assembly I would let them know that we considered such jokes to be in very poor taste, a rather mild rebuke which, I always suspected, they accepted with a secret, swaggering delight.

As the alerts continued to come almost every night, the singing and story telling stopped. Even the bridge games were discontinued. We simply became accustomed to going to sleep in stages. First stage, bed in bedroom; second stage, dozing fitfully on a chair in the cellar; third stage, back to bed if possible.

> Air-raid followed air-raid. Sometimes they were shorter, sometimes longer. Sometimes there were two during one night, sometimes there were none. The shelter grew more and more gay. The morale was high, but some of us lost weight. Then the air-raids stopped altogether. The long sit-down war began. Life went on in our home as if no war existed.

We were into that strange season of muffled cannon that was called the Funny War *(Drole de Guerre)* in France, the Phony

War in the United States and the Sit-Down War *(Sitzkrieg)* in Germany. Through it all, the children kept coming in, pouring in now not in groups anymore nor directly from Germany but moved as individuals from one underground drop to another. By the spring of 1940, we had sixteen hundred children in eleven Homes all over France, with a twelfth about to be opened.

The one mass operation inside Germany involved six hundred children who were to be gathered up in a carefully coordinated effort and whisked to a staging area in Norway—which meant with the full knowledge and tacit cooperation of the Norwegian authorities. On April 9, just before the rescue was to be effected, the war erupted again with the surprise invasion of Norway and Denmark. On May 10, the *Drole de Guerre* came to an end on the Continent with the invasion of Holland and Belgium. From there, everything went fast. A month to the day after the German army began to roll, Paris was evacuated. In that month, our children discovered what it was like to go about their schoolwork with the sound of gunfire off in the distance and the roar of planes overhead. They were able to find out what it was like to feel the floor shaking beneath their feet during the great air attack on Paris that killed fifteen hundred people. In one Home, they witnessed a German plane crashing within sight of their classroom window. In another, they watched an adjoining building burn to the ground. And, when the German army was within ten miles of us, they found out what it was like to be on the run again.

During that month, we had a choice of spending our lives in the shelter or going about our normal routine. Where there had previously been so many alarms without air raids there were now frequent daytime air raids without any alarms. The new rule was that everybody who was outside was to get inside at the first sound of antiaircraft fire, and those who were already inside were to go on with what they were doing.

> During the last days at Tourelles, a place nearby was bombed but we were not hit. I also witnessed a fight in the air between a German and a French fighter. I felt mad and wanted to cry but

was unable to. Just as I had felt during the persecution of my family and other people.

—Young boy

As we followed the advance of the German armies across the map in the morning assemblies, I explained the military strategy and tactics. For two reasons. To begin with, they had a right to know what was happening. Beyond that, I wanted them to understand that *nothing was happening accidentally.* Because if nothing happened accidentally, they could not look upon themselves as helpless pawns of fate.

With everything crumbling around them, I considered it more essential than ever to hold the great vision of a triumphant future before the children's eyes. Accordingly, we insisted that the smallest as well as the largest task be performed with the utmost skill and dedication. When a new coat of blackout paint was applied to the windows, it had to be done with scrupulous care. The paper strips were to be pasted across the windows not merely as a protective measure but also as an exercise in taste and artistry. For we had a great task to perform. As the inevitable survivors, it had fallen to us to preserve the culture of a civilized life—the highest impulses and the most noble aspirations of mankind—from being destroyed by the barbarism of war. "Hitler has no future," I said, again and again. "We have a future." I repeated that so often that my younger son, Georgie, the rascal, would amuse his comrades by clasping his hands behind his back in a fairly good imitation of me, and rattling off my favorite speech, bad French accent and all. "Hitler is not all-powerful. From Hammerfest on the northern tip of Norway to Gibraltar on the southern tip of Spain, Hitler cannot hold one front with everything and everybody against him. Hitler is doomed. Time, *mes enfants,* is on our side."

The present very clearly was not. The final battle for France was fought in Montmorency two days after we had joined the swarm of humanity—ten million strong—choking every road leading to the south of France in a frantic attempt to get away from the German army.

With the fall of Paris, on June 10, 1940, the Montmorency period had come to an end. Not the story of the children; in many ways their story was only beginning. But the Montmorency period was over for them, and for me. It is only when something comes to an end that it is possible to look back and see what was done and, with the passage of years, make an assessment on where you have succeeded and where you have failed.

Epic stories are born only in retrospect. While the Montmorency Homes were in operation, it was no more than a modest story of children who wanted to survive, and whom I thought I could help to survive. Nothing so remarkable about that. The child who dies of pneumonia wanted to live too. The doctor who treated that child wanted to help him live. It happens every day.

I didn't do enough because nobody did enough, but some things were done. I was forty years old when Paris fell. I am now seventy-two. A child who was ten is now in his midforties. There are those who survived and found their lives, exactly as we had wished for them. There were those who survived into a vague, disquieting sense of guilt that they should have lived while so many died. There were those who did not survive and should have survived, and there is a bitterness about that which the years will not swallow.

The story of the children moves from Montmorency to Nazi-occupied France and, as it moves with me, to the United States. In Nazi-occupied France, the Underground workers of the OSE risked their lives every day—and suffered terrible casualties—to save the lives of these children. And they will not talk of it. The two Underground leaders—a famous psychologist in Paris and an incredibly brave woman in Berlin—were my dear friends, and they have remained my dear friends, but on this one subject they will say not a word. Not then. Not now. Fate had placed them in a position where they were forced to make desperate choices every day, such desperate choices that even now, for history's sake, they cannot bear to talk about it. When life and death rides on every choice you must make, you remember only those whom you did not save.

And that is the bitter irony of it: Those who did the most feel

3. On the Threshold

To be perfectly frank, I took on the job originally for a limited time and for the most practical of all reasons; to put aside a little money. I was myself a political refugee. As a leader of the Social Democrats in Austria and a member of the Diet and the Town Council of Vienna I had been forced to flee the country at the time of the Dollfuss putsch. On February 12, 1934, seventeen thousand government troops and Fascist militia had turned their guns on the workers in the street and raked homes in the workers' sections of Vienna with their artillery, slaughtering thousands of men, women and children and turning Austria into a clerical-Fascist state. For the intervening four and a half years I had worked in the Underground from Switzerland to Spain.

It was not as a political man that the OSE wanted me, of course, but as a teacher. As an eighteen-year-old freshman at the University of Vienna I had organized four hundred of my fellow students into a group called Spielkameraden (playfellows), which went out into the streets to join the kids running wild in the streets of postwar Austria. The theory was that once we were able to win the children's confidence we would be able to rechannel their energies or, at the very least, be in a position to arrange for their care and feeding. One way or another, I had been involved with young people ever since. As a teacher, as a leader of Socialist youth and as a child psychologist.

We had been scheduled to leave for the United States in about three weeks when the OSE approached me. The boat tickets were already in my pocket. Since there were four of us—myself, Lene and our two sons, Gustl, twelve, and Georgie, seven—it did seem like a prudent idea to have enough money to see us through the early months in a strange new country.

The OSE Union ("The Osay") was founded in 1912 by a group of Jewish doctors in Saint Petersburg (Leningrad). The initials stood for Obsczestvo Sdravochraneniya Eryeyev, which translates into Society for the Health of the Jewish Population. For the Czarist authorities to have granted a charter which permitted a Jewish organization to hold meetings, recruit members and establish medical institutions at a time when any public gathering was looked upon as subversive was the best possible testimony that the founders of the OSE were men of considerable influence and, even more significant, men whose loyalty to the Czar was beyond question. The first great expansion of the OSE's activities came during World War I. Not only had the Eastern Front completely destroyed the most compact Jewish communities in the surrounding countries, but hundreds of thousands of Russian Jews had been driven from their homes along the border areas by the traditionally anti-Semitic Russian military. Amidst all these disasters came the Czarist order of May 5, 1915—familiar to everybody who has seen *Fiddler on the Roof*—compelling 150,000 Jews to leave their villages, literally overnight. Among the men, women and children who had to be evacuated in less than twenty-four hours were entire orphanages. To care for these refugee children, the OSE eventually set up twenty-four hygiene stations, served regular breakfasts to 25,000 children in school kitchens and established twenty-six summer colonies which accommodated more than 2,500 children.

When refugee children were dying like flies in the hospitals of Kiev in the days immediately preceding the Revolution, convalescent homes were set up in Poland, Latvia and Lithuania, financed for the most part by the American Joint Distribution Committee. Meanwhile, a group of OSE workers in Berlin, in cooperation with the JDC and a special Paris Aid Committee, was sending food supplies and medical aid into Russia and setting up institutions for about ten thousand children. At this

stage of its history the OSE reached its most energetic heights
—and its most Revolutionary fervor—as thousands of Jewish
intellectuals joined with the doctors to stir the political consciences of the Jewish masses.

Ironically, the success of the Revolution resulted in the expul-
sion of the OSE from Russia. With the acquiescence of and
indeed at the insistence of Jewish Bolsheviks, the liquidation of
all purely Jewish organizations was ordered as contradictory to
the unifying aims of Leninism.

The new headquarters were set up in Berlin which, irony upon
irony, offered by far the most hospitable environment for Jews
during the 1920s. When Hitler came to power in 1933, the OSE
was forced to leave Berlin and move to Paris where, with Albert
Einstein as the figurehead chairman, it set up its new international office. By 1938, the OSE in France consisted mostly of
well-established and completely assimilated Russian and Polish
Jewish doctors. Rather conservative. Perfectly content with the
status quo. Not particularly committed to humanitarianism or
culture. The same kind of men, one might say, who had been
considered safe enough to be granted a charter by the Czar. Their
principal activity was running a little convalescent home in
Montmorency for the sick or undernourished babies—six years
old or under—of Russian and Polish refugees who had come to
France years earlier and had not been able to adjust to their new
surroundings.

The official of the OSE who phoned to tell me they were
looking for a director was Dr. Aron Lourié, a relative of Lene's.
(Lourié had been a member of the Duma [Parliament] of Russia
in the early days of the Revolution, as a member of the Constitutional Democrats, the liberal splinter party which stood about
halfway between the Bolsheviks and the Mensheviks.) I couldn't
have been less enthusiastic. I wasn't interested in Russian or
Jewish refugee children as such. My concern had always been
with youth and human misery wherever they were found. Besides, I was an educator, not a pediatrician. No, there was
certainly nothing attractive enough about such an offer to tempt
me to cancel our voyage to the United States.

On the other hand, there was the question of how we were

going to live once we got there. Having enough money had never been a problem for me before. My wife's family owned a famous sanitarium in Vienna, so famous that Lene and our two boys had been able to remain in Vienna in safety for almost four years, slipping across the border from time to time to meet me. She was, to put it simply, considered too valuable by the Austrian government to be harmed.

On March 11, 1938, Hitler marched into Austria. The next day, the blackshirts broke into her mother's home while the boys were there and demanded to know where they had hidden their millions. Except for Lene and the boys, the whole family was arrested. The Nazis wanted her on the outside so that she could run the sanitarium for them, too. Three months later, word came to the Underground via Holland that the Germans were going to arrest her anyway, not for anything I had done in Austria, curiously enough, but for what I had done during the Civil War in Spain. Before the Nazis could move, we were able to get Lene and the boys across the border and onto a train for Paris.

The call from Lourié had come to me in the resort town of LaBaule, on the Atlantic coast, where I had been making ends meet by running a summer camp for children, something unique in France during those days. Before we had opened the camp in LaBaule, however, we had spent two months in Paris, and that's where I had discovered what it meant to worry about feeding a family. The four of us had lived together in one room, cooking our meals on a *Spiritus Kocher* (a little stove) that Gustl had brought with him from the hiking movement. Shopping for food had become an adventure of saving a franc here and another franc there. I had no assurance of a job once we landed in America, for my English was, at best, primitive. And Lene no longer had an income. Or, for that matter, a sanitarium. In order to get Lene's brother out of the concentration camp, her parents had been required to sell the sanitarium to a Nazi for about the price of a *Spiritus Kocher*, which was only to make it "legal." The sale of any property by Jews was taxable at a rate of about 90 percent, which was itself only another legal maneuver since no Jew was allowed to take more than ten marks (five dollars) out of the country. Legal. Logical. Systematic. Fortunately, Lene had bought our boat tickets at the French Lines office in Vienna ahead of time with money she wouldn't be allowed to take out of the country anyway. She had also had the foresight to buy round-trip tickets so that we could cash in the return tickets when we were in the United States. The way the profits from the camp had been disappearing, it was beginning to look as though we would have to cash them in immediately upon landing if we were going to find out what American food tasted like.

So why not leave a few months later in order to take advantage of this unexpected opportunity to put a little money aside?

I met with the Board of Directors in the OSE office in the workers' quarter of Paris, and then—by mutual agreement—took the train to Montmorency alone to make a personal inspection.

At Number 2 Rue St. Denis I found two ordinary, ramshackle one-family cottages surrounded by a little garden. Inside, there were a few rooms off a large hallway, and although the rooms varied in size they were all equally overcrowded and dirty. Every room was packed with beds, and many of the beds had two children in them. In the smaller rooms, there were as many as eight or ten children; in the largest room, maybe fifteen. Altogether, fifty children piled on top of each other.

"Forget it," I told them when I returned. "The place is impossible."

The leading officers were Dr. Lazar Gourwitch, the international secretary of the OSE; Dr. Joseph Millner, the French secretary (who had a brother in the State Department in Washington); Dr. Eugene Minkovsky, the chairman, who was a famous psychologist, and Dr. Julius Brutzkus, the treasurer.

Brutzkus wanted to know what I had against the place.

"I don't want to discuss it," I said.

"I don't see why we can't at least discuss it," Brutzkus said, rather mildly. "Why should we not be friends?"

"It is absolutely the worst run place I have ever seen. It's dirty. It's run-down. It's just impossible, that's all."

Another shrug from Brutzkus, the kind of philosophical shrug that belongs to the Russian Jew. "So why wouldn't you want to change it?"

Brutzkus was a big man with a walrus moustache. He had been

Minister for Minorities under Lenin for a time even though he was a Menshevik. Inevitably, he had been exiled with the rest of the Mensheviks but still . . . for a Menshevik to hold such a post in the Bolshevik government was ample testimony to his ability to hold onto the affection of old friends.

It was easy to see why. Although I didn't know Brutzkus any better than the others, I found his frank and open manner very attractive. "Are you telling me you would give me full power to change it?" I asked. "To do anything I want?"

Of course they would. Why did I think they wanted me, because they suspected they were running such a palace? To prove it, they were willing to take my word for it that there was room in the cottages for no more than thirty-two children. And since each child was there, on the average, for only a month, I should be able to reach that figure through a process of natural attrition within a couple of weeks. "And," Brutzkus said, "we are not necessarily thinking solely in terms of a convalescent home anymore." Certain OSE members, he said, dropping the first hint that the status quo men were considering doing something again, were thinking in terms of refugee children from Germany and Austria.

That's all that was said, and it put an entirely different face on the matter. Before I gave them a definite answer, though, I wanted to talk it over with Lene and the boys. Lene, no longer the incorrigible optimist she had been in Vienna, was against staying in France any longer than necessary. She had discovered what it was like to live under the Nazis; she knew what it was like to have relatives carted off to the concentration camps. And I was, after all, on the wanted lists in Germany, Austria, Italy and Spain. "Hitler will come here and you will be caught and killed," she cried. "And the children and I will be sent to the concentration camp."

Since the Czechoslovakian crisis had coincided with our stay in LaBaule, there was a certain amount of logic to what she was saying. The crisis had begun in July with Hitler's demand for the Sudetenland and had come to a head with Neville Chamberlain's meetings with Hitler in Berchtesgaden and Godesberg in the second and third weeks of September. When Chamberlain left Godesberg it was with Hitler's ultimatum that Sudetenland must be turned over to Germany by the following Wednesday.

On September 28, 1938, "Black Wednesday," I received a telegram from Léon Blum, who had been deputy premier of Chautemps' coalition government, requesting me to come to Paris immediately. As I arrived at the railroad station in LaBaule, workmen with brooms and buckets of paste were already posting a general mobilization order. In Paris, I found the same call to arms posted everywhere. "We must expect to be at war in two or three days," Léon Blum told me gravely. He wanted to know whether I would be able to set up housing in LaBaule for the children of the Socialist refugees living around Paris and of our French comrades who would be called up by the army within the next few days. A hundred children at the minimum, to begin with. Of course I could. With the summer coming to an end there would be plenty of houses available.

Thursday was a hectic day of meetings with government officials and refugee committees and of rearranging our own plans for returning to Paris. There was a late train to LaBaule which left around midnight and arrived at five o'clock in the morning. When I boarded the train, the Paris station was still jammed with people trying to get out of the city. When I got off at LaBaule I walked into a strangely empty station and saw, to my bewilderment, that the mobilization orders had been posted over. A very quick war, it seemed. Over in five hours. And not a soul around to explain what had happened.

Munich had happened, Lene told me when I arrived at the house.

It is still difficult to describe the emotions that came over me as she told me about the sellout of Czechoslovakia at Munich. An overwhelming sense of relief that was immediately followed by a sickening feeling of shame at what had been done and, yes, that I should feel so relieved.

Relief and shame mixed with bewilderment and despair. Bewilderment because everything Léon Blum had told me had led me to believe that Daladier had gone to Munich with every intention of holding firm. Despair because I did not really believe that Munich would prevent war; I believed in my heart that it would only weaken the line of defense in Western Europe and make an even worse war inevitable.

Léon Blum was one of the great political thinkers of all history; there is no man I have ever admired more. Having said that, I must also say that the doctrinaire pacifism of the European Socialists—peace at all costs—had rendered them incapable of recognizing that this was no ordinary conflict between nations but a collision between two philosophies of life to which there could be no political solution. The history of the Socialist movement in Austria had forced us to fight for survival while holding onto pacifism as an ideal; I had been arguing the necessity of making a stand against Hitler so consistently for five years that some of my old comrades were no longer speaking to me.

Americans are still criticized for being so slow in understanding that Hitler was a force of pure evil. But how could they have been expected to understand what Europeans whose very borders were being menaced refused to understand? There are a hundred examples I could give. In 1935, at the very time of Hitler's first territorial demand in the Rhineland, I spoke of the danger of war at a conference of Socialist Democratic Youth in Copenhagen. A cold, disapproving silence fell over the audience. The next afternoon, I was at a luncheon being given in honor of a few of us by the French Minister of Commerce, who was a woman, when the news came over the radio that Hitler had just marched into the Rhineland. "This means war," I said. Immediately she disagreed. "Why should this mean war? The Rhineland is German. We should have given it back long ago."

I agreed with her about that. Absolutely. The Rhineland did belong to Germany and it should have been given back when the democratic regime was still in power. If Hitler were permitted to march in and take it now, whatever was left of the democratic movement in Germany would be discredited. Hitler would have undisputed control and a much larger war would be inevitable. "This will not mean war, small or large," she snapped. "Because we will not fight any more wars." With undeniable passion and sincerity, she said: "My husband died in the World War. My son is now eighteen, and he will not die in another one. There can be no war if we refuse to fight. If the Nazis occupy France itself we will not resist."

"But you are giving them permission to go ahead," I protested. "You are inviting the very thing you hate the most."

Not only wouldn't she recognize what I was saying, everybody else at the table became angry with me, too. They did not want even to consider the possibility that the choice between national resistance and national surrender was not theirs to make. For the lady it turned out to be far more tragic. Whatever she had told her son, or he had promised her, when the time finally came that the terrible choice had to be made it was he who had to make it, not she. He died in World War II.

Those who were caught up in the middle of it could be just as blind. My wife's brother Alex was a passionate mountain climber, and during my years in the Underground I would arrange to meet him in Switzerland from time to time to hear the latest news from the family. The last time we met he said, in complete exasperation, "Ernst, why are you so crazy? All you have to do is give up this political work of yours and say you support the government, and I am sure they will let you return to your family." Of course they would have. As a defecting leader of the opposition, I would have been such a prize that they would have sent a royal coach and greeted me with a brass band.

"Alex," I sighed, "you are not a political man, you do not understand. But you will find out very soon how important it is to fight fascism, to fight these Nazis who are taking over the country. I am more afraid for you than you are for me because you are such an innocent that when the time comes you still won't know what you are fighting for."

Six months later, the Nazis arrested him and shipped him to Dachau, where he suffered terribly before we were able to get him out to New Zealand.

And even at that late date, the lesson was lost on those who were not actually suffering. The first time I returned to France after Hitler had occupied Austria I told Léon Blum, who had just become Premier, some of the stories that had come to me through Underground sources about the beatings and public humiliation of Austrian Jews, which were far worse than anything that had occurred up to that time in Germany. All the while he was listening to me, Blum's eyes were saying very plainly: "Papanek's a nice fellow. Why does he think he has to tell me such lies? We are willing to help the man anyhow."

I tell these stories for two reasons. First, to set the historical backdrop, but also for a reason that is more directly related to my decision to accept the offer from the OSE. With events at Munich having eliminated any need to find homes for children in LaBaule, we prepared to return to Paris to wait out the three weeks before our ship would be sailing for America. For some reason, the equinox weeks—March 21 and September 21—are always exceptionally rough on the Atlantic coast. Our house was right on the waterfront, and as I looked out at the ocean and saw the wrecks sticking up so symbolically on the suddenly placid waters, I could not help but reflect that if the oceans of Europe also seemed suddenly becalmed, rougher winds yet were brewing just beyond the horizon and a time of greater wreckage lay ahead.

And so while I may have been basing my argument to Lene solely on the opportunity it would give us to save up some money, I also had the queasy feeling that this was not a very good time for a man who had done so much talking about standing up to Hitler to be running off to America.

What risk, I asked Lene, could there be in staying for a few more months?

We made a deal with the people at OSE. If they were willing to hire me with the understanding that I would remain for only six months, I would be happy to get their program organized for them.

Before the month was over, the "Night of the Broken Crystal" completely altered our course. On November 7, 1938, a young German Jewish refugee walked into the German Embassy in Paris and mortally wounded the third secretary, Ernst von Rath, in the mistaken belief that he was the German Ambassador. To compound the tragedy, von Rath was an anti-Nazi, quite possibly the only anti-Nazi left in the entire German diplomatic service. Upon the death of von Rath two days later, the Nazis loosed a pogrom upon the Jews of Germany that was reminiscent of the worst days of Czarist Russia.

And I will insist upon making a note here: The Jews of Germany were utterly defenseless. The first Nuremberg Laws in 1933 had forced all Jews to turn in their firearms upon penalty of death. The bravest and most vigorous of the young men, the war veterans in particular, had refused to live in a country where they were not allowed to defend themselves. Fifty thousand of them had streamed out of the country within the year. To Palestine, to South America, to South Africa, to the United States. The exodus was so great that it had been necessary for the Jewish Community to organize a more orderly emigration. By the Night of the Broken Crystal, there were old Jewish men and young Jewish men, but very few between their late twenties and early forties left in Germany. As for a young man of eighteen, he had been doubly disarmed, having been instructed since the age of thirteen as to his helplessness and inferiority.

On the night of November 9, all Jewish males who could be found were taken out of their homes and beaten by successions of roving bands. The murders ran into the hundreds. The synagogues were burned. Private homes were ransacked and set on fire. Every shop that was run by a Jew was wrecked and looted. The broken glass of the shop windows, the splinters of glass that covered the sidewalks the morning after, became the symbols of the carnage. The broken windows in the streets and the broken crystal glasses in the homes. *Kristallnacht* it was called by the Jews of Germany to convey the message that something far more precious than glass was shattered that night—something having to do with the dignity of the human spirit and the fragility of human trust.

For two nights, the beast of Nazism went ravening through the streets of Germany in full view of the entire world, and to all intents and purposes the world averted its eyes. When the beast was penned, the Jewish Community of Germany was fined one billion marks for its sins. Other edicts were issued to exclude Jews entirely from the economic life of the country, expropriate what remained of their property and banish them from schools, resorts, parks and all other public meeting places.

No longer could we be content to wait for Jewish parents to bring their children to France. It was now up to us to go and get them. Minkovsky, the famous psychologist who was also a war hero, was placed in charge of that phase of the operation. And then, at last, the OSE people turned to me. We would now, quite obviously, have to accommodate more than the thirty-two children in the one Home we had to start with, no? No! We would now only be able to accommodate twenty-four, because I was going to take the largest room and convert it into an office for myself. And did they want to know why? "Because I don't want to make this only a shelter for terrorized children, I want to make it a great Children's Home. To make a GREAT Children's Home, you start with administration. Everything else will follow."

With the rescue operation already being organized, it was necessary to find a suitable shelter quickly. They found it only three miles away. The Villa Helvetia was a rambling vacation hotel which in better days had catered to a wealthy Swiss clientele, *Helvetia* being a poetic name for Switzerland. For our purposes, it was perfect. Big enough to take care of eighty to one hundred children once we had broken it down into smaller rooms, and with spacious grounds, covered with huge old trees, for the youngsters to roam in.

The Baroness Pierre de Gunzbourg, the French wife of a Russian-born aristocrat who had made a fortune as an armaments manufacturer in Strasbourg, gave us the forty thousand francs we needed to rent it for the duration. (The exchange rate was thirty-eight francs to a dollar in those days, but with the cost of living figured in they could almost be used interchangeably for our purposes.)

"Forty thousand," she warned us, "and you'll never get another penny out of me."

It was really very funny. The Baroness was an imposing woman, with hatchetlike features that she refused to make the slightest attempt to pretty over, and a warm, beautiful heart that she was always trying to hide. She had become interested in the OSE because of the work we had been doing with convalescent children. We hadn't just been phasing those children out, I want you to know. We had introduced an educational program—working with both the children and their parents—that was progressive by any standards and completely new to France. What had impressed her more than anything else was the casework-oriented approach Lene had developed whereby the parents were given a special diet for each individual child plus written advice on how to handle the child's medical and emotional problems.

Impressed or not, the Baroness wanted us to understand that she was a completely assimilated Frenchwoman who wasn't giving us the money because the children were Jewish but only because they were children who happened to be in danger. "If you can do what you say you can do, here is the money," she said. "But I will tell you right now, here is also where it will end."

Three weeks later, she gave us another forty thousand francs to buy a castle on the outskirts of Montmorency. Before the year was over, she had bought castles for us all over France at a cost of more than a million francs and was serving very actively as the chairman of our Board.

The Baron de Gunzbourg would always joke with me about it. "What am I going to do with all those castles you're getting my wife to buy?" he would ask. "When the war is over the children will all return to Germany and I will be stuck with them."

There would always be children in need of an institution, I would assure him.

"No, no," he would sigh. "I will be the Castle King of France. I am resigned to it. The taxes alone will make a poor man of me. Nothing can save me from my fate now except a return to the Age of Chivalry."

He was hitting too close to the truth there for comfort. The castles were such a godsend to us not only because they were so large but also because the aristocrats who owned them were only too happy to find someone who would take them off their hands. They were ancestral castles, out of another age. The last ornate reminder of a style of life that had disappeared.

The first group of children arrived from Germany and Austria early in February, 1939, thirty-odd youngsters between the ages of five and twelve. Most of them had come across the border holding tightly to the hands of Frenchmen or Frenchwomen who had volunteered to bring them through customs on their family passports. Since none of the children spoke French that well, they had been instructed to smile if they were spoken to but to say nothing that might give them away. The poor little things were so terrified in the aftermath of the Night of the Broken Crystal that few of their benefactors were able to coax a single word out of them even after they were safely in France.

For us, it had been a race against time to get the old wooden hotel ready. As far as the remodeling of the house was concerned we had to partition off the old rooms, which also made it necessary to put in some new doors and windows, paint the outside, redecorate the inside, strengthen the foundation and patch up the roof. Since we were going to need new furniture anyway, we decided to build our own. Chairs and tables staggered in size to fit every age group. And because I was determined that we would be as self-sufficient as possible—for educational reasons that far outweighed the financial ones—we drew up plans to construct a complete tailor shop in the basement.

We had eight weeks to get it all done and no money to hire skilled workmen. I passed the word among the political refugees who were sitting all over Paris going crazy that we had plenty of work for them and that while we wouldn't be able to pay very much, we would be serving good meals and they would be working for children.

We had a hundred positions to fill, counting the double shifts, and as soon as the unions agreed to waive their rights we filled every position and had a long waiting list. Except for the Jewish intellectuals from Poland, who had a tradition of learning a trade, few of our workers had ever held a tool in their hands before. But they worked day and night—literally, day and night—and if some of the work wasn't very good at first, it improved every day. They were working for the love of the children and they were happy for the chance to be working, and that meant they were working with enthusiasm. A medical doctor who was well over fifty prescribed "fresh air and exercise" for himself, as his way of volunteering to cart the rubbish away in a wheelbarrow. Another doctor became a mason, and a pretty darn good one. Lawyers became carpenters, professors became painters, former ministers of state became roofers, writers became laborers. One of the professors, who is at Carnegie University now, was one of our most—uh, exuberant painters. He comes to visit us once a year and never fails to say, as if for the first time: "Ho, did we cheat you! We could not all paint." To which I answer—the ritual is unfailing—"I knew it. Number one, the painting was so lousy; and number two, it took you clowns three times as long as any ordinary lousy painters."

Nobody thought we could have the Home ready in time. But we did. We did it by working like hell through the final night and by leaving the decorating of their rooms to the children themselves. When the guests of honor arrived from Paris the next morning to officiate at our grand opening, the representative from the Office of the Interior came upon an unshaven, unkempt workman sleeping soundly on a bench in the garden. It was the architect who had drawn up the blueprints for us, stayed on to oversee the work and then pitched in himself through the final night to get the job done.

The children had spent a couple of busy days themselves. By the time they arrived at Helvetia, they had already been processed through OSE headquarters in Paris, brought to the Rothschild Hospital in Paris for a medical examination and taken by train to the railroad station at Enghien, a little town five miles away, where they had been picked up by their group counselors and driven in by bus.

They filed into the large dining hall, took their seats quietly and dutifully and waited to be told what to do next.

I have always felt that when it comes to creating a feeling of community spirit nothing can compare with group singing. The only question was what songs would a group of children who had grown up under Hitler know? Looking at them sitting there so stiff and silent, I knew the song I wanted to start with. The song of the Kinderfreunde (Friends of the Children), which is the youth organization of the labor movement. "We are young, the world is open," it begins. "Oh, you beautiful spacious world." The directress of Helvetia, Margot Cohn, was an excellent piano player and singer. We began to sing, Margot and I, hoping for the best, and some of the other adults picked it up. The children looked at us and looked at each other. And then, very timidly, one of the older children began singing. And then another. And another. This was four years after the labor movement had been crushed in Austria, you understand, and six years after it had been crushed in Germany, and still almost half these children knew the song. To me, this did more than simply break the ice. It told me that in the privacy of their own homes the old values and traditions had been passed on.

When the singing ended, I explained that they were now going to have a little snack to eat and then go outside with their counselors and play until lunch was ready.

A moment of silence. A somber-eyed, redheaded girl, about nine years old, raised her hand tentatively, and when I encouraged her to speak up she asked, in a sweet, tremulous little voice, "Are Jewish children also allowed to go into the park?"

We were annihilated. It was all we could do not to rush out and throw our arms around her. What made it even more annihilating was that every other eye was turned up toward me waiting just as anxiously for the answer.

When we did go outside, they just stood around waiting to be told what to do. They didn't ask any questions. They didn't even wander around aimlessly. They just followed whatever instructions or suggestions came their way. And so, at least, we knew what our first task was going to be. We were going to have to show them how to play. We were going to have to teach them how to be children.

With all future transports, I always tried to be at the station so that I could greet them in a way that would show them they were already a part of the Home. But whether I was on the scene or not, we would always have some of the other children come along to help the newcomers load their belongings onto the bus and, in the course of the conversation during the ride back, to let them know what we were like and what, in general, they could expect at the Home. In that way, the kids who had met them at the station would also have a sort of vested interest in showing their new friends around, and each of the newcomers would have an immediate contact within the established group. Someone to play with, you might say, and to show them how to play.

Once the operation was underway, new transports arrived so frequently that we opened the next Home, La Chesnaie (The Oaks), in Eaubonne three weeks later, and the fourth Home in the complex, Villa Les Tourelles (The Little Towers) in Soisy, three months after that. The next month, we opened three different castles down in the Creuse, a Department (county) in the middle of France, and from there it became a matter of buying them as fast as we could find them and having new directors and staff people trained.

4. Those Who Came

Despite this general policy of assimilating each incoming group of children into the established population, there were three groups so distinctive that they never lost their identity:

The Orthodox, which was the only group we didn't try to break up.

The Cubans, who were not Cubans at all but rather the children of middle-class Germans who had rented a luxury ship to take them to Cuba.

The Robinsoner, who were the children of political refugees who were already in France.

The Orthodox

The minor complaints that arose from time to time within the OSE came from those members who felt that while somebody should certainly be doing something about these children, it should be somebody else. To their way of thinking the OSE already had a job: taking care of convalescent children.

The charge most often leveled against me personally was that I was not paying enough attention to Jewish culture and tradition, which from their point of view was certainly true. I had only the haziest notion of the dietary laws and knew nothing at all about the ritual. On Passover, the Joint Distribution Committee had sent us some literature in both Yiddish and German, and that was the full extent of our observance. The fact that my own two boys had received no instruction at all in the Jewish religion was something so foreign to the Board members' experience that when it was suggested to me that the boys who were turning thirteen should have Bar Mitzvahs another member snorted: "Why do you bother to tell this goy about such things? He doesn't even know what a Bar Mitzvah is."

And that was how I learned that in the privacy of their offices I was referred to as The Goy.

My main source of strength came from people like the Baroness de Gunzbourg. Educationally, we were breaking new ground, and there was a segment of the wealthy, liberal Jewish community of France that was not only following what we were doing with great interest but was willing to back its interest with cash contributions. Although, to be sure, only after they had made it clear—in much the same manner as the Baroness—that they were acting out of humanitarian rather than narrowly Jewish impulses. Baron Guy de Rothschild and his wife, who represented the younger branch of the family, had contributed money for the upkeep of Helvetia but only with the stipulation that none of it could be used for "special privileges." All that ritualistic stuff, they had said, meant nothing to them.

At that, they knew a great deal more about it than we did. The young Baroness was from Austria, which made us great friends immediately. During the opening ceremony at Tourelles, where the Chief Rabbi of the Orthodox Community was among the guests, she whispered to Lene that she should not be serving cheese and meat hors d'oeuvres from the same platter since cheese was a form of milk and there was no sterner injunction in the dietary laws than the one against mixing milk and meat. Milk and meat during the same meal we knew about. The rest of it—cheese was really considered the same as milk?—was news to us.

Although one or two children in the first few groups had come from Orthodox families, the main Orthodox contingent was made up of about forty children who were transported in one solid group from an Orthodox orphanage in Frankfurt. The

rescue of these children was one of the great early accomplishments of the OSE. The large Orthodox community of Frankfurt
had been pushed into a tiny ghetto which had very quickly
become all but uninhabitable as the Orthodox Jews of the entire
surrounding countryside were shipped in to join them.

The Guy de Rothschilds were willing to put up the money to
support the Orthodox children with the same stipulation against
"special privileges," only this time I found those terms unac-
ceptable. This time the Board was treated to the spectacle of The
Goy arguing with the young Baroness that it was absolutely
essential to provide kosher food for these children, not merely to
make them feel welcome but as the best possible way to demonstrate our respect for the beliefs they and their families had
been suffering and dying for.

It wasn't a question of money for the Rothschilds, needless to
say. It was a matter of principle. We were finally able to hit upon
the right formula without compromising the basic principle by
agreeing that if we bought kosher food for everybody nobody
would be getting any special privileges.

As it turned out, we were completely mistaken in one of our
basic assumptions and rather arrogant in another. We had all
been assuming that the kosher meat was going to be more expensive and we discovered that, in Montmorency at least, it
wasn't. The arrogance came in thinking that the choice was
entirely ours. I wouldn't say these children weren't frightened
when they arrived; they were, after all, primarily between the
ages of eleven and thirteen with perhaps a few who were
younger. More than anything else, though, there was a group
consciousness which translated very easily into suspicion. But
that was to be expected. We had never before had a group of
children who were tied together by such a powerful common
background or had traveled together from the original point of
departure.

On the first day, everything went fine. Everybody ate kosher
food, and there was a great deal of joking about it among the
other children.

On the second day, two of the Orthodox girls volunteered for kitchen duty. I passed through the kitchen once and saw that they were in deep and earnest conversation. The next thing I knew I was being informed by a breathless messenger that the Orthodox children were not going to be eating dinner.

And why did they not want to eat?

"Because they say this is not kosher meat they're getting."

Well, that was a relief. I had been afraid it might be something serious. All I had to do was go down to the kitchen and set their minds at ease. I could guarantee that it was kosher meat, I told them, because we had bought only kosher meat. Their spokeswoman was a thirteen-year-old girl, Elfriede, a very good-looking girl who wore her hair in long braids. "Yes," she said. "We appreciate very highly that you tried very hard, but it is not kosher because you used the same pots in which you cooked the other food."

I apologized for my ignorance and promised to have a special set of pots by morning. Which, of course, solved every problem except the one facing us. Wasn't it possible, I asked, for them to eat the meat just this one time even though it had been cooked in the wrong pot?

"No," she said. "It is not. We will eat the vegetables but not the meat."

And then, seeing how upset I was, she said: "Don't worry so much. We didn't eat meat for three years in Germany because we could get no kosher meat there. One more day isn't going to bother us."

We were all very favorably impressed by them, and yet the more I thought about it, the more I could see that the same kind of firm stand in other areas of our communal form of life could give the director of a large and very diverse institution a great deal of trouble. More trouble than he was really looking for or, being such an obliging fellow, deserved.

We soon realized that mixing the Orthodox and non-Orthodox children was not going to work. For one thing, the Orthodox Community took a most understandable interest in them, and our philosophy of progressive education openly challenged their

completely authoritarian approach. To say nothing of the coeducational aspect of it. According to religious law, Orthodox boys
and girls are not supposed to mix together in any way, either in
school, at play or in the synagogue.

It was so impossible in so many ways that the obvious solution
was to have a special Home for the Orthodox. The Gunzbourgs
once again put up the money so that we could buy a beautiful
white brick-and-stone castle in Eaubonne, about three miles
from the most distant of our Homes in Montmorency. At about
the same time, the Rothschilds decided (for reasons which I am
sure had at least as much to do with being a Rothschild as with
the question of "special privileges" for the Orthodox) that they
would be much more comfortable if they supported one Home
completely and had full authority over it. Guy de Rothschild—
who, incidentally, was badly wounded in the early days of the
war—set up a Home in a castle in de la Guette, near Paris. We
organized it for them, trained a director for them, sent them one
hundred of our children, supplied the counselors and teachers
and, on certain special occasions, had the children visit back and
forth. I myself spent considerable time in de la Guette discussing
policy with the staff and contributing any other kind of advice
and assistance that might be requested. Once the Rothschild
imprimatur was on it, though, it was their Home, not ours. So
completely that although it was the twelfth OSE Home in everything except name I am still unable to regard it as anything
except a spiritual descendant.

(Not that I would want you to think we were opposed to the
creation of the Rothschild Home. Quite the contrary. We were
hoping, as they would say in Austria, to "make school" on it. The
name Rothschild means something in America, I know, but in
Europe it is a name that can part the oceans and still the waves. It
was our fond hope that another wealthy family or two might be
inspired by their example to underwrite a Children's Home in
their own name.)

Before the home at Eaubonne was opened, I thought it wise to
meet with representatives of the Orthodox Community of Paris,

led by Chief Rabbi Lange, and work out a formula that would be acceptable to both sides. (And also—now that the Rothschilds had removed themselves—to solicit their financial support.) Since we had to find a compromise between two philosophies that were essentially irreconcilable, I brought out the basic conflict immediately. "This is to be a Home for Orthodox children," I declared, "not an Orthodox Children's Home."

Few of the Board members could see the difference, but Rabbi Lange understood exactly what I was getting at. "It is all the difference between living as Orthodox and not living as Orthodox," he said, "and I cannot accept it."

"But I'm sorry," I said. "I cannot direct an Orthodox Children's Home because I'm not Orthodox."

When the Board still wasn't able to see why that should make any difference, I explained: "As things stand, I take my authority to educate these children from the Board of OSE and from the Ministry of Education in France. If it became an Orthodox Children's Home, I would be taking my authority from God."

And once again, Rabbi Lange was in complete agreement.

It would be impossible to conduct a system of progressive education under such conditions, I emphasized, not only because I would be obliged to follow all the Orthodox rules and rituals but because I—and every counselor and teacher who took his authority from me—would be acting as an agent of God. "I doubt whether it is really necessary to belabor the point that when the student is obliged to look upon his teacher as an agent of God, the spirit of free inquiry goes right out the window."

I was making my stand wholly on the issue of education. On everything else, as I was sure Rabbi Lange would be able to see, I would therefore be willing to compromise. He agreed that it had to be a Home for Orthodox children and I agreed to give the Orthodox Community the right to appoint the resident director, subject only to my approval. In day-to-day operations, all educational matters were to be under my direction and they were to refrain from offering any suggestions except by invitation. All other questions, such as the dietary laws and observance of holidays, were to be in the hands of the resident director—which meant in the hands of the Orthodox Community.

Three directors came and went very quickly, the first two because we could not abide their interference with our educational approach, and the third because he could no longer stand having everything he wanted to do vetoed by the Orthodox Community. The fourth was a woman, Mme. Koffsky, who came to us complete with husband. In many ways, we had more difficulty with her than with any of her predecessors, and yet I was reluctant to ask that she be removed because in the matter of education she had demonstrated a capacity for being influenced and because I despaired of getting anybody better.

Her worst quality was her strict schoolmistress air, which was completely at odds with everything around her. Her predecessor had been a beloved figure, Boris Ginodman, a French citizen who had taken part in the Russian Revolution. Although Boris was a teacher by profession, he had been everything in his rich and varied life from a master carpenter to a professional ballroom dancer. It had been, in fact, the Orthodox Community's violent reaction to his decision to instruct his boys and girls on the finer points of ballroom dancing that had caused him to throw up his hands and resign. I kept him on to teach the boys at Montmorency carpentry—although we already had an excellent carpentry instructor—because what better model could there be for boys whose future was so uncertain than an intellectual who could also work with his hands. Especially when it was someone like Boris, who demanded from them nothing less than perfection. He was an artist, really. I always wanted to make Boris the director of one of the new Homes, but he was rather lazy in some ways and he didn't really want to leave Montmorency. He loved the children, and they loved him. In the letters I have been receiving from the children for over thirty years, it is Boris who is mentioned most often.

The children, I must say, were surrounded by love, and though I wouldn't want to go so far as to say Mme. Koffsky didn't love them too, she was wholly incapable of communicating it. The children, unfortunately, were not so incapable of communicating their dislike of her.

The great revolt came during the *Drole de Guerre,* directly after Rabbi Lange, who had become the chief Jewish chaplain in the French army, had come out to Eaubonne in his army uniform to pay them a visit. It turned out to be a very unhappy one. Mme. Koffsky returned from driving the rabbi back to the station, took one look around and put in a frantic, semihysterical call to me. And with good reason. Her door had been kicked in, her bed had been turned upside-down, her furniture had been smashed and her clothes had been ripped to pieces.

By the time I arrived, the children had all become very good children again; little angels tucked safely into bed.

I called in the members of the council who had been elected under our Constitution to aid in the running of the Home. The only piece of unbroken furniture was a table, so I sat myself on top of it and let them gather around me in a semicircle and try to make me understand how they could have done such a thing. What had happened, it seemed, was that Rabbi Lange had lectured them severely about their behavior, expressing particular disappointment in the way they had been falling away from Orthodox strictures in regard to coeducational activities. "We were very much offended by what Dr. Lange told us," their leading spokesman said. "He is our spiritual leader. We believe in him and we want him to believe in us." Rabbi Lange had been given a completely misleading picture of what had been going on, they insisted, and the only person who could have given him such a picture was the directress. "So some of us got mad and broke into her room and wrecked her furniture."

I thought I knew exactly what the rabbi had been lecturing them about, although it pleases the participants to this very day to think that I didn't. There had been a Rosh Hashanah (New Year's) party at Les Tourelles a few days earlier, and the Orthodox had returned home at eleven, as was their practice, although a couple of hours of dancing still lay ahead for the others. The boys lived at one end of the castle in rooms of various sizes, and the girls lived at the other end in one large dormitory. The New Year's party had been a great release after the nights in the air raid shelter, and it was still too early for some of the gayer spirits to simmer down. After everybody was in bed, six of the big boys, covered by sheets, invaded the girls' dormitory—a monster ghost with three boys under one sheet and three one-man ghosts. Each of the ghosts gave off a hopefully unearthly glow from a flashlight being held under his sheet, and all of them were all making the moaning and howling sounds that are well known to be the normal form of nocturnal ghostly discourse. And if that weren't enough to make any normal thirteen- or fourteen-year-old girl's blood run cold, the monster ghost was clutching a dummy that had been whipped together out of wood and rags and was easily identifiable by the tassel pinned to its head as a female toward whom no good was presumably intended.

Some of the girls screamed, which was really the only decent thing for them to do after the boys had gone to all that trouble, some of them giggled—and what kind of a way is that, Mme. Koffsky had undoubtedly asked the rabbi, for Orthodox boys and girls to act?

The Orthodox boys and girls gathered around me apparently felt they were in trouble enough without telling me about that earlier escapade, which was perfectly all right with me. I didn't care what the reason was and I wanted to keep on not caring. The only issue here was that they had taken the law into their own hands. Like Nazis.

"This is intolerable," I told them. "This is the method of Hitler!" If they had a grievance against the directress, I reminded them, they also had a duly elected council through which they could have presented it to her. If they had not been able to find satisfaction there they were then entitled to lodge a complaint against her with me, on either a formal or informal basis. If they had done that, they might have been able to find out what had really been said to the rabbi. Instead, they had chosen to resort to the tactics of the Hitler Youth. All right. "Since you did not see fit to use the democratic methods of protest that are available to

you under the Constitution, all your democratic rights and privileges are suspended and all your elected councils and committees are dissolved." Indefinitely.

The children argued strenuously. It did no good. They had
scorned democratic methods and therefore they had lost the use
of them. Actions have consequences. Evil actions have evil
consequences.

Mme. Koffsky didn't consider that to be any punishment at
all, as I discovered the next morning when the OSE Board
informed me that she had appealed to them over my head. They
were in complete agreement with her that some "real punishment" would have to be meted out to the culprits.

What did she mean by punishment? I asked her. "What do you
want me to do, hang them? Tell me, what do you think we should
do with them?"

No, she didn't want to hang them. She wanted the ringleaders
to be sent away.

"What! Do you think I would send German children who are
alone here—who have no parents—do you really think I would
send them away?" I am usually a professional when it comes to
dealing with disciplinary problems, but it was impossible to keep
the anger and contempt out of my voice. "Where should we send
them, back to Germany? Is that what you want?"

No, that wasn't what she wanted either. "You can send them
to one of the other Homes, for all I care. I don't care where they
go as long as they're thrown out of here."

I had never been so appalled in my life. "That you, the director
of the Orthodox Home, would want to send an Orthodox boy to
a non-Orthodox institution!"

It was not the relationship between Mme. Koffsky and one
boy or the whole group of children that was involved anymore. It
was the relationship, so suddenly and nakedly revealed as to be
embarrassing, between Mme. Koffsky and Orthodoxy. Her
husband was not really that Orthodox. He was only as Orthodox
as she made him be, which meant that he was pretty Orthodox
when she was looking at him. What did it say about the roots of

her commitment if out of sudden pique or, even, justifiable anger she would demand that the Orthodox life be taken away from young boys who had been placed in her care? What kind of an Orthodoxy could it be for her if she used it as a way to punish people? She punished her husband by forcing him to observe, and she would punish these boys by preventing them from observing.

Nor was she alone. When the Board requested a meeting with the Orthodox Community, the Orthodox leaders supported their directress. More, I suspected, to show me where the true fault lay, than because they agreed with her. I was the famous Papanek who didn't believe in punishment and I could see now where such foolish ideas led, couldn't I? They were right in one respect. I didn't like punishment for the sake of punishment under any circumstances. I also thought the punishment that was being asked for in this instance was both idiotic and wicked. All I could do was insist that I had punished them enough by taking away their democratic rights, and nobody else seemed to think that was any punishment at all. The Board laid down an ultimatum. One boy would have to go as an example—Friedman, the boy who had kicked down the door.

I could lay down ultimatums too. The moment the first boy was taken out of Eaubonne I would resign.

The whole tempest came to an abrupt end two days later when the Board members, who had come down to conduct their own investigation, discovered that the children were absolutely shattered by the revocation of their democratic rights. But while the ultimatums had been hanging there, side by side, some of the Orthodox children—including all the ringleaders—had become so outraged at learning what Mme. Koffsky wanted to do that they themselves were asking to be transferred.

"You will stay right where you are," I told them. After all they had suffered did they really believe I would permit them to turn their back on everything they believed in out of some childish spite against a teacher? Was it possible, I wanted to know, that they would permit themselves to be defeated so easily? In addition to which I wanted *them* to know that this attitude of self-righteousness didn't sit very well on them. "If it is maybe not such an Orthodox thing your directress wants to do to you," I told them, "it was maybe not such an Orthodox thing you were doing when you broke her door down."

Even with those who insisted that they were not so Orthodox anymore, I could not bring myself to permit them to make that formal a break. And while it may have been nothing more on my part than the respect the nonreligious man somehow feels he owes the more deeply committed, I think it was something more. Their parents were still my clients. Their parents were dead. Where did I go for permission?

On the other hand, it was always understood that any child who decided he would like to become Orthodox would be transferred to Eaubonne on request. About a dozen did.

On the whole, the Orthodox children, accustomed as they were to the solidarity of the ghetto, found it very difficult at first to adapt themselves to a larger community. We tried to give them status on their own terms—and also fill a need of our own—by having them organize, and indeed conduct, the religious celebrations for the other Homes, and having them invite the non-Jewish children to their own services at Eaubonne. I had never heard of the Oneg Shabbat, which welcomes the arrival of the Sabbath with dancing and singing, and when they told me it was celebrated at Eaubonne every Friday evening, I asked them to organize it for all the other Homes. It became a permanent fixture and an enormous success.

Despite everything, the Orthodox children were always the most confident of their ultimate triumph and the least scarred by their persecution. They knew who they were and they knew what they were being persecuted for. They did feel different, they did feel special, they did feel that they had been chosen by God to fulfill some Almighty purpose. In one sense, they didn't have to win over anybody or anything. They won by *being*.

On another level, however, there was an overcompensating drive in them that made them want to prove to the other children that even though they walked around in skullcaps and prayer shawls and lived by the Book, they could hold their own in more worldly pursuits. When it came to the classes in agriculture, their vegetables always seemed to grow bigger and better than anybody else's. When they went to the workshops they worked hard to show they could become competent carpenters and shoemakers and brickmakers. And athletes. Our own "Olympics" were held very shortly after the Great Revolt, and with Eaubonne having been shorn of its representation on the Sports Committee it became necessary to do a bit of legalistic maneuvering and allow them to be represented by one of the teachers so that they would be eligible to compete. Not that we thought we were doing them any great favor, you understand. The Orthodox had never played soccer in their lives before coming to Montmorency, and since we really had some good players on the other teams everybody expected them to be the pushovers. To the astonishment of everyone except perhaps the Orthodox boys themselves they got every break in every game and won the championship. It was enough to make a believer of you.

The Cubans

By the time the Cubans came to us they had been on the front page of the world's newspapers for three weeks and had been wandering around the ocean on the German luxury cruiser, *St. Louis,* for five. Aboard the ship were 907 men, women and children who had been granted exit visas from Germany upon the surrender of all their material possessions. Some of them had come directly out of concentration camps and many of the others had been in concentration camps earlier. Their passports—stamped "J" for Jew—carried the notation that they could not return to Germany. After the Cuban government had refused to permit them to land, every other country, including the United States, turned a deaf ear to their pleas on the grounds that it could not be expected to make good the promise of another government. They were, then, 907 penniless souls adrift upon the empty seas, with no country willing to offer them refuge and no country to which they could return.

Our own interest in the *St. Louis,* in the beginning, had been largely educational. With new shifts of children coming in weekly, it would have been impractical to set up a firm curriculum of study even if my own pedagogic instincts had carried in that direction. We had begun, instead, by dividing the entire student population into three groups according to age for classes on "general culture and social studies," a wide-ranging but very tightly integrated series of discussions in which as many academic "subjects" as possible were extracted from one central topic.

In order to encourage student participation, the topic of the week was drawn from their own activities or common experience or, where it was relevant, from the headlines of the day. The sinking of the American submarine *Squalus* off the coast of New England was perfect. We began—geographically—by charting the distance between us and the sunken submarine. We then computed the quantities of oxygen that would be necessary to sustain the trapped men. This exercise in simple mathematics uncovered such a prevalent weakness that classes in math were scheduled on the spot. The dramatic rescue of more than half the crew by the use of the diving bell—the first time a diving bell had ever been used for that purpose—led quite naturally into a discussion of water displacement and hydrostatic pressure, and to courses in both elementary and advanced physics which were embraced with enthusiasm. Through it all, the courage and tenacity of the trapped sailors remained the main focus of our interest. We were citizens of the world and we retained our humanity. The parallel that existed between the sailors and ourselves required no special laboring on my part. Nor did the lesson that could be drawn from it: However desperate the situation, brave men do not give up hope.

The dismal story of the *St. Louis* broke in the headlines just as the inspiring story of the *Squalus* was running its course. And here, of course, the parallel was even closer. The passengers were, by and large, middle-class Jewish merchants, businessmen and professional men who already had their visas and affidavits to the United States. They had been so anxious to get out of Germany while they were waiting for their quota numbers to come up that they had been more than willing to accede to the demands of the Hamburg-American (Hapag) Line that they buy round-trip tickets to make the one-way trip.

The *St. Louis* was not the first ship of the Hapag to make that voyage; not a few of the passengers already had relatives in Cuba waiting for them. The *St. Louis* became the ship to go sailing blindly into its appointment with history because there had been a shift of power within the government of Cuba, and the new President refused to honor their visas on the grounds that they had been obtained illegally.

We picked up the story for our lectures on general culture while the ship was still waiting outside Havana for permission to land. To get our bearings, geographically, we began, again, by charting the voyage of the *St. Louis* from Hamburg to Havana. We then explained how a group of islands in the Caribbean had come to be called the West Indian Archipelago, an explanation which took us, in turn, directly into the story of the discovery of America. Once the historical background had been covered, we were able to move on to the current inhabitants of the islands, the structure of their societies and the state of their culture. From there, we explored the possibilities that existed for our children to emigrate to that part of the New World themselves and, as a natural extension, the ways in which they could begin even now to prepare themselves. By popular demand, classes in English and Spanish were started immediately.

During those first few days, the passengers didn't seem to be in anything approaching the peril of the submarine men. Negotiations were in progress to clear up whatever legal difficulties surrounded the visas and, it seemed to us, if Cuba wasn't willing to let them in, why would they be negotiating?

In point of fact, the passengers of the *St. Louis,* like those who had preceded them to Cuba, had bought the visas from Hapag along with their tickets at a price which seemed to fluctuate according to what the traffic would bear. I heard of individual cases later where as much as 1,000 marks ($400) had been paid. Superficially, then, the Cuban authorities were on sound legal grounds; the visas had been bought and paid for. Realistically, they were engaged in a profound and shameless betrayal. The trafficking in visas had not occurred between the passengers and some minor functionary at the consulate; it was a deal between Hapag and the Cuban government. And a good deal it had been for everybody. Thousands of Jews had been able to get out of Germany, the Hapag had profited mightily from the full passenger loads and the round-trip tickets, and the visa money had been spread around among high government officials in Cuba and Germany.

The passengers from the *St. Louis* were not being permitted to land because the Cuban government, at the very highest level, had upped the ante. To back them up they had the most powerful of all economic arguments: the Law of Supply and Demand. In the six months following the Night of the Broken Crystal the flight from Germany had reached such epidemic proportions that refuge, which had hitherto been only a luxury item on the world market, had become an item of scarcity. Four days after the *St. Louis* left Hamburg, the British had cut off the main port of entry by announcing that immigration into Palestine was to be severely curtailed at once and completely stopped in five years, a policy shift which was being enforced with such enthusiasm that by the time the *St. Louis* reached Cuba, a solid barrier of refugee ships lay outside the three-mile limit. With Palestine closed, a domino effect had come into play. One after another, the gates had crashed shut all over the world.

Cuba wasn't closing itself off. The new leaders simply wanted to renegotiate the deal in light of the more favorable economic indicators. Not that they were suffering from any delusions about the prospect of extorting more money out of the passengers. The negotiations were taking place with the American Joint Distribution Committee, with whom the original arrangement for using Cuba as a way station to the United States had been made. The escalated terms called for "the Joint" to post a $500 surety bond for every passenger, with the private understanding that the "bond" was never to be returned and an even more private understanding that those officials who were in a position to be most helpful were also in a position to become independently wealthy. All the Joint would be buying for its half-million, pending a satisfactory payoff, was the right to have the passengers interned in a concentration camp on the Isle of Pines.

Why these negotiations failed—how indeed they could be permitted to fail—is a matter that will be taken up later in an entirely different context. Suffice for now to say that after the *St. Louis* had been tossing outside the harbor for six days the Cuban government ordered it to leave. For the next two days, while the negotiations were grinding on to their final collapse, the ship cruised up and down the coast of Florida. Telegrams of encouragement and promised aid came in to the passengers. Telegrams of desperation went out from a hastily formed Passengers Committee to Franklin D. Roosevelt and other American leaders. For all the good it did them, they might as well have floated their messages out in a bottle.

At last, with the food and fuel running short, the Hapag ordered the captain to bring his ship back to Germany. The captain, a remarkable man who had come by degrees to identify wholly with the plight of his passengers, defied his orders. For three days he sailed in a circle to give the Jewish organizations around the world as much time as possible to find some country, somewhere, that would take them in.

Even as the ship was steaming along the coast of Florida, I was saying along with everybody else that Roosevelt would never fail us. The *St. Louis* was scheduled to proceed on to New York anyway to pick up passengers for a Caribbean cruise. Eighty percent of the passengers were on the quota list to enter the United States. If Cuba didn't relent, the solution was obvious. The United States would, of course, waive the waiting period and permit them to enter immediately. And yet, all the time the feeling in my little finger was that the children were going to end up with us. No, it wasn't a premonition. It was more like a feeling of historical inevitability. In a time adrift, these were children who were adrift; their course and ours were coming too close together not to reach an intersection. Although my confidence in Roosevelt remained unshaken, I found myself asking Gourwitch, the international secretary of OSE, to contact the Joint just to remind them that our facilities were available and we were eager to help.

A week later, after Roosevelt and everybody else had failed us, I received a telegram from Morris Troper, the European director of Joint, asking me how many children we were prepared to take. By that time, Hitler had turned the wanderings of the *St. Louis* into such a propaganda bonanza that it had become a matter of overriding importance to settle all the passengers somewhere, quickly, not only for their own sake but for all the Jews of Europe. "The hypocritic democracies criticize us for the way we treat the Jews," the Germans were crowing. "But when they themselves are put to the test, it can be seen that they don't want the Jews any more than we do."

Troper, who was headquartered in Paris, had managed to coax and cajole the governments of Belgium, France, Holland and, finally, England into making an attempt to work out some formula for distributing the passengers among their respective countries. While the details were being ironed out, the *St. Louis* was directed to head toward Antwerp.

Eventually, a series of agreements was worked out with each of the four countries whereby the adults would be interned in detention camps—detention camps were a growth industry in those days—or have their support guaranteed by either the JDC or a relative who was a citizen of the sheltering country. It was the children who were the final stumbling block. None of the countries *liked* the idea of putting people in concentration camps. They had no stomach at all for locking up children, and even less stomach for taking them away from their parents.

Humanitarian considerations aside, children with nothing to do can cause trouble. Inside a camp or outside. And grow up in a very few years to cause even more trouble.

Well ... if we weren't in business to handle precisely that problem, what were we in business for?

With the *St. Louis* already docked at Antwerp, the French government finally accepted Gourwitch's assurances that we would be able to take care of whatever children came along with their allotment. Once the deadlock had been broken the other countries yielded too.

Dr. Gourwitch phoned me in high glee: "You have sixty new children. Do you think you might want to take them in?"

As far as the morale of the children already at the Home was concerned, the call didn't come a moment too soon. The jubilation that had followed the reading of Troper's telegram had given way during the long delay to a mixture of cynicism and despair. Their favorite refrain during those days, picked up from the adults around them, went: "Nobody wants us. All countries are closed to us. And now even France. So how can you complain about the Nazis?"

And still, it is interesting to note, there was very little criticism of the United States and none at all directed toward Franklin D. Roosevelt. Never mind that when the United States was finally heard from it was in the form of a message to the German government reiterating an earlier request that no more refugees be permitted to leave the country without valid papers. Roosevelt remained above politics and beyond criticism. Our faith in him was that blind, unquestioning faith which knows only its own need to believe.

From Antwerp, the 227 passengers who had been allocated to France were placed on an overnight freighter to Boulogne. Gourwitch, Millner (the French secretary of the OSE), and I met them at the pier with mixed emotions. Very mixed. If it was our happy assignment to welcome them to French soil, it had also fallen to us to inform them of the harsh terms on which they were being accepted. All the adults were to intern themselves in a camp at Le Mans, a good one hundred miles west of Paris, and pledge that they would make no attempt to leave. Those who had children would not be allowed to come to Montmorency to visit them, and while there was no such restriction against the children making the trip to Le Mans, they would have to visit their parents not in the city but inside the camp.

To give them one final day together, we had reserved all the rooms that were available in the best hotel in the city. After we had finished breakfast, Gourwitch and Millner remained in the hotel restaurant with the adults to break the bad news to them. The restaurant remains with me in all its splendor—a grand and spacious place with hanging chandeliers—because I can still remember thinking that it seemed to be the fate of these people to be tormented amidst the grandest of surroundings. My job was to gather the children together in the meeting room down the hall and explain the ground rules to them. And I did it badly. We had decided on the way to Boulogne that it would be easier on the children if I could persuade them to want to join the Home voluntarily before I made it clear that they would not be able to remain in France under any other conditions. A terrible idea, even if I had been able to pull it off. As it was, I found myself stressing the attractions of the Home so heavily and skirting the other part of it so delicately that it came out sounding as if they could come or not as they pleased.

One of the oldest boys in the group, a fifteen-year-old named John Windmuller, was quite clearly their leader. "Let us understand what you are saying," he interrupted. "Do we have a choice to stay with our parents or do we have to go to this children's institution?"

"You have to go to the children's institution," I said.

"Then why have you been trying to make it seem as if we have a choice when you know that we have none?"

"I guess it was because that's what I wanted you to think," I confessed. You can't be dishonest with children at any time. To take the odor of dishonesty upon oneself as the very first impression can be fatal.

John Windmuller was an amazing boy. He had managed to

cross the border after the Night of the Broken Crystal by performing a professional job of forgery on his passport and had
lived in Holland for six months in what amounted to a concentration camp. He had rejoined his family on the *St. Louis* when
the ship stopped off at Boulogne, the same city to which he had
now been returned, thirty-seven days later. Having been away
from his parents for so long, it was very painful for him to have to
leave them again. Having spent six months as a man in a concentration camp, it was equally painful for him to agree to live in
a children's Home.

I didn't know his history then, of course. I only knew that if
John Windmuller was against me, they would all be against me.
Fortunately, as I would have occasion to observe many times
through the years, he had not only a brilliant mind but the rare
ability to see what had to be done and the even rarer ability to
proceed at once to do it.

"If we have no choice," he said, accepting my apology without
a backward glance, "then we have no choice. We don't want to
go. But we will go."

Only one girl insisted that she was going to remain with her
parents, even if they had to return to the boat and be taken back
to Germany. By the next morning, she too was fully prepared to
accept the inevitable.

We were very fortunate in another way. The other children
eased the transition for them far better than even the best trained
or most openhearted adults could have. They had reached out to
them all the way from Montmorency by sending their full ration
of chocolates and candy to Boulogne with me, along with instructions not to pass them out until we had boarded the train
and were on our way back to Paris. At Helvetia, a tremendous
welcoming reception awaited the newcomers, complete with
songs and pictures and pageants. Everybody participated and
everything was geared to the theme spelled out on the huge,
hand-painted poster that hung from the rafters above the circular staircase: FORGET THE PAST AND FOLLOW US INTO A BETTER
FUTURE.

The hit of the day was the band from the Petite Colonie. The youngest children played only one-tone instruments, cymbals, tambourines, drums and bells, and so musically their performance was not impressive. But it was the little ones themselves who captivated the Cubans with their well-scrubbed brightness and their eagerness to please. The little ones, in turn, were so awed by the sheer size of their new comrades that they gathered around the bigger boys and girls to ask how old they were, and their eyes opened wide in unabashed wonder when they heard there were some who had reached the ripe old age of fourteen or fifteen.

The Cubans, incidentally, were called exactly that—the *Kubaner*—from the very first, and though they didn't like it and never became completely reconciled to it that was the way the others thought of them. The staff had already picked it up from the children by the time they arrived, and there was not a thing that could be done about it. Thirty years later, I met the daughter of the man who had been the head of the Passengers Committee and discovered that the children who went to England were called the Cubans by their English playmates, too.

The only problem that confronted me personally was, as usual, housing. With the opening of the new Home at Eaubonne we had embarked upon the kind of rebuilding job at Helvetia we would have liked to do originally if there hadn't been such a rush to get the place ready. Since Eaubonne wasn't prepared for complete occupancy either, we were so tight for space that the children who were still in Helvetia had volunteered to move into tents and turn their rooms over to the Cubans. As much as their generosity touched me, enough work had been done at both Homes by the time we returned so that nobody had to pitch any tents on the lawn—which I suspect came as a terrible disappointment to them. The boys moved right into Helvetia, and the girls were sent to Eaubonne while the wooden Annex alongside the big house was being remodeled for them. It was an arrangement the girls found considerably less than enchanting:

> None of us had any Orthodox background and we resented everything from the Kosher food, which didn't taste any different than the non-kosher food, to the prayers before and the prayers

after. We resented everything, and made ourselves and every-body else miserable. (How we pestered you to take us away from there to be in Helvetia where the rest of our group was!) Once we moved into the little house in Helvetia, I think we were very happy and I always felt especially after growing up there was nothing better that could have happened to me.

The Cubans, with their intellectual backgrounds, were bril-liant students and they quickly became the political leaders of the institution.

One last thing must be said before I leave the story of the *St. Louis.* Dr. Brutzkus was always convinced that the survival of the European Jew lay elsewhere than in the Western world. In fact, he had been in contact for a long time with some of his old friends in the Russian government about the establishment of a colony near Siberia that would ultimately absorb 1,000,000 people. When that project fell through, he turned his sights southward toward Ethiopia, whose exiled emperor Haile Se-lassie was perfectly willing, in the event of his return to his throne, to establish a colony for 600,000 to 1,000,000 Jews. After the crisis brought on by the closing of Palestine—at the very time that the *St. Louis* was wandering around in the middle of the ocean—Brutzkus asked me whether I would be willing, if events allowed, to go to Ethiopia long enough to set up a school system. Under the circumstances, it was impossible for me to say no although, very frankly, I felt that Ethiopia was an impossible solution for middle-class people from mostly urban back-grounds. Like everybody else, all my thoughts were turned to —and attuned to—the modern, expanding countries of North and South America.

And that, looking back, was possibly the greatest mistake that was made. Once the emergency surrounding the *St. Louis* was over, whatever interest existed in the colony in Ethiopia faded away. Haile Selassie's offer to provide asylum was never known to the millions of European Jews who might very well have found Ethiopia a more attractive alternative than those of us who presumed to speak for them imagined.

There was yet another reason why it would have been better if the agreement between the four countries had never been made. Before the Belgian government agreed to allow them to dock, the younger bloods aboard the *St. Louis* had ·formed a sabotage committee. Their objective was to take over the ship or set it afire in order to force the Law of the Sea to do for them what the conscience of the civilized world had shown itself so unwilling to do: mobilize a rescue operation. The only reason they hadn't forced the issue was because the captain had given his word that he would not take them back to Germany. More remarkable still, their trust had not been misplaced. It was unbelievable, but a German sea captain had entered into a conspiracy with his first officer and his chief engineer to scuttle his own ship. Their planning had to be done in complete secrecy. It was not even considered safe to let the leaders of the sabotage committee in on it, because the firemen, like the firemen on most German passenger ships, were Gestapo.

As the ship was approaching the North Sea, the captain and his first officer charted their course so that they would enter the English Channel at low tide during the night and run the ship aground on one of the many sandbars between Dover and Plymouth. Once the ship was on the sandbar, the chief engineer, who had displayed unsuspected talents as a conspirator, was going to blow one of the engines (which would give the captain a convincing alibi for having veered off his original course) and set it afire (which would keep the Gestapo men occupied). The tugboats out of Plymouth would have to wait for both daylight and high tide before they could pull the ship free. By that time the chief engineer would have worked so furiously to "fix" his damaged engines that only one of them would be operating, and that one so faintly that it would be necessary for him to request permission to limp to an emergency port, as he was fully entitled to do under the Law of the Sea, while also making it clear to the British authorities that he would not be able to move the ship at all until the passengers had been removed.

There was the genius of the plan. Once the passengers were on English soil, the onus would be squarely on the British government to either grant political asylum, in accordance with its long tradition, or to take the unthinkable action of herding them onto a British ship at gunpoint and shipping them back to whatever fate awaited them in Germany.

You never know, of course, what would have happened if you had walked the untrod path. As it was, events could hardly have been more disastrous. Of the passengers who were allocated to Belgium and Holland, only the merest handful survived. All who went to Holland and most who went to Belgium were placed in detention camps, and after the German army had overrun the Lowlands they were shipped, sooner or later, to the extermination camps. Those few who did manage to flee before the German armies were either trampled under the onrushing juggernaut or died on the beaches of Dunkirk. That's right, Dunkirk. The long, tormented journey for many of the passengers of the *St. Louis* came to an end at the water's edge on June 5, 1940, a year to the day after they had been ordered out of the harbor at Havana. They pleaded repeatedly for space in the armada of small civilian boats that was evacuating the British and French armies. The last words that many of them heard before they were cut down in the final cross fire between the Germans and the British was that there was no room in the boats for any of them.

As for those whom we had greeted at the pier in Boulogne, they didn't fare much better. Most of them ended up in the concentration camp at Gurs, which under the Vichy government became the doorway to Auschwitz. And because the Cubans were generally older than the other children, a disproportionate percentage of those who were taken from our Homes after the fall of France and placed on freight cars for Auschwitz were the children of the *St. Louis*.

Those who went to England fared best of all, I suppose, and even they didn't do that well. The ultimate destination for almost all of them was still the United States. With the outbreak of war, the passenger schedules were cut back so severely that it became impossible to book passage when their quota numbers came up.

With the invasion scare that followed the fall of France, all the men from the *St. Louis* were interned on the Isle of Man, not as Jews but—if you can bear it—as German nationals; that is to say, as enemy aliens. More than a year passed before the eighty-odd refugees from the *St. Louis* who had become eligible for immigration into the United States were allowed to book passage on the *Arandora Star,* a converted troopship that was carrying prisoners of war and other German nationals to Canada. Two days out of England, the ship was torpedoed and everybody aboard was lost.

Of the nine hundred passengers who were aboard the *St. Louis* when it sailed out of Hamburg harbor with its colorful streamers flapping and the ship's band playing the traditional German song of leavetaking, it is extremely doubtful if as many as one hundred lived to see the end of the war. It was as if something had gone so terribly wrong the moment they set foot upon the luxury ship that nothing could ever set it right again.

The Robinsoner

This was a small group of about thirty, all of them children of Social Democratic refugees, and almost half of them Gentiles. They came to us directly from a summer camp that had been run by the Red Falcons, the worldwide organization of Social Democrats for children between the ages of twelve and fourteen. The only significance to their name—and unlike the Cubans it was the name by which they preferred to be known—was that the camp happened to be located in the little French town of Plessy Robinson, near Paris.

At the heart of the group were fifteen boys and girls (my own son Gustav among them) whose parents had been leaders of the Socialist party in Austria. They had been brought together the previous winter by Marianne Pollack, the wife of the former editor of the *Arbeiter Zeitung* (the largest Socialist newspaper in Vienna), and a figure of prominence in her own right in the journalistic and political life of the movement. I had asked her to do so shortly after I took over the Petite Colonie, ostensibly in my capacity as chairman of the Socialist Youth of Austria but also, I must confess, so that Gustl, who had only recently turned twelve, could meet boys and girls of his own age and interests.

How should I describe the Red Falcons? It would not be fair to dismiss it as nothing more than an instrument of political indoctrination. Nor would it be entirely accurate to say that political orientation was not the fundamental reason for its existence. Perhaps it would be best to let Gustl describe it himself, as he did in a long autobiographical essay he wrote for his English class at Haaren High School a few months after we arrived in New York:

> I went away from our first meeting in high spirits. Marianne had turned out to be very nice and had discussed with us our plans for the future of our group. We had decided to meet every Thursday and to make excursions on Sunday. Those days were the days I was waiting for during the rest of the week. With every meeting we knew each other better and better till a certain place had unconsciously been assigned to everyone. Whenever somebody had to talk about a certain subject Herbert was chosen, he really was the spiritual leader of our group whenever Marianne was not present. Around him formed a circle [of four others] to which I also belonged. Although we were really a minority, through our matter of fact attitude toward continued discussions, we made the rest, although unconsciously, feel that they were not grown-up if they were not of our opinion. . . . Still, we all loved those weekly discussions and songs and our excursions. And we steadily built to improve ourselves and our community. A proposal to spend the summer vacation together in a little town near Paris was enthusiastically accepted. . . .

It may be worthwhile to compare the interests and activities of these highly politicized children with those of the Cubans, who were to become their great rivals for leadership at the OSE Homes.

> At Robinson, we spent the best summer vacation we ever had. Our day began theoretically at seven in the morning when we were roused. Naturally nobody got up immediately and it was a quarter to eight when we finally assembled in shorts to make our

morning exercises, after which we had roll calls, we sang a few
songs and the one that was leading it for the day, we changed
every day, spoke a few words; somebody's birthday, something
happening in the world or the anniversary of a date in the fight for
freedom gave the topic.

Not that the activities were always so overpoweringly inspira-
tional. "Once Madeleine and Bruno had stayed at Helmut's bed,
who was sick, to keep him company while the rest of us played
and another time Gerhart had had a fight. Both of these were
mentioned during roll calls."

The high point of the summer came with the decision to put on
a play of their own creation—"the idea struck like a bomb-
shell"—for the entertainment and edification of their parents and
a few privileged guests. If the form the play would take became a
matter for heated discussion, the theme was never in doubt. "We
finally decided upon a speaking chorus on the flight of twelve
refugees from Germany and a play titled 'The Dream of a
Dictator.' In the latter, the figures he [the dictator] was dreaming
of appeared as shadows on a screen. This we had to rehearse in
the dark. We therefore went into the woods, after sunset, and put
linen sheets between two trees. Then illuminating it with pocket
lamps we rehearsed until late in the evening. Our performance
was a great success. Really the climax of our vacation.

"One day we were having a game in the woods. When I
returned, all excited and worked up, I expected to find the rest
arguing about the mistakes made in the game so far and the
chances of winning for either side. But when I entered the room
everybody was silent and downcast. Cheerily I remarked: 'Well,
what's the matter, anybody die?' As the only answer Herbert
gave me the paper. One glance at the headlines and all my
cheerfulness was gone. I was as downcast as the rest. 'HITLER
AND STALIN MAKE PACT.' That evening we were in bed as soon as
possible. After a short goodnight we were all asleep. Funny how
a certain state of mind can influence your body. Never before
and, up to now, never after have I been in such despair."

It is not really so surprising that children who had been forced to leave their own countries because of the political activities of their parents would have a healthy regard for the influence political events can have on their lives. And yet, for children of that age to have the political acumen to be able to see at a glance that with his back door protected Hitler would very soon be attacking the Western democracies was remarkable. Remarkable enough, at any rate, to put them miles ahead of some of the more respected political journalists around the world.

It was at the Villa Les Tourelles, which had already been rented but which opened one day after the declaration of war, that the Robinsoner boys and the Cuban boys first came into contact with each other. They were both such extraordinary groups of children, in such completely different ways, that they had only to look at each other to start battling. The Cubans might not be Orthodox Jews, but they were conscious, and even self-conscious, Jews with what I would call "a Jewish intelligence." The Robinsoners' contact with Jewish life had been so limited that they had only a minimal sense of their identity as Jews. "Matzohs at Passover," a Robinson girl wrote later. "And for some of us the first matzohs of our lives. Very strange, like cardboard but not so bad with butter and jam."

In one very important way, however, the Robinsoner were very much like the Orthodox. They knew who they were and why they were in exile. They were anti-Fascists. Many of their parents had fought in the Spanish Civil War, and most of them had been in the Underground. All were totally committed Socialists who had transmitted to their children a vision of social justice through political action. The Robinsoner were, one and all, internationalists and revolutionaries. They were burning to make a new and better world.

The parents of the Cubans, on the other hand, had identified completely with Germany and its institutions. They had rushed to serve the Fatherland in World War I. They were inordinately proud of the Jews who had served Germany well in the arts and sciences. They were, in short, archetypical of the middle- and upper-class German Jews whose proudest boast had always been that they were not Jews who happened to be living in Germany but Germans who happened to be Jews. Their children were middle-class, sheltered and bourgeois to the bone. The fix they were in was that they still couldn't understand how the Germans could have turned on them so completely.

The conflict can be shown most clearly, I think, through the girls. The Robinson girls came to us directly from the camp, as brown and hard as hickory nuts. The relationship they had established with their boys was based on a pact of frankness and equality. The Cuban girls were conventionally feminine, conventionally flirtatious and utterly innocent of politics. Amidst the turmoil on the *St. Louis,* puppy-love romances had sprung up which were being played out, in one way or the other, in Montmorency. The following excerpt is from the *Diary and Remembrances* of a thirteen-year-old Robinson girl. As valuable as it is for its description of both the crisis atmosphere under which the Robinsoners came to us and the almost instinctive hostility that sprang up between them and the *St. Louis* girls, I cherish it mostly for the way in which the little girl keeps peeking through the political thickets:

> Every day [at Robinson] we went out through the iron garden gate of the Youth Hostel to look at the posters. There were many of them: one class after the other of the French army was being called up but still the war had not been declared. People came all day long to look at the notices. We were told that our parents had decided we should go as a group to the OSE Kinderheim that Gustl's father was running somewhere north of Paris. One day, one of the counselors from there had walked all across Paris in his heavy boots, on his day off, to visit us in Robinson. A few days later big black taxis came for us. A whole bunch of us got into each taxi with our stuff and rode all the way through Paris sticking our heads out of the open roofs of the taxis and singing. Herbert was in the same taxi as I, and I was delighted, but only secretly. When we heard that only the boys would stay in Tourelles, we were terribly upset. The group could not be broken up, it was impossible, and there would only be the few of us girls among so many strangers. We promised each other to keep the solidarity of the group. We got beds near each other in the small annex of the main building at Helvetia, where the older girls stayed. Upstairs,

but not in the same room as the really big girls. . . . But of course, the group had broken up and our boys were not with us. We were just a small remnant of something important, and we tried to hold our own, but the real fight between Robinsoner and Kubaner was in Tourelles. You could tell it from the tones of contempt between us and them. The Kubaner did not know anything about politics—unimaginable! Politics was the most important thing, and if you didn't know it, you didn't count. They had bourgeois ideas about boys too, and the big girls laughed at the way we felt about our boys. They didn't know about friendship between girls and boys, in the same way we had discussed this in Robinson.

We got back at the big girls by putting things in their beds, folding their sheets up wrong, and rushing in at night with sheets and flashlights to scare them. But they only laughed. In games we could be good in a way which they weren't, they didn't care about ballgames with the same sort of passion.

Medical examination by Lene and shots, and X-rays. One girl fainted from the shot; what a coward, but then she did not know much about life, she wore a corset, so what could you expect? Regular social dancing for the big ones every week, very bourgeois but since it meant our boys were coming over, we said all right.

Looking back, I would say there was more hostility on their part than ours, because we were just a bunch of immature kids who didn't think. I am sure we didn't think at all. I don't know how we could have gone to [high school] and had such a lack of interest in anything intellectual. We thought these kids were just odd and had nothing in common with us. Later on, after we had fled south, we mixed more with them, I think. Even then . . . The only one we all sort of took in was Hilde, and I don't know why.

—Cuban girl

Immediately, the Cubans and the Robinsoner became the two contending political factions around whom the rest of the institution rallied. Unfortunately for the Robinsoner, the Cubans had already been on the scene for three months and they were running the show. For all the political sophistication of the newcomers, they had no chance whatsoever of overthrowing them. John Windmuller had been overwhelmingly elected as the

president of the Children's Parliament, and he was so popular
with every group that the Robinsoner could not have defeated
him even if they had wanted to.

For my own part, I liked nothing better than to have them
sharpen their axes on each other. We didn't ask them to like each
other necessarily, although there were instances where firm
friendships were formed. We didn't even ask them to work
together. The only thing we requested of them was that they
respect each other; and although we had every expectation that
our wishes would be followed, the only agreement that could be
reached in certain instances was "an agreement to disagree."
Herbert Schiller, one of the leaders of the Robinsoner, was never
willing to come to any accord. Schiller's father had been a union
leader in Austria, and Herbert had some very strong ideas of his
own.

In competing with each other, the children found it necessary
to understand each other. That was the important thing. The
Cubans do not know it but they would not be the same people
they are today if the Robinsoner had not come along to stir their
political and social consciences. The Robinson children would
never believe it but they would not have become the men and
women they are if the *St. Louis* kids had not been willing to
accept them into the life of the institution as legitimate rivals.

The Orthodox, whom neither of them would have come into
contact with under normal circumstances, taught them both an
entirely different lesson in the richness and variety of the human
race.

As distinctive as the three self-contained groups were in
themselves they also formed a part of a community that was
constantly interacting and endlessly evolving. The Orthodox,
who originally had far more respect for the Gentiles than for the
assimilated Jews, learned the lesson of tolerance, too. Because of
the time they spent in Montmorency, they came to understand
they were unique in an entirely different way from the way they
had thought they were. At first, the Orthodox had no interest in
participating in the institutionwide politics. When it came to
electing a president for their own Home at Eaubonne they

simply elected their most intelligent boy, Ernst Valfer, and let it go at that. But John Windmuller had free passage into every group. He and Ernst Valfer became good friends, and then close friends. They influenced each other, and since they both had searching minds were drawn into bull sessions with the sons of the Socialist leaders.

Of all our children, who do you think became a professor in labor relations? That's right, John Windmuller. Ernst Valfer, the leader of the Orthodox group, became an industrial psychologist. And while Herbert Schiller, the son of the union leader, never lost either his involvement in politics or his gift for leadership he also managed to find the time to become the owner of a very successful electronics company.

The vast majority of the children didn't belong to any group. They were just kids, with individual personalities and talents but no particular coloration. They came to us in small groups and large groups, from different countries and, on occasion, from other organizations. But always they would come to us from the Paris office, fully sponsored, duly processed and right on schedule.

Except, of course, for Emil Geisler, who came alone.

5. A Community of Children

Every meal was a joy.

"Bon appétit, les enfants," I would call out, in general benediction.

"Merci, Ernst," would come bouncing back at me from the mixed choir of lively, eager children. A hundred youthful voices, and always there was a cheerful, chirrupy music to it.

And then we would all dig in with gusto.

In the other Homes, the director or whatever adult happened to be in a particularly expansive frame of mind would do the honors.

"Bon appétit, les enfants."

"Merci, Margot."

Lunch was a special joy with a flavor of its own, for it was during lunch that we held our birthday parties. Nobody's birthday ever went uncelebrated, and with better than a hundred kids to a Home we were not often deprived of a suitable occasion. The ritual was unfailing. After the main course had been finished, a friend of the birthday boy or girl would come marching in with the cake, complete with lighted candles. Everybody would jump up and sing a rousing chorus of "Happy Birthday," followed by the inevitable burble of laughter and applause. And then would come a couple of booming hip-hip-hoorays, the rattle and clatter of silverware against glass, wood or crockery, and resounding cries of "Speech . . . speech . . ."

It was always understood that the invitation to a speech was exactly that. An invitation and not a command. If the child who was being honored wanted to respond with a few well-chosen words of derisive appreciation or unabashed sentimentality—and humor won out over sentimentality by about a hundred to one —the floor was his. If not, he just blew out the candles and was lifted up on the shoulders of his friends so that he could be saluted with another round of singing. Finally would come the presents. Small, inexpensive gifts from his friends and his counselor and, on the really great occasions, a package which his parents had been able to send out to him.

Many times, there were two or even three birthdays in the same Home and we would usually have the bearers of the cake march in together, holding the cakes high so that the candles shone like sparklers. To make it even more impressive, we would sometimes seat all the birthday children at the same table.

Birthdays aside, we celebrated every Jewish and French holiday and anybody else's holiday that seemed good to us. Bastille Day, July 14, was one long roundelay of celebration. We held our own festivities in the morning for ourselves and some invited French guests, went to Montmorency in the afternoon to join the French schoolchildren in their celebration and, in the evening, were able to sit back and ooohh-and-aaahhh over the fireworks displays exploding in the skies above Paris and its immediate environs. We loved celebrations so much that when no country had an acceptable holiday coming up we would put on a play or a circus of our own. The world was a festival. Even the morning gymnastics, a feature common to all our Homes, were conducted in the form of games and accompanied by songs. We did so much singing and dancing that a visitor from the United States once told me with a smile that he had come to inspect a children's institution and had found that we were really a Strauss operetta.

He could not have been more mistaken. We were not a Strauss operetta. Neither were we one big theater party. We were a community of very special children with very special problems. They had come to us, strangers and afraid, and we had to make them happy again. Not merely by creating a well-ordered home.

Not with parties or songs. When I speak of making them happy, I am not talking in terms of *amusing* them. Our task was to create an atmosphere in which they could develop and bloom again.

As must be evident by this time, everything was on a first-name basis. I was "Ernst," Lene was "Lene," and all the teachers and counselors were also addressed by their given names. This did not come about by any accident. In greeting each new group I would immediately introduce myself as Ernst, and as soon as one of them called me Mr. Papanek—which would be as soon as the first child, or on a good day the second, addressed me—I would say, "Then I will also have to say 'Mister' to you and 'Miss' to her." My tone conveyed the message that if they wanted to make us both sound that ridiculous there wasn't very much I could do about it. "In my own family," I would then say to clinch it, "my children have never called me anything except Ernst. We in this institution are also a family. A much bigger family, to be sure, but based upon the same kind of mutual loyalty and respect."

The use of the first name, as the most outrageous symbol of our permissive policies, was one of the things that kept the Orthodox Community in a permanent state of discontent. Nor could I say that I was surprised. The conventional relationship between child and parent, as I had reason to know, has a way of becoming sacrosanct even to people for whom nothing is sacrosanct. Especially as it is seen in the rosy afterglow. In the Social Democratic movement there was a conscious policy of having children and adults address each other by their first names, but even there it did not extend to the child's own parents. Parents weren't supposed to be comrades, they were supposed to be . . . well, parents. Consider my friend Otto Gloeckel. Otto Gloeckel had spent his entire life fighting for the rights of the children. Under the Emperor, he had been one of the prime movers in the formation of the Free School Society to give the children of working families an opportunity to go on to high school and college. As the first Secretary of Education of the Austrian Republic he had reorganized the school system along such progressive lines that even today the very words *Austrian School Reform* shine forth as a model of enlightenment.

"The poor children of Papanek," Otto Gloeckel would sigh whenever he visited us. "They have no father and no mother. They have only Lene and Ernst."

If the use of our first names by our children was looked upon by our most enlightened friends as an affectation which could very well undermine the foundation of family life I could hardly be astonished to find the somewhat more traditionally oriented people of the OSE Board viewing such a familiarity between the director and his charges as an assault upon authority itself. But it's all convention really, isn't it, and therefore purely arbitrary. If King Henry VIII had ordered all his subjects to cut out the baby talk and call their parents by their given names think how quaint it would sound to hear grown boys and girls saying Mama and Papa. And if the Founding Fathers had come out of the Constitutional Convention with a resolution calling for children and their teachers to address each other by their first names, think how unbearably stiff and undemocratic it would sound for a little pipsqueak of a ten-year-old to insist upon calling his teacher Mister.

But words do carry their own symbolism, and as a practical politician I would be the last man in the world to underestimate the importance of symbols. With the Social Democrats, the exchange of first names was exactly that, a conscious symbol of the children's full status as comrades. And so it was with us. We were a community of children and adults, sharing a common danger and engaged in a common experiment.

I have always felt that the community can support the individual to a far greater extent than has ever been suggested. If we were to be a true community, if community living was to be given a fair chance, authority had to be based on something far more meaningful than Mister or Sir or, heaven help us, Herr Direktor.

It is the relationship between children and adults that primarily determines the atmosphere of an educational institution. The children had confidence in us only after we had earned their confidence. Lene did not say, "This won't hurt a bit," and jab them with a needle. She said, "This is going to hurt." They clenched their teeth, and the next time they were asked to expose their arms they did it bravely and willingly. And when she told them something wasn't going to hurt they believed her.

We did have random incidents of impudence and disrespect as individual children struggled to come to terms with this wholly new relationship. Of course we did. Most of our children were from countries where authority had always meant Authority. In not one instance, however, did it persist to the point where I was forced to take action. The other children viewed that kind of behavior as such a breach of trust that they very quickly took the offending child aside and put an end to it.

Comradeship with children didn't mean that we were placing ourselves on their level. That would have been dishonest, which would have violated the very basis of community, and it would have also made us look ridiculous, which would have been fatal. We were equal in the respect we felt toward each other and in the loyalty we owed each other. But the adults were still adults with adult rights and responsibilities, and the children were still children with only the rights and responsibilities that they were equipped to handle. They shared in the running of the institution. They did not run it and we did not insult either them or ourselves by pretending that they did.

And I tell you that there is not less respect in the end, there is more. The walls of our houses were never marked up with crayon or pens. Vandalism was nonexistent. There were never even any drawings or graffiti in the lavatories, something that any educator can tell you is so unheard of that in a normal situation they would be appointing committees to find out whether their children had descended directly from heaven or were merely suffering from some rare form of creative stultification.

No, familiarity does not necessarily breed contempt. During our early days in the United States, at a time when I needed a job very badly, I was asked to take over a home for problem children in Putnam County, New York. Lene and Georgie had driven up with me and as we started back, Georgie said with commendable firmness, "You cannot take this job, Ernst." I had already turned it down because they had a policy of discrimination, but Georgie had no possible way of knowing that. All Georgie knew was that we had come up with high hopes of becoming solvent again.

"Oh? Why can't I take it?"

"Because you cannot direct a children's institution where the children say 'sir' to you."

For Georgie, at the age of nine, it was inconceivable that you could approach people with whom you were living and sharing the exhilarating experience of education on such a formal and nonegalitarian basis.

For Georgie it was a matter of taste, style and philosophy. For the children of the Kinderheim in Montmorency, it was a great deal more than that. For the children of Montmorency, it was a form of therapy.

> Prior to that day in 1939 when a group of us drove into Montmorency, calling an adult by his first name was a completely foreign thought to me. Being able to freely call you Ernst was possibly one of the first steps into a new kind of world, where every child in its own right was listened and talked to, and where trust and communication between people could help us overcome many doubts and inner conflicts. . . .
>
> —Letter from a girl, thirteen at the time
> of Montmorency, received on the occasion
> of my sixty-fifth birthday

I must now tell you about Eugene, who would have prescribed an entirely different brand of medicine. One day I received a phone call from Theodor Dan, the Menshevik leader who had been exiled by Lenin. "I have a young man here who does not speak French or German," Dan began. "Could you take him as one of your staff?"

Excellent credentials if you happened to be looking for someone who didn't speak those languages. What else couldn't he do? And then Dan explained to me that this young man Eugene had been the editor-in-chief of *Komsomolskaya* (Communist Youth) *Pravda* before he had found it necessary to flee Russia for his life. I tell this story here because it helps me make two very salient points. Eugene had been only six or seven years old when the Russian Revolution started, which meant that his entire education had been in Bolshevik schools. The Bolsheviks had allowed him to become a member of the Komsomolsk and then an officer and finally editor of its newspaper. And when the first purges started and Tukhachevsky, the Marshal of Russia, was executed, Eugene wrote a front-page editorial in which he said: "Until yesterday you told us Tukhachevsky was a hero. When you now tell us that he is a traitor you must also give us a reason why he is a traitor."

Within an hour after the paper came out, the entire editorial staff was arrested. Except for Eugene. By sheer luck Eugene had stepped out of the office a few moments before the GPU came storming in and he didn't stop moving until he was in Persia. After working in the Persian Underground against Stalin, he had come to Dan with a wild-eyed scheme for uniting all anti-Stalinist elements, from monarchists to Trotskyites to Mensheviks, into a single unit that would work within Russia for the overthrow of the common enemy. Having listened to the plan, Dan advised him to get a job in France so that he could apply for legal status as a political refugee without running the risk of being shipped to a detention camp.

To me, this young man stands as one of the wonders of the human spirit. To me, he is proof that tyranny can never triumph because the inquisitive and rebellious spirit of youth can never be broken. Here was a young man who had been raised by the Bolsheviks, trained by the Bolsheviks, taken into the Bolshevik Establishment and raised to what was probably the highest position it was possible for a young man of his age to attain. And still, at the critical moment, he had dared to face the man whom he had been programmed to look upon as all-wise and whom he knew only too well to be all-powerful and tell him that he was a tyrant.

Despite what I have just said, I must also admit that Eugene was a terrible disappointment to me. Dan had assured me that he could speak English. I discovered that he had learned his English from a teacher who had never been out of Russia. My English wasn't good; his English wasn't English. I hired him as a handyman so that he'd have a job, hoping he would pick up the language quickly and never doubting that his strength of character would shine as a beacon light for every child who came into contact with him to follow.

His work was unsatisfactory from the first and deteriorated rapidly into nothing. I would find him sleeping in the barn, and when I would admonish him that he should not be sleeping when there was work to do, he would agree with me every bit as wholeheartedly as he had agreed with me two days earlier when I had caught him back in his bed—and would agree with me again two days later when I found him asleep under a tree. A very agreeable young man, and a very poor worker.

One day I ran across Theodor Dan in Paris, and Dan said, "Did you know, Ernst, that Eugene believes you are completely crazy?"

I said, "No, I didn't. Why does he believe I am crazy?"

"He says when he does not work you only tell him that he should. You never punish him, you never hit him, you never take a franc off his salary. And so naturally he thinks you have to be crazy if you believe that's any way to get any work out of him."

That wasn't all. "It also seems that your theories on education offend him. He tells me you never punish the children. You never hit them. How do you expect them to learn anything," asked Dan as proxy for Eugene, "unless you hit them?"

So that explained Eugene. "He believes that if you let children make such a sucker out of you, why shouldn't he make a sucker out of you, too?"

Despite a lifetime of conditioning, Eugene had been able to challenge Stalin, who had the power of life and death over him. And still he was unable to question an educational philosophy which taught that children were able to learn only out of fear.

And he was so wrong. Life would have been much easier for me if I had been a sucker, because I would have been filled with self-pity for the way my good nature was being abused. And also very angry with myself for allowing it. When you are a sucker you are allowed to take a lot of time off to nurse your wounded feelings—a week to be angry here and a week to sulk there—and while you're indulging yourself you are also not working. I am not a sucker because I believe children should not be beaten. I can prove it by the thousands of children I have taught.

Eugene was not able to see, as any child would have understood at once, that if I was willing to allow him to use me that way it could only be because he had ceased to be that important to me. He had been sent to me because he needed a job, and I was willing to put up with him.

He disappeared when the war started and I never heard a word about him again.

6. The Invisible Wound

The average child gained ten pounds during his first two weeks with us, which was just about right, because they came to us, on the average, ten pounds underweight. Building them up physically was the least of our problems; in each of the dining rooms, there was always a long list posted of the children who were on special diets. Their shrunken and shriveled self-esteem, their battered image of themselves, wasn't so easily handled. These were children who came to us in a kind of psychic shell shock. They had seen their parents murdered and beaten and humiliated and had themselves been systematically terrorized and publicly loathed. In a strange country, they were strangers and afraid. In the truest sense of the word, they were orphans. By simply conditioning our acceptance of them upon slavish obedience and faultless rote scholarship we could have turned our Homes into authoritarian showplaces that would have warmed the cockles of Eugene's heart and given future generations of Prussians something to shoot at.

The sad truth was that many of them longed for a strong authoritarian hand. Having been excluded from the higher ranks of German society, they would have been only too delighted to have a go at a bit of Hitler Youth for themselves. Many of them, girls included, found the elitist trappings of the Hitler Youth so attractive that it was by no means unusual to find a group of newcomers exchanging the Nazi salute with an enthusiasm that was positively chilling.

For any kind of child, the punitive system of education espoused by Eugene can only be stultifying. For our children, clutched at by guilts and anxieties that were beyond their understanding, overwhelmed by feelings of worthlessness, it would have been the most destructive thing that could have happened to them.

By 1938, *Rassenkunde* (race-ology) had become such an important part of the German and Austrian school curriculum in even the elementary grades that an ambitious teacher with a suitably sadistic turn of mind might hope to carve out a very nice career for himself. During one hate session, just such an instructor had ordered one of our ten-year-old girls to stand up in the back of the class (where the few remaining Jewish students had been consigned) so that her classmates could pick out the characteristic Jewish traits which, as any good Aryan should know, were splattered all over her. To get things going, her nose was mentioned most unflatteringly. Also her curly black hair. And then, because she happened to be short and pale, her shortness and paleness. "I was shaking all over," she told me while she was recounting her ordeal. "I was so frightened I thought my knees were going to give way under me." Most of her classmates, to give them their due, were almost as horrified as she was, which wasn't so much of a comfort either since it only served to drive their teacher into a frenzy. When nobody was able to come up with any further evidence of her conspicuous Semitism—her mouth and eyes being rather indistinguishable as mouths and eyes went—he leveled a finger at her and shouted: "Can't you see her deceitful look!"

How does a ten-year-old girl react, emotionally, to having such hatred and loathing heaped upon her? Which is by way of asking: What is the psychic damage done? Where are the unseen wounds?

In the larger sense, to jump the question, everybody reacts pretty much the same to persecution in the beginning, adults and children alike. *They dream of escaping; they hope to survive.* Whether they had pinned their hopes on Hitler's early overthrow or on emigration to another country was a matter of individual temperament or, perhaps, of age. By the time you have achieved a certain age, the seasonal cycle has crept into your very bones. After the winter will come another spring, and that's a form of optimism and, therefore, of escape in itself. My mother-in-law was not the only one who chose to believe that it was only a matter of sitting in Vienna until Hitler and all his works were washed away. They could not bring themselves to recognize, those optimists who pinned their hopes on the quarterings of the moon, that the weather was turning cold and bloody and no spring thaw was going to come.

The optimism of youth, of course, takes far more fanciful and dreamy forms. Where the old man hopes for an uprising that will overthrow Hitler, the young boy dreams of leading it; a dream so unrealistic that not even he—alas—can hold onto it for very long. The only thing it does for him, in the end, is force him to confront his own pitiful weakness and, in confronting it, to despise himself for it. But human nature will not permit so young a mind to surrender itself without putting up a better battle than that. Locked in as he is, trapped, the dream now takes a completely opposite form. Having admitted to himself that he has no chance of storming the enemy camp he can only dream of finding salvation by escaping, as it were, into it. Increasingly, he identifies with the oppressor. The longing for acceptance, which is a powerful force at that age anyway, pushes to the surface. His admiration for the glitter and swagger of the Hitler Youth is no longer suppressed. He secretly begins to resent his parents—and this is what holds the most peril for him—for having saddled him with "the burden of difference."

I didn't ask to be born a Jew! the mind cries out as the enemy camp beckons more and more invitingly. *It's not my fault!* it wails as the gates clang shut.

Since tyranny did not begin with Hitler, the invisible wound of the persecuted is not exactly a startlingly new phenomenon in mankind's march across the pages of history. What Hitler did was to apply the psychology of terror on a scale so massive as to be unprecedented and to apply it, systematically, against children.

In a study published in Copenhagen, Irma Kessel, a Danish psychologist, made an invaluable contribution by setting down her conversation with a six-year-old Jewish girl in Germany during Hitler's first year in power. "Ruth changed completely in a short time. She became ambitious, peevish, pale and was seized with an intense interest in arithmetic and writing. 'Will the teacher be very happy,' she asked, 'if I know so much? If I can write up to a hundred will the teacher tell the principal and then will the principal be glad? And if I can write up to a thousand and write all the letters and read all the names, do you think Adolf Hitler will like me a little bit too and forget that I'm a Jewish child?' "

And, later: "All the Jews have to get out of Germany soon. Adolf Hitler has a long list of all the Jews and he goes down the list and chases them all out. I'm so scared when they're coming to me. And what if there's no room in any country? Once I said Heil Hitler on the street and an S.A. man slapped me in the face and he said I should go to Palestine because I'm a dirty Jew.... Maybe if I'm very good and study very hard, Adolf Hitler will let me be a German child and like me too."

A pure laboratory specimen of the incubation of self-hatred as only a six-year-old who has not yet completely resolved the distinction between fantasy and reality could have expressed it.

The second phase, after it has become unmistakably clear that there is no escape and no acceptance, is *hopelessness and despair.* If you were looking for a laboratory specimen of "no escape and no acceptance" where would you look except on board the wandering *St. Louis.* The following excerpts are from a long, forty-thousand-word letter written to his mother by Max, a fourteen-year-old boy from Hamburg, shortly after the ship was finally allowed to land in Antwerp. The boy, whose father had been taken away by the Gestapo even before the Night of the Broken Crystal, was being sent to Cuba to wait for his quota number to come up, at which time he was supposed to join an uncle in Miami. The letter, written at a fever pitch, is remarkable for its cool photographic detail of every phase of the journey from the time the first instructions were received at the Hapag office to the ultimate disposition of the passengers.

Notice in this description of the fifth and final day in Havana Harbor how he remains aloof from the cycle of escalating hope, gradual deflation and the final descending hopelessness. Pulling himself further and further away until it is as if a wall of ice has descended in front of him.

> The rented motor boats carrying the relatives and friends of the passengers came out again [in the morning] and still the police would not permit them to come close to our ship. The wife with the children were on our boat, the husband and father down in the little boats. Or the parents were on board ship and their daughters down in the boat. But this time they were waving and shouting to us that the Parliament had voted in favor of us and the bill was now up for the President's signature. They were shouting that we would very shortly be allowed to land. Manana. It was still Manana. The words were of little consolation to us. They had the opposite effect. We had been disappointed and frustrated too often. Nothing made any impression any more. We would not believe anything. When they came again at noon and the evening, it was the passengers who were shouting to them, "Manana. Manana." We know it is very bad for us. At last the passengers did not want to see the boats anymore. The unrest increased. Many people had nervous breakdowns and were crying uncontrollably. People shouted and cursed, many women and children cried because they saw their fathers down in the boats and could not get to them. It was like being in a witch's castle. I, myself, tried very hard to keep calm because after all I had experienced since October 28th made me indifferent to this kind of situation. It was really unimportant what was now happening. I was only sorry that you had spent your last savings to buy me a ticket and that your great sacrifice was all in vain.

But a few pages later as the ship is passing so close to the coast of Florida that he can see the skyscrapers and white beaches of Miami ("... so close that we could almost touch it and easily could have swum over to it") the wall of ice melts away and out comes the cry of despair:

> My Uncle is here in this beautiful Miami! I am supposed to immigrate there. I am so close and still so far away but also all others were moved because it came clearly to our minds what kind of worthless cargo we must be that everyone refuses to

accept us. Slaves had it better in former times. People were even willing to pay for them and here we had even offered to pay additional money for each and every one of us and in spite of that nobody wants us. Are we really so bad and so rotten? Are we really the vermin of mankind that we are treated this way? Why are we treated like outcasts? Are we no longer supposed to be even human beings? Has the world now finally reverted to the so-called Law of Nature where it will permit only those whom it believes to be the fittest to survive? Are they finally engaged in a fight to exterminate those whom they look upon as unfit, as Nature itself eliminates the weaker and most helpless types of animal and plant life? Then please tear off your mask. Do not call yourselves human beings anymore with intelligence, courage and a higher morality. You are worse than animals because they fight only when the natural instinct for self-preservation forces them to it but you believe you are great heroes when you fight the weakest of your own kind.

The residue of Phase 1, the dream of escape, is passivity, self-hatred and a smothering sense of worthlessness and guilt. "I did not bear these persecutions proudly," wrote Peter, a six-teen-year-old German boy. "I shall never forget this cowardice. Not because I am ashamed that I was cowardly but because I hate my humble, submissive spirit. I was so frightened, and I cannot get rid of this fear. I never feel safe; I don't even feel safe from my fear."

The significant thing here is that this was not a boy who had sat passively by to wait for his fate to overtake him. After Hitler occupied Belgium (where Peter's family had fled) and all Jews were being shipped to Poland, Peter escaped from the police agents who had come for him by climbing out the kitchen window. After the fall of France, he was picked up by the OSE Underground in Paris and smuggled over the demarcation line to the castle to which we had repaired in southern France. Two days after he arrived, the French gendarmes swooped down and shipped everybody they could get their hands on to Auschwitz. " 'But,' I said to myself, 'I saved myself in Belgium, why should I now in France let myself be taken to Poland?' " Once again, Peter went out the back window. This time he hid with a farmer for six weeks before deciding to try to escape into Spain. "I was arrested in the railway station at the border for I was not legally there. They were planning to send me to Poland, but I was cleverer than the police. I tore all my documents up and said I was a Rumanian, as Rumanians were not to be sent to Poland." After a week, the Quakers were able to get him out of prison and place him temporarily in a children's colony. "Then I went with a hunter who was going to the Pyrenees. He left me in the middle of the Pyrenees after we were in Spanish territory. I didn't know what route I should follow so I summoned all my courage and decided to go straight ahead." After walking for five days and nights he found himself in Barcelona. There, he was put in touch with a Spanish doctor who was part of a doctors' Underground railroad (which had been formed, as we shall see later, as a result of Georgie's stomachache during our own escape through Spain). As soon as his strength had returned he was placed on a train to Vigo, from where he was to be smuggled into Portugal. Again, trouble. The Spanish conductor, who was supposed to be safe, demanded to see his papers. Peter, resourceful as ever, fended him off by pretending to be deaf and dumb and—sheer masterstroke—eager to ask him all kinds of questions in sign language.

Not exactly a boy you'd have thought of as cowardly or submissive. But, then, you'd have had no way to know about those terrible disloyal thoughts that had been in his mind back in Germany and Belgium. He had dreamed of escaping from the burden his parents had placed upon him and he had escaped, in a manner of speaking, by leaving his parents behind. And if he hadn't escaped into the enemy camp, he had shown a nice little talent for pretending to be something other than he was, hadn't he?

In his seven months of wandering through Europe, Peter had not allowed himself to dwell overmuch on the fate of his family. Ducking the police, finding a bed and a meal had taken all the energy he could spare. "I had no fear during all that time," he said, "because I had nothing to lose. There was only deportation to Poland." An odd way to put it. So completely at variance with everything else he has to say about himself that it has the solid ring of truth to it.

Once he was safe in Lisbon, though, he felt utterly empty. Something far more depressing than the normal letdown that might have been expected. And then he realized what it was. The running was over, and he was alone. As wave after wave of loneliness washed over him, he knew with a certainty beyond question that his parents and his little brother were dead. His first five days of freedom were spent in a locked hotel room, crying.

When he came to see me after he had been in the United States for a few months, he was suffering from chronic headaches and a noticeable eye tic. Any kind of noise startled him. He found it difficult to fall asleep. The psychic damage had been in the making for five years, and it was too deeply embedded to be wholly excised.

Wasn't his courage apparent to himself, you are entitled to ask. Didn't he appreciate what it had taken to do what he had done? Of course he did. We know he had acted without fear only because he told us. We learned how resourceful he could be only because he boasted about it. But that had been before he was forced to absorb the shock of the destruction of the rest of his family. In that context, the courage he had discovered within himself became the new burden he hadn't asked for.

Having shown so much cleverness in saving himself, how could he ever be sure that he might not have been able to save the rest of his family if he had not jumped out the window and deserted them?

The mind is very clever when it comes to finding a solution for an impossible dilemma within the structure of the dilemma itself. Who jumps out a window and deserts the people he loves? Only a coward. And how can you blame a coward for being a coward? That's the way he is, that's all. A courageous boy might have been able to help them; a fearful boy, never. Better to be meek and full of fears. Better to throw up a barrier of pain between what you say and what you feel. Better to keep the mind occupied in a meaningless search for extraneous sound. And always be on guard. Relax for a minute and you'll find yourself out. Asleep, you can't protect yourself.

With a more passive boy, the wound would have been so deeply embedded that the symptoms would have been less visible and largely unarticulated. Whether it would have been more or less destructive over the long run, who can say? All children are different. Every life turns on its own events.

The residue of Phase 2, hopelessness and despair, is an acceptance of oneself on the oppressor's terms. If you were a small-town German boy like Siegfried, who had been brought up to believe in the glory of the Fatherland and the superiority of all things German, you were caught in a hopeless bind.

Siegfried's father had been a minor war hero and a fanatic admirer of the Kaiser. For as long as Siegfried could remember, the walls of his home had been covered with poems attesting to the strength and goodness of the German character:

> Virtue and pure love
> Who cherishes and loves it
> Let them look in German land
> Where both reside
> May I long live in this land!

He could also remember how he and his younger sister had watched the parading of the Jungvolk, the Hitler Youth and the League of German Girls, admiring their uniforms, thrilling to the martial music, envying their boisterous camaraderie as they chanted the slogans of the superrace. Wishing to belong to such a marvelously exciting organization and feeling always the presence of some unknown enemy in the crowd waiting to denounce him as a Jew.

The first time Siegfried was insulted by a gang of neighborhood boys he deliberately challenged the biggest and oldest of them, a boy at least three years older than himself, and was given a brutal thrashing. That didn't stop him. He continued to attack boys much older than himself whenever the words *"Jude verecke"* ("Die, Jew!") were flung at him and always with the same result. The day finally came, however, when he was challenged by a boy his own age, and this time it was Siegfried who left a beaten and bloodied opponent behind him. And yet, even as he was running home to tell his father about his great victory, he was aware of a curious and indefinable discomfort, a feeling of compassion even for the Aryan who had been beaten by a Jew. The next day a gang of Nazi Youth grabbed Siegfried outside his school, forced him into their clubhouse and held him down while the boy he had defeated in honest battle was instructed—to their mutual degradation—to "paddle the Jew." That done, they shaved Siegfried's head and threw him out into the street amidst a shower of jeers and insults.

Siegfried knew that it would have been fruitless for his father to go to the police. A year or so earlier when his father had gone to the station to report that his daughter's bicycle had been stolen he had only succeeded in getting himself held overnight "for questioning." But still, Siegfried had always looked to his father as such a source of strength and protection that he was overwhelmed by a feeling of helplessness which, together with the humiliation to which he had been subjected, brought to the surface his suspicion that Jews were so weak and cowardly that Hitler was justified in demanding that they be eliminated completely from the future of the Fatherland.

The fact that his father had been resisting the best efforts of the local Nazi leader to close down his shoe store could only serve to confuse him further. Stickers were pasted on the window identifying the owner as a Jew. Party members were stationed in front of the store with cameras to warn prospective customers away.

In that regard, there was one incident that had left a particularly deep impression on Siegfried. A passerby who had absent-mindedly paused to look in the window became so panicky when he turned to find his picture being taken that he picked up a rock and heaved it through the window and, in case anybody still had any doubts about whose side he was on, sent forth a stream of anti-Semitic epithets. "I hope," he shouted before he marched off, "you got a picture of *that,* too."

Through it all, Siegfried's father kept insisting that all they were witnessing was a temporary aberration in the noble German character that would pass with the passing of Hitler.

Nothing could shake him. The Hitler Youth were assigned to march on the store each day, breaking the window as the spirit moved them, piling trash up in front of his doorway and shouting their daily quota of insults. The few old customers who continued to patronize the store were publicly labeled "Jew lovers" and either fired from their jobs or threatened with summary dismissal. As a final blow, the party distributed pledge cards all over town binding the signers not to shop at any Jewish store, and held them to their pledge by publishing their names in the morning paper. Siegfried's father was still not beaten. Instead, he shook his fist and promised that he would "beat them" by cutting his prices so drastically that his business would actually increase.

Siegfried's reaction was entirely different. Having learned that the only thing worse than losing was winning, Siegfried had stopped fighting. At home, he had become increasingly unmanageable. His feelings about his father were in a turmoil. On the one hand, he was proud of his father for standing up to the Nazis; on the other he despised him for making the rest of the family the target of the daily vituperation. In his heart, he attributed all the qualities he found admirable in his father to his German heritage and all the qualities that were tormenting him to his Jewish blood.

As the Nazi leader continued to close his grip on the town, "WE DO NOT SELL TO JEWS" signs were posted in all the butcher shops and grocery stores. A few store owners were willing to take an order by phone and deliver it after dark—for a price. "After a while, even they became afraid. My sister and I were sent to other parts of town to buy food, one store one time and a different one the next. The storekeeper would always ask us if we were Jews, and we would deny it. All the way home we would not look at each other.

"In November, 1938, father planned a picnic. We were unable to use any of the recreation grounds or parks. But it was my birthday and since we could not hold a gathering in our home [the authorities took exception to this kind of congregation] father planned a visit to Aunt Martha who lived about thirty-five miles away. On our way there we could see signs and placards, strategically placed on the new streamlined roads warning: JEWS ENTER THIS TOWN AT THEIR OWN RISK. JEWS AND DOGS FORBIDDEN.

"The party was a pleasant affair. We forgot for the moment our troubles and I was given the extra treat of being allowed to remain for the weekend. Father and mother and sister started for home."

The following Monday was the day von Rath was shot. Wednesday was the Night of the Broken Crystal.

"It was the last I saw of my parents and little sister. They had been taken away after I allowed them to return home without me while I hid in safety with a Gentile friend of my aunt. I could only imagine what had happened."

What a tangle of guilt, weakness and self-loathing can be found in that single word *allowed*. I am not going to attempt to untangle the strands here. That's a game anybody can play. Enough for our purposes to point out that he was able to impute a weakness to himself only by presuming a strength he did not have. Again the split. As always, the confusion.

Intellectually, Siegfried was aware that there had been no reason for him to ask his parents to stay, and even less to insist on returning with them. He also knew how stupid it would have been not to have "allowed" his aunt to hide him where the Nazis would be least likely to look for him. But we are not dealing with the intellect. We are dealing with the emotions, and emotions travel on a separate wire. As long as the family remained intact, the emotional upheaval was held in check. It was death and separation that pulled the plug out, and we were a community of children without parents.

7. The Torn Fabric

The haunting and sometimes unbearable vibrations from the past were one of the problems we had to address ourselves to. In every possible way that we could think of, we sought to instruct the children that:

1) We were living in a time when very bad things were being done to many people, Jews among them.

2) This had come about as a result of a combination of historical and political events and was not directed against them as individuals

3) They were not being individually punished for anything they had done or for any congenital defect in themselves or their character.

One of the greatest virtues of a children's institution is that it does not have to impinge upon the primary loyalty that is owed to the parents. We *respected* their parents. All their past loyalties, great and small, were accepted and respected by us. The job description for everybody who dealt with the children on a professional level emphasized that periodic progress and development reports were to be sent to their parents or—if we had their names—their next of kin, using an incident from the child's daily life wherever possible as a point of departure. We asked the children to write home weekly. We didn't demand it. If they missed a week, it became the duty of their counselor to write a chatty, news-filled letter. By very deliberately setting out to act as

if we were taking our commission for their care not from the OSE
Board but from their parents, we were constantly reinforcing the
parents' worth and dignity in the child's eyes, reaffirming their
continuing concern about them and acknowledging where the
primary vested interest lay.

Mail call was always treated as a great event. As soon as the
mail arrived from Paris, all activity came to a halt for twenty or
thirty minutes. If classes were in session we didn't wait for the
next intermission, we made our own intermission. Mail call!
Everybody out! There would be another class tomorrow.
Brothers and sisters, of whom we had our share, would automatically seek each other out to share their letters.

As mixed as their feeling about their parents may have been,
the ties of blood, the host of conscious and unconscious memories, held firm. Children know more than they know. They
understood how powerless their parents had been to protect
them. If they could remember acts of cowardice, they could also
remember, as John Windmuller did, how his father had dragged
himself to the door on the Night of the Broken Crystal to present
himself to every new band of roving thugs so they would take
him down to the yard for another beating before they had a
chance to look around and decide to take his sons.

In the children's letters, which we censored only to make sure
they hadn't written anything that might get anybody on the
receiving end in trouble, the shock of separation came through in
many ways. Sometimes it took the form of nothing more than
chatty reassurances: "When we arrived at the home, they gave us
a very warm welcome. There, I forgot something! We also took a
trip on the bus, that was grand. The home is very nice. The
children are very kind to us. The house is very beautiful. The
walls are decorated with painted flowers, and there are curtains
on the windows. The food is good. Only there is too much milk in
the coffee, but that does not matter. For about two days we were
in the Rothschild Hospital. Now don't get worried and don't
think I am sick. Everybody was there and nobody was sick. I shall
explain it to you. This is done to avoid the spread of any possible
illness among children at the home [Girl of twelve, Vienna]."

Even more often, it was in the concern for the safety of the parent: "It's swell here. I wish you were here too. I can imagine what is happening to you now [Boy of twelve, Vienna]."

"Imagine, I haven't had any news from you for three weeks. You can realize how upset I was. This morning I was woken up with these words: You've received a letter from your parents. You can imagine how fast I was out of bed. My dear parents, don't worry so much about me. The Lord helped us get out of Germany, let us hope that He will also bring us together again. We must be strong! I'm not homesick any more. Most of the children still have their parents in Germany and they have to stand it [Girl of fifteen, Vienna; parents in South America]."

At other times, it was the fear and longing that came through most clearly.

"Dear Mother, I dreamt that you came here in your gray dress. And when you came in you began to wait for Auntie [Girl of seven, Austria]."

". . . Is Daddy with you again? [Boy of seven, Berlin—father in concentration camp]."

"I ask you again whether Ernst and Leo [brothers in concentration camp] have come back. Some day you will answer, at last, by saying yes. But this time it has been no [Girl of nine, Vienna]."

There was even a reversal of roles whereby the child, from his position of comparative safety would become the morale booster and mentor. As with a fourteen-year-old girl who came to the decision that the future of the family lay in South America. ". . . Last Wednesday we had our first Spanish lesson. Today we have another. I thought it would be impossible for you to study Spanish in camp, and since the pronunciation and spelling are identical, I decided to write you everything I learn and add a few remarks about the pronunciation whenever necessary. In this way you will be able to learn Spanish with me. Please, keep these notes. Each of you is to send me the sentences from the first lesson and ten sentences from the second lesson when you write. Let us hope I will be able to help you learn Spanish this way. The pronunciation is very easy, and I hope you will be able to learn a lot in spite of the insufficient explanations. Well, now get to work!"

Other children took the initiative in attempting to open up new avenues of escape: "Unfortunately, my dear Mother writes to me that she got a refusal from Australia. Couldn't you help her to go to the United States, Uncle dear? [Girl of twelve, Ludwigshafen]."

Although we did not open the incoming letters, the counselors were available when advice or comfort was needed. And since parents were not always able to shield their children from their anxieties the mail could be upsetting: "Father writes that he arrived safely in Shanghai. There are no work permits there, alas, and food and lodgings are dear. Our little family is scattered to the four winds. I don't know what will happen to us now."

"There has been fine weather since last week, so we don't go to Loquai Park to sit on the bench for Jews but we go to the roof of Lilly's instead. As for you, you don't have to do that sort of thing any more."

"Your father will soon go to England, but I shall stay on with Rose in Stettin. Don't worry about me, my precious jewel, I will be all right."

". . . and when you say your prayers pray that we too find some possibility, whatever it may be, to get away from here."

The saddest letter came to a nine-year-old girl from her fourteen-year-old brother who in his own helplessness and despair presented his little sister with a set of practical and moral conflicts that were far beyond her capacity to handle: "Write very often to your poor Mother, as often as you can, so she won't be worried. If you can do anything, help your dear mother, for you know what your mother has had to suffer for you. If mother could get the immigration visa, it would mean deliverance from Dachau for your father. Daddy must at all cost get out of there soon, for you know that poor dear father is very delicate. Show your tears and ask for help, for there is no other help to be expected. Say that you still want to have a father and that you still want to see the rest of your family. I imagine that if you could only get a visa, father would be delivered from that torture. How unhappy he must be to stay imprisoned so long and not be present when you, dear sister, and I left. He must think of mother, too, how she must be tormenting herself and going about without food or sleep, getting weaker every day. I am sure he is thinking of us all. I don't want to write anything more because I am crying already and besides I don't want to make you suffer. But look around and see whether you can't help your mother."

That was one of the risks. We considered the correspondence so important that after war had been declared we called upon the Red Cross for help in getting it reestablished. Many children did not receive answers for as long as six months and still they continued to write weekly. Some children never received an answer and they were still writing when we left Montmorency.

When the first shipment of children from the OSE Homes was en route to the United States through Portugal the train stopped at Gurs. By that stage of the game, it wasn't only the Cubans who had parents or relatives there. Prisoners had been shipped in from concentration camps all over Europe, and Gurs had turned into the hellhole of France. From the time they heard they were going to stop, all the children on the transport had begun to save their bread ration. Those who had no parent or relative at Gurs gave their bread to someone who did.

After they had arrived in the United States, Edith, a thirteen-year-old German girl who had been able to see her parents for the first time in two years, told me that her mother had looked better than she had expected but that her father had looked so old and pale that she had scarcely been able to recognize him. "I should have begun to save my bread earlier," she said, sadly. "Do you think, Ernst, it will be possible to send them something from here in America?"

Admittedly, the texture of any relationship that is held together through correspondence is frailer—or, at least, very different—from what it would have been under normal circumstances. What was important was that it was kept intact at a time of their lives where to be estranged from their parents was to be estranged from themselves and all human society.

When the child is no longer a child the need is no longer there, something I was remarkably slow to appreciate.

One day the bell rang at my apartment in New York, and outside there was a big blond young man who looked like an all-American football player. In very bad and halting German he said, "I see, Ernst, you do not recognize me."

I will forget a name far more often than I will forget a face.

With him it was the opposite. The name I recognized immediately, Erich. He had come to this country with the first group and had been placed with foster parents in Connecticut. He was still in Connecticut, he told me. He had, in fact, married a girl from one of our Children's Homes. They had known each other casually in France, met again in the United States at one of the get-togethers the children arranged among themselves, seen each other briefly and then lost track of each other. He had gone out with other girls, she had gone out with other boys, and somehow when they were both ready to get married they had gravitated back to each other as the most natural thing in the world. A very interesting story but not the reason he had made the trip up from Connecticut. He had come to ask for help in tracing his parents. The last letter he had received from them had come from Poland just before the *blitzkrieg* and now he was suddenly overwhelmed by a yearning to find out for certain whether they were still alive.

"If we can find them, do you want to try to bring them over here?"

"Yes."

"To live with you?"

No. He didn't want that at all. He just wanted to know they were safe and being taken care of. "I don't know if you'll understand this, Ernst, but I would not want to live with them. If they were in California and I was in New York, I'd be happier than if we were all in New York."

He was right about one thing; I didn't understand. A year later, when we had a big get-together at my apartment to celebrate my tenth year in America, I deliberately turned the conversation to Erich. To my astonishment, I heard his sentiments being overwhelmingly endorsed. They all wanted to do whatever they could for their parents; very few of them thought it would be possible to reestablish a relationship on anything approaching an intimate basis. Generally, they agreed they would be satisfied to know that their parents were alive and safe. Whether it was in this country or not was immaterial. "But I don't worry about them," one boy said. "They sent me away so I wouldn't worry. Why should I make their sacrifice meaningless?"

To me, that was such a cold and callous attitude that I was really shocked. But now that he had carried the day, it was Erich himself who entered the first mild demurrer. Yes, there was one thing that did worry him. Did I remember that he had been sent to the Rothschild Hospital for a minor operation a few weeks before the war? Well, in the last letter he had been able to send out he had written that the operation had been successful. "I still find myself wondering from time to time," he said, "whether that letter ever got to them. It just doesn't seem right that they might be alive somewhere and worrying about an operation that took place more than a dozen years ago." It wasn't even the worrying that seemed so wrong to him, it was the *not knowing*. "If in the last ten seconds of my life the Angel of Death appeared to tell me he would deliver one message for me to anyone in the world, I would tell him to let my parents know, wherever they were, that the operation had come out all right."

Although not a word was said I could see by the solid nodding of heads around the room that they could identify completely with that sentiment too.

A cold shiver went up my spine. What was so eerie to me was that he was talking about his parents' right to know about the thirteen-year-old boy they had sent to the Children's Home in France. He was granting them no vested interest whatsoever in the twenty-five-year-old man who was sitting right across from me. He recognized, as I could not, that their paths had diverged so widely that those with whom he had once suffered the most terrible of times would now be, if he should run across them, no more than strangers to him.

And yet, I could recognize that if it was an attitude which troubled me, that was my problem, not theirs. My problem has always been that they are all eighteen or nineteen to me. It is amazing to me that I see them not as I saw them last in the Homes in France but as I saw them for the first time after the war. My problem was that I had become a prisoner of my own fiction. For them, life had gone on. Which was, after all, what I had wanted for them. I wanted them to take their losses realistically, hadn't I, and was not this the reality of their lives?

8. The Educational Task
—It Had To Be Great!

I feel splendid and am very happy to be out of Germany. I am here with about 57 children in a wonderful home close to Paris, approximately 10 miles from that city. We have an enormous park with two lawns where we play during our free periods. The food is excellent and I have already gained 11 lbs. and have become much taller. But that is also because of the change of climate.

Early in the morning we have gymn. After Breakfast we have classes until twelve. We have physics, French, English, German, drawing, mathematics, geography, social studies, etc. We also have games during part of our free time. In the afternoon we have class for one hour and then we are free.... There are four big houses for the children; all of them belong to the Union OSE, which is a wonderful organization. Our director also teaches gym and crafts. Now we are making pretty leather things. Before that we did basket weaving and we'll soon have a workshop for carpentry and book-binding. Next time maybe I'll be able to write part of my letter in English and you can do the same if you like with your whole letter.

—Thirteen-year-old Orthodox boy from Frankfurt

Our first educational goal was to assure the children, explicitly and implicitly, that nothing that had happened to them had been their fault. The second was to convince them that the persecution they had suffered was not their inevitable fate as Jews. The third was to create an educational system that would return them to the world with a sense of pride, accomplishment and social consciousness.

Our basic philosophy of education descended directly from the *"Arbeitsunterricht"* or study-project method of the Viennese school reform, which views the schoolroom not as a cage in which children are lined up in neat antiseptic rows to be fed their daily ration of facts and figures but as the center of a child's intellectual and social world. Once the teacher comes down off his pedestal and the student is unbolted from his desk, the child becomes an individual who is fully capable of participating in and contributing to his own education. The underlying concept here—particularly valuable to our children—is that the child who is given the opportunity to discover for himself where his talents and interests lie will be far better equipped to adjust himself to the more complex problems that will arise later on in life when he has only his own resources to fall back upon.

There was a hard-core group within the OSE that believed that the creation of a complete school system was carrying things far, far beyond the purposes for which the organization had been founded. That particular objection we were able to meet by a stroke of sheer luck. In order to preserve its identity when the international headquarters were moved to Paris, the initials had been made to stand for Organisation pour la Santé et l'Education (Union for Health and Education). Now, I knew as well as anybody that if the word *education* had to be justified as anything more than a repository for the final "E," it would have been something as inconsequential as the dissemination of information about health and hygiene. Never mind. The word was there and history was about to make honest men of them.

A far more serious objection arose around me and, more specifically, my plans to emigrate to the United States. How, asked the opposition, was it possible to justify adding such a massive expense to an already overstrained budget in order to install an educational system that would have to be dismantled after only one year. If the children were going to be sent to the French public schools in a year anyway, why not send them immediately?

The answer to that was easy. The first year was the one that counted. Because of that I had guaranteed to extend my stay for a full year with the understanding that I would be given a free hand to do whatever I thought had to be done. To take the children away for the better part of every day would be bad enough. To take them away and turn them over to a school system which was run along the strict authoritarian lines of the French school system would be to undercut me completely.

Far outweighing the opposition from within the OSE, fortunately, was the enthusiastic support that came from the wealthy liberal Jewish community. I was not, after all, an unknown quantity in the field of progressive education, and I was proposing the most massive experiment in progressive education ever attempted—saturation treatment, twenty-four hours a day. The opportunity to become a part of such an experiment was so appealing to so many people that an independent fund-raising committee was organized by the Baroness de Gunzbourg, with her daughter Philippe, a remarkably beautiful young woman, serving as the chairwoman. The contributors were free to come out to Montmorency any time they wanted to and see for themselves how their money was being put to use. They *were* a part of it. And when they told their friends about it, their friends wanted to become a part of it too.

In this connection, there is something else that should be said. The intellectuals in France, native and refugee alike, had very bad consciences about a great many things, going even beyond the residual guilt that all intellectuals carry. The refugee intellectuals, who were very uneasy about being out of their own suffering countries, had been willing to work like hell around the clock to get our first Home ready for the children. They were as convinced as I was that they were participating in something that was so important that it had to be *great* if it was going to be anything at all. The French intellectuals had bad consciences

arising out of the pacifist philosophy that left them so impotent
to combat the spread of Nazism. If writing a check could ease
their consciences we were happy to be of service.

We saw it happen, one way or the other, over and over. Most
notably, perhaps, when the Baroness de Rothschild, who had
contributed money originally only with the proviso that it must
not be used for anything smacking of ritualistic privilege, came
up from de la Guette with a group of her children during our
Chanukah celebration to lead the singing of the Jewish marching
songs. Something happened to her as she was leading the five
hundred massed children in those stirring Chanukah songs, and
the very air around us seemed to tingle. Now, the young
Baroness had an excellent voice for an amateur. That's all she
was, though, an amateur. By any standards, she was a good-
looking woman. But for sheer beauty she could not touch the
young Baroness de Gunzbourg. She was dressed all in red, her
personal trademark (the name Rothschild deriving from *rothes
Schild,* which means "red shield") and suddenly with the cool
autumn sun upon her and an unusually soft breeze rustling
through her hair she was positively dazzling. I had heard her sing
a few times before and her voice had never approached such
richness. Something remarkable had happened to her. Something that had exalted and transformed her. You could see from
the glow within her own flesh and spirit that for the first time she
really believed that she was doing something *great.*

And she was. There was one song in particular. A Hebrew
song with a beautiful melody. It begins with the words *Ochra,
ochra, onete omee,* and, in translation, goes on to say, "The little
stone which the architect scorned as unimportant and the
workers threw away because it was too small became the cor-
nerstone of the great temple that was built in honor of God." Or
so they told me. Yiddish I would have understood, Hebrew no.
John Windmuller and Ernst Valfer translated it for me because
they understood immediately how perfect it was for us, and it
became our second theme song, along with the song of the
Kinderfreunde.

Not that I would want to overstate the opposition that came

from the top leadership of the OSE, either. Many of the leading figures were solidly behind me from the beginning, Brutzkus in particular. As for the others, once they saw the enormous amount of interest we were creating within the French community, their opposition very quickly faded away. And when the leading educators of France, England and the United States began coming in to study what we were doing, they were as proud as anyone else. It was, after all, their organization. They were as eager as anybody else to be associated with something *great*. It was almost as if everybody connected with the OSE came to recognize at almost the same moment that they had taken on something so far beyond what they had originally committed themselves to that to be anything less than *great* was to fail.

And, also, that we did not have the right to fail.

9. A Shoe Shop in Orinda

We did not completely escape the supervisory eye of the French school system. Because our children were going to be entering their schools the following year, the Ministry of Education demanded that we follow their syllabus closely enough so that they would be prepared to take the examinations for the *certificat d'études,* the national exams that are given to all French students. The first and foremost casualty of our new curriculum was my grand design for integrating all instruction around one central theme. Not that we abandoned the idea completely. The principal difference, really, was that I no longer had to search for a new topic almost every week; I could wait for something that was of such obvious and overwhelming interest to us—like the sinking of the *Squalus* and the voyage of the *St. Louis*—that it more or less forced itself upon me.

Within that shifting framework, learning remained a cooperative venture. The classes were small and autonomous. Since we did not have attached seats and desks, something which was so unheard of in France as to be scandalous, our kids were able to do what anybody with good sense would do on a warm summer day—hold the class outside. It was squatter's right, first come, first served. On any given day, you could walk through the grounds and see small groups of children clustered around a teacher on the grass or seated around a table or, perhaps, up on the porch. And not necessarily around a teacher, either. Where there was a child who was unusually bright or innovative—and we had our share—the class might very well have been turned over to him. And if the discussion would benefit from a trip into town, they were perfectly free to jump into the truck and ride off.

The same freedom of movement held for every group activity. If a class or a group of friends wanted to carry their lunch outside to continue a discussion, or for no other reason than that they felt like eating outside, why not? They were the ones who had to carry their food and chairs outside, not us.

After school, their time was their own. We did not believe in stealing it from them by assigning homework. Well, perhaps I had better clarify that. In the lower classes we found that the children were easily able to cover everything in class, and so where there was an individual child who didn't quite understand something, it was assumed to be the teacher's fault. Being the teacher's fault, it was also the teacher's responsibility to bring the child up to par by tutoring him privately.

In the upper two classes where the syllabus was more demanding, the teacher would sometimes arrange to meet with her whole class after hours to go over the work that hadn't been covered. Whether you want to call that homework or call it an extension of the class, the fact remains that no teacher was allowed to assign extra work unless the need was so compelling that she was prepared to give up an equivalent amount of her own time.

If, on the other hand, the children wanted to study on their own time, that was entirely up to them. And they did want to. Once the compulsion of homework and the pressure of marks have been removed, children will insist upon learning out of the sheer pleasure of learning. They have a need to learn. We didn't ask them to do any extra work, and we couldn't have stopped them from doing it. Well, you may be thinking, these were Jewish children who had come to us instilled with the Jewish respect for education. You are mistaken. In later years, I became the director of Wiltwyck, a home up in the woods of the Hudson Valley for emotionally disturbed juvenile delinquents who had been sent to us by the New York City courts. Mostly, they were black. To a great extent, they had to be taught how to read and write. No value had been placed on education in their homes. They were at Wiltwyck because very little attention of any kind had been paid to them. No homework was assigned to these children, either, and I was forever complaining that they were working too hard. I shouldn't have. Children enjoy working too hard. What they don't enjoy is being told to study when they would rather be doing anything but. What they don't enjoy is being forced to memorize a lot of names and dates to be written on a test paper and forgotten.

Whatever they wanted to do, the children's leisure time was their own. In a community where everybody knows everybody else, one of the most important rights is the right to be left alone. Otherwise, the same community that supports a child can impose itself upon him. When a child felt the need to go off by himself and think the long, long, thoughts of youth, it was understood by adults and children alike that his privacy was to be respected. If two boys were wrestling around, nobody came running to break it up. If they were wrestling, it was fair to assume that they felt like wrestling. It was all right to watch them if you wanted—that was your business—but you didn't disturb them. Any more than they had a right to disturb you by wrestling around in a room where you were reading or studying.

With us, where the school and Home were one, there was always that problem of continuously reaffirming the strength of the community without losing sight of either the individual the community was there to serve or the very real world that lay outside. To make the children happy was one thing, but to turn the Homes into "islands of happiness" was to be avoided at all costs. Just as we refused to disguise the fact that their parents were in mortal danger and that their own situation was precarious, we impressed upon them constantly that the Kinderheim was only an episode in their lives, a temporary respite in which they were being given a chance to prepare themselves for the new life that would be opening to them. The immediate reality was that we were living in France. Since everybody had been attending a daily French class almost from the day of his arrival, I would have preferred, all things being equal, to have conducted all our classes in French. Things being as they were, I was confronted with a head-on collision between two of my basic purposes. Language, as I discovered very quickly, was such a powerful emotional tie to home and family that the children, and particularly the older ones, were simply not prepared to abandon the German tongue.

Another reality was that many of them had not attended school on anything like a regular basis for two years. Obviously, we were not going to turn them into eager students again by forcing a language upon them that was, at best, strange to them and, at worst, threatening. We began, therefore, by conducting all classes in German, with a follow-up discussion in French. After two months had elapsed, the French language began to predominate. By degrees. At first, it was only for gymnastics and drawing, which require a minimum of abstract thought, then for geography and French history and, at length, the natural sciences and mathematics. From there, it was easy enough to set apart one day a week when all classes were to be conducted exclusively in French and, by the time the school year had come to an end, three days a week.

Within that general timetable, I was never unmindful that the ability to learn languages varies markedly according to age. With the little ones, from three to six, we didn't even bother to hold classes. At that age, they don't so much learn a language as absorb it from the air around them. In no time at all, they were chattering among themselves as naturally as any other little French kids.

Sometimes they picked it up so naturally that, like any other children of that age, they overreached themselves. At the end of our first year in France, two days after the beginning of the war, to be precise, we put on a circus to which more than two hundred French citizens and officials had been invited. The circus was an enormous success, far beyond anything I had anticipated, and the hit of the day was Hans, a little scene-stealer from the Petite Colonie. The circus was supposed to end with an enormous ballet number, and there were so many ballet dancers that I was afraid the stage, which had been constructed of heavy cardboard mâché, was going to collapse. As the dancers pirouetted into their final bows, Margot's piano broke into the "Marseillaise," the French national anthem, and the smallest of the children from the kindergarten class—materializing it seemed from out of the air—stepped between them waving small French flags. A smash ending and, considering the audience (which had obviously been considered), a smash hit. To little Hans, who was a little devil anyway, always in the middle of everything, the first taste of an appreciative audience proved to be so heady that as soon as the applause began to die down he stepped forward, front and center, and began to sing out the words. Loudly and exuberantly. Pumping his little flag back and forth to the march tempo of the music. But it was the words . . . The words that were rolling out of him so proudly and defiantly sounded for all the world like French, the zest and spirit were undeniably French, the accent and phonetics were perfect. It was, to give our little devil his due, as close as it was possible to get to French without actually hitting upon one certifiable French word. And quite understandably too. The words of the "Marseillaise" tend to ringing denunciations like, "The filthy blood of the oppressors will soak the battlefield," and such other declarations as might be expected to move an army of revolutionaries to action and mystify a six-year-old. No matter. What made his performance so irresistible was that the more evident it became that he had no idea whatsoever what he was saying, the more evident it also became that he was blissfully unaware that he didn't. (What made Hans himself such a striking figure was that he had come to us only a few months earlier with such a headful of lice that his head had been shaven clean. The hair had been so slow in growing back that only the finest of fuzz kept him from being completely bald.)

After the first stunned silence, there were smiles and chuckles, roars of laughter and, at the end, a thunderous ovation. Little Hans became famous forever after and was pointed out to visitors as The Boy Who Sang the Marseillaise. A legend in his own time. Good-natured chap that he was, he took it all in stride, never doubting for a moment that he had brought the house down by the sheer brilliance of his rendition.

That was how the little ones learned the language. Naturally and without question. Within six months or so, German became nothing more than a second language to most of them and by the end of the year no more than a foreign language they had once known.

The other children of the Petite Colonie, those between seven and ten, picked up the language without too much difficulty from their daily contacts but since they don't absorb it through the pores at that age, we thought it advisable to reinforce the environment with daily classes for a few months. Within a short time, Georgie was even dreaming in French. He continued to dream in French long after we had come to the United States and he was speaking English fluently.

No matter how fluent they became they continued to speak German among themselves, even after the war had begun and there was no hope, realistically, that they would ever return to their homes. You could almost state it as a Law: Much as immigrants will cluster together in their new country, young people who are brought to a new country in a compact group will cling to their old language, their *own* language, for years.

I didn't interfere. How could I? Their private lives were their own. If their behavior conflicted with my goals, life is, after all, a patchwork of unresolved conflicts. I try to practice what I preach. I am a realist.

It was, I can say, the sole area in which we did not fight the refugee mentality wherever it reared its head. Few things made me angrier than to hear the children say, as they sometimes did when things weren't going exactly as we had hoped, "Well, what can you expect? We are only refugees."

"What do you mean!" I would snap back. "We are human beings like everybody else. I have no complaints about how I am treated in France, and the French have given you no reason to complain, either."

I meant it. If I had one overriding concern it was that we should not become a self-imposed ghetto. To give them a better

understanding of French people and institutions, we planned
excursions and trips and exchanged visits with the children of the
village.

The Great Paris Excursion was one of our biggest events. The
preparation for the trip took weeks. After breakfast, we would
gather in the big assembly hall. The route we were to travel was
studied and sketched. Photographs of every landmark, every
house, every monument that was on our itinerary were hung on
the wall behind me, alongside a detailed map of the surrounding
area. The background and historic significance of each was
minutely discussed. Finally, on the night before the excursion, a
movie of Paris was shown.

On the appointed day, more than fifty cars, running
predominantly to black limousines, descended upon us. Our
volunteer chauffeurs for the trip were the distinguished members
of the OSE Board, the even more distinguished members of the
Board of Honor, and a few friends and well-wishers.

For everybody, young and old alike, Paris is a woman. An
ageless woman with an infinite variety of charms. For us, she was
a wise old lady who wrapped her bountiful arms around us and
welcomed us with a smile. The names and pictures came to life.
The children greeted each new landmark as if it were an old
acquaintance. You could sense the growing feeling that we were
finally becoming a part of Paris, and therefore of France. For
weeks afterward, we continued to talk about Paris, retracing our
steps, reliving every scene; verifying and validating the total
experience. We read her poets and sang her songs and learned
her language with a wholly new sense of understanding and,
indeed, belonging.

Before I had ever been to Paris I knew it better than I knew my
own city. I know it better even now than I know San Francisco
though I have been living here for fifteen years. I am certain that
if I should return to Paris today, as I returned during my service in
the army, I would find within myself the sense of nostalgia that
can only be experienced when you are walking through the streets
of a city that you know like the back of your own hand.
—Ernst Valfer

The educational benefits resulting from the Great Paris Excursion were twofold. Psychological and cultural. It was only with the establishment of the family as a social institution, you know, that the period of childhood was prolonged long enough for the upcoming generation to inherit the vast cultural and scientific storehouse of mankind. For our children, the umbilical cord had been broken. With us, where school and Home were one, the cultural continuum that would have been absorbed unconsciously around the kitchen table had to be imparted by a kind of artificial insemination.

In addition to our plays and festivals and trips, the older children organized their own programs every other Sunday afternoon. They invited guest speakers for discussions on youth problems and movements, assimilation and Zionism. At other times, they would opt to forgo the speakers and entertain themselves. They recited the *Malade Imaginaire* by Molière. The airs and choruses from the *Barbier de Seville* and *Le Mariage de Figaro* were sung and played. They arranged a concert and—culture being where you find it—a ping-pong tournament.

The visits to the studio apartment of N. Aronson, who is generally regarded as second only to Rodin among French sculptors, made the deepest and most lasting impression. To see a form emerge beneath the quick and expert hands of a sculptor of that caliber is exciting enough in itself. But Aronson left them something beyond a mere exhibition of his craft to remember him by. As he conducted each new group of refugee children through his studio, he attempted to describe for them the pride and passion that impel a man to hurl himself against an art form where every new achievement can only permit him to glimpse the vast and dimly envisioned possibilities that are forever beyond his reach.

Many students were so inspired that immediately upon their return they asked us to schedule seminars on every known form of art. Some of them returned to Aronson's studio again and again.

One of my fondest remembrances goes back to the day when you made it possible for me to join the older ones in a trip to Paris where we visited the studio of N. Aronson. The autographed reproduction of one of Aronson's sculptures has accompanied me ever since; through a period of hiding in the convent, and later when we walked into Switzerland. I have taken it with me to Argentina, and to this day it is one of my favorite mementoes. And now that painting means so much to me, I often think back to that exciting day when I was introduced to the world of Art.

—The birthday letter of Henny Bienstock,
a girl of Eaubonne and artist of renown
in Los Angeles.

In an educational system which is truly geared to keeping instruction as close to life as possible, one also has to be mindful of the backgrounds of the children, the special circumstances under which they had come to us and the living conditions that probably awaited them. These were not children who had been sent to a boarding school by indulgent parents. They were children who would have to go out into the world to earn a living, possibly in a strange country, probably without any family tradition to guide them and certainly without any parental connections to smooth the way. For those, like Emil Geisler, who were bored to death by academic studies, vocational studies were provided first on an apprenticeship level and then as they became more proficient, on a professional one. By professional we meant exactly that. Able to earn a living at it. Our goal was to turn out skilled artisans.

For that matter, a great deal of attention was paid to manual instruction with all the children. More attention perhaps than to anything else. Since our aim was to turn out complete men and women, not intellectual snobs and certainly not intellectual cripples, the preapprentice course, in which the boys received elementary training in the use of basic tools and the girls were taught how to sew, was always looked upon as our most important single course. So important that it was mandatory for even the older boys and girls who were being definitely pointed toward college. And it was just as well. When the war came and we had to reinforce the dirt barricades with bricks, the older boys already had the basic skills required for a crash course in brick-making. (And manual skills once learned are never completely forgotten, as I discovered with a grandfather's pleasure a few years ago while watching Gustl teach his wide-eyed nine-year-old son the remarkable craft of carpentry.)

Manual dexterity was developed in the younger children through lessons in drawing and painting, cutting and modeling. From there, they moved into the preapprenticeship courses, beginning with two-hour classes given twice a week and, as they became more proficient, into three-hour classes three times a week. After that, they were ready for the professional courses. For the girls, the choice lay between horticulture (at Tourelles) and dressmaking (Helvetia), and since all vocational students had both a major and a minor, it really came down to which one they preferred to spend the most time at. At the beginning of our second year, cooking courses were opened in the kitchen of each Home, and if that doesn't sound very professional I can only say that it wasn't the way we had planned to do it. We had ordered a fully equipped kitchen and were just getting ready to have it installed in the cellar at Helvetia when the war intervened, making it necessary to convert the cellar into a bomb shelter.

For the boys, there was a somewhat wider choice between joinery and carpentry (Tourelles), shoemaking (Eaubonne), tailoring (Helvetia) and horticulture. We were also about to offer a course in leather tooling and polishing (which had previously been available at Eaubonne on only an arts-and-crafts level) when the real war caught up with us.

Nor was their academic work overlooked. Just as the academic students were encouraged to appreciate the pleasure of working with their hands, the vocational students were exposed to the pleasures of the mind. We proclaimed that our goal was to encourage our future workingmen to reach the highest intellectual level they could attain, and as pompous as that may sound we meant every word of it.

With some of the boys, where the interest in one trade was overwhelming, the second trade amounted to little more than training in rudimentary principles. In other cases, we assigned the second trade ourselves and insisted upon a complete and thorough training. Our shoemaker apprentices, for example, had sixteen hours a week of shoemaking, twelve hours of horticulture and from eight to twelve hours of academic subjects. Our thinking there was that if they should eventually find themselves in a stultifying kind of factory work we would have provided them with an alternative way of earning a living or, at least, a more pleasant way of supplementing their income or, at the very least, a hobby that would get them out into the fresh air.

For vocational and academic students alike we handed out progress reports every three months. In lieu of grades, there were twenty-four different evaluations (twelve positive and twelve negative). The most important part of these reports as far as we were concerned were the personal comments, which were aimed at encouraging the child to keep working rather than at merely passing judgment on work that had already been done. Social adjustment, which was only one of the many categories, was judged as to manners, cleanliness, politeness, helpfulness, comradeship and cooperation. Under a special heading, as a category unto itself, we noted in which direction the greatest progress had been made and where improvement was still most urgently needed.

For our own use, psychological and health charts were kept up to date on every child as a kind of instant profile on his social and intellectual development, his adjustment to the shock of separation and his ability to adapt to his new surrounding. A visiting English physician who spent some time at the Homes studying our methods informed me upon his departure that the most severe criticism he could offer was that our evaluations were too modest. "What to you is an optimistic prognosis," he said, "I would call successful therapy."

There was one other set of records we had to keep. The Ministry of Education insisted that we submit grades to them, on a scale of 1 to 10. We kept them on an A to E basis so that our books would be in order in the event of an inspection—a pitiful show of independence, to be sure, and other than that, pure clutter. The children were never aware that the grades existed and we in the administration ignored them.

If I now seem to dwell overmuch upon grades for a man who has just disclaimed any interest in them, bear with me. The war started a couple of weeks before the next school year was to open, and in what may have been an excess of prudence we did not feel justified in sending the children off to the public schools until the new term had begun in January. Thereafter, one-quarter of the children of school age attended the public schools of Montmorency, Soisy and Eaubonne, and the others attended our own centralized school at Les Tourelles. Seven of our children finished at the head of their class, three others were second and two were third. In one class the top five students were ours. In addition, seven of our brightest children, four girls and three boys, were sent to an excellent private high school in Enghien. The girls, who were children of political refugees, had attended school in Paris for about a year before coming to the Home and could handle the language with ease. At the end of the term they ranked first, second, fourth and ninth in their class.

> We were all in separate classes, mostly according to age, and we felt lonely, even though the work was not difficult. During the recess, we stood and shivered in the open sheds next to the school and tried to make friends with the French girls who were much older. After a while we got regular gas masks and took them to school every day, but the French girls kept their knitting in the olive drab canisters and did not take the masks as seriously as we did.
>
> —Hanna's diary

Two of the boys—Friedman, the instigator of the Orthodox revolt, and Windmuller—were sent for an entirely different reason. Each of them had missed so much schooling in Germany that they were far behind others of their own age. Nevertheless, I felt they were intelligent and secure enough in their identity so that they could only benefit from being thrown in with the brightest French children in their own age group and forced to sink or swim. Being among our oldest children, they were not at all fluent in French. Never mind. Knowing them, I had every confidence they would more than hold their own before they were through. It was of critical importance as far as their futures were concerned that they learn the subtleties and nuances of the language under pressure and in the real world into which they might very well be thrown far sooner than any of us had anticipated.

For with the declaration of war, our situation had changed drastically. Everything was now up in the air. Lene and I canceled our ship reservations again. Indefinitely. It was the older boys who were in the most immediate danger, though. An edict issued on the day war had been declared directed all enemy alien males, sixteen years or over, to turn themselves in at a detention camp. (I had turned myself in after a reasonable delay, the worst mistake I ever made. But that's another story. I mention it at this time only to make the point that all Germans and Austrians were considered to be enemy aliens, prima facie, regardless of the reason they may have left their country.) Windmuller and Friedman were both over fifteen. Unless the French authorities could be brought to look upon them not as Germans but as Frenchmen, they—and eventually all our boys—would be interned, an indignity so profound in the light of everything we had been telling them as to stamp an ineradicable wound upon them. From an even more practical standpoint—psychology being somewhat of a luxury when survival itself is at stake—they would be sitting there for the SS to scoop up when the German army captured the country. For if my experience in camp had done nothing else for me it had shorn me of any illusions I might have had that a country being run as badly as France could possibly win a war.

It was not only our older boys I was so worried about, then. Unless the French could be convinced that it would be in their interest to protect our children after the war was over, they were all in mortal danger. Nor did I believe that I was shooting in the dark. France had been bled white of its young manhood during World War I. Its birth rate was the lowest in Europe. With all its other problems, the government had become acutely aware that when this new round of bloodletting came to an end its population problem was going to be staggering. And so, if I seem to have been overly pleased at the high marks achieved by our children it was not out of any personal need to prove that we could beat the traditional schools on their own terms, on their own grounds. *Here are exactly the kind of French children you will be needing,* I was saying to the government. Do not treat them as political enemies, see them for the potential national resource which they are. Those who remain in France after the war will make good Frenchmen and Frenchwomen for you. Those who leave will be eternal friends of France wherever they may go.

The 75 percent who continued to attend classes on our own grounds were divided fairly equally between those who had arrived so late that their French still left a great deal to be desired and, of course, the vocational students. Included among the vocational students were a scattering of village children whom we had accepted with absolute delight after we had been informed that their parents felt that our mix of the manual and academic was exactly what they wanted.

A few of our boys were also being sent to highly specialized vocational or professional schools. One boy went to the School of Mechanics at Suresnes. Oskar Stammler, who may well have been our most brilliant mind, was attending a school of cinematography. Another boy was going to a school for graphic arts, and two others to a preapprenticeship school for electricians.

Ernst Weil, better known as Jumbo for exactly the reason you might suspect, had expressed a great deal of interest in becoming, of all things, a chef. His disappointment when we were unable to install the special equipment at Helvetia had been so great that we were sending him to the Cordon Bleu in Paris, the most famous training school for chefs in the world. In order to attend their classes, he had to leave us every morning before dawn—excellent training, I must say, for a man who would be owning a string of bakeries in San Francisco one day.

I can still recall arriving in San Francisco some years ago for a conference, switching on the television set in my hotel room and seeing the familiar face and figure of our own Jumbo in living

color as he instructed the good housewives of the city in the art of
pastry making.

We have a nice little contingent of alumni in San Francisco
and its environs; among them Albert Baer, who was invariably
called the Brown Bear in Montmorency to distinguish him from
his brother who had red hair and was, of course, the Red Bear.
The Brown Bear settled in San Francisco, went to work as a
salesman for Canada Dry and in due time married a German girl
who had been in a concentration camp. We had kept in touch
with him through the years, as we had kept in touch, to varying
degrees, with many of the others. But after fifteen years or so,
correspondence has a way of becoming desultory or, at best,
haphazard. When Lene and I found we had a chance to stop over
in San Francisco during one of our trips we arranged to meet Mr.
and Mrs. Brown Bear for a late dinner.

"You will never guess what I am doing now," he said, as soon
as we had exchanged greetings. "I own my own shoe shop."

He was right. I would never have guessed it. "Not in a
thousand years. How did it come about that you are the owner,
and a very proud one I can see, of a shoe shop?"

Very simply. He had suddenly come into a windfall in the
form of reparation money paid by the German government to
his wife. "You will never know how mad I would get when you
made me work in the shoe shop," he smiled. "You will never
know how much I thought I hated it." From the day he had
departed from France he had not given shoemaking a second
thought, he wanted me to know, except perhaps to remark
absently upon the increasing shoddiness that seemed to be
overtaking the product. Not until he and his wife began to realize
that the reparation money had given them the one chance they
would probably ever have to do something for themselves. And
then he hadn't even thought twice about it.

"Now I know why I learned to repair shoes in the Kinderheim," he had told her.

He had opened a shoe store in Orinda, outside San Francisco,
not only to sell shoes but to repair them. At first it had been a
struggle. And then, slowly at first and then in a rush, the repair

work had begun to come in. "Nobody wants to repair shoes anymore," he said. "As far as I know, I am the only repairman in all of California who works with modern machines." Apparently, he did his work surpassingly well. Inevitably, when you do good work the word gets around. The very best, most expensive shoes were being shipped to him from all over the country. The people who buy really expensive soft-leather shoes are anxious to keep them for as long as possible, it seems, because the longer they wear them the more comfortable they become.

By the time we had finished eating he had become so enthusiastic that even though it was well past midnight he insisted upon driving us out to Orinda so that we could see his shop and inspect his machines for ourselves.

Now, some of our children have become very successful. There are doctors, male and female. Professors, male and female. Youth directors. Electronic engineers. Businessmen. A city planner. A rabbi. I could go on and on. Except for the two youth directors, I cannot say for certain they would not have ended up in the same or reasonably equivalent professions if there had never been a school in Montmorency. And even with the youth directors, I cannot be absolutely sure.

But there is a shoe shop in Orinda. . . .

10. Coadministration

The preamble of our Constitution read:

"All the children and adults who live in the children's homes of the OSE Union form a community that directs the life of the homes by co-operating democratically in the administration. This community is a part of the great community of all human beings. It is proud to live among the French people and is conscious of belonging to the OSE Union, a center organized to help the Jewish people.

"The democratic rights as well as the duties of the members of the community are the same in both our small community and the larger ones. The liberties and the rights of the members are limited by voluntary commitment to all other human beings, to the nation in which we live and to the association we belong to."

To say that children learn better in an atmosphere of freedom does not mean that learning is an act of pure freedom. In order to adjust themselves socially, in order to learn how to learn, they have to be willing to submit themselves to voluntary restrictions. Anybody who believes that permissive education means permitting children to do anything they want to do knows very little about education and even less about children.

Once when the entire staff had to go to Versailles for a meeting with the Ministry of Education, members of the Board and of the central administration in Paris volunteered to come out—along with some of the more distinguished supporters of the institution—to take care of the children for the day. A pedagogue's delight! In they came, loaded down with candy and cookies and soccer balls and games of every description, their hearts overflowing with love, purity and inexperience. The eyes of their little angels lit up with a malicious gleam at the very sight of them. The children did love them, make no mistake about that. At any other time, they would have gone out of their way to please them. But their roles had been changed. The old, dear friends were now substitute teachers and that meant that they were to be tested and provoked; tormented, preferably in the most "angelic" and "innocent" ways, out of their minds. Thus it has been written in the Great Book on the War of Generations.

We came back just in time to rescue as harried and bewildered a group of kind hearts and gentle people as you are ever likely to see. Should I admit to the malicious pleasure that arose momentarily in my own breast at the relief with which they greeted us and the haste of their departure? We pedagogues were so greatly appreciated that it was weeks before a murmur of advice or complaint was heard from Paris.

Love is not enough. You have to know what you are doing.

While we were expressing our loathing for Prussian discipline, we were also striving to develop the positive aspects of companionship, democracy and fair play through a system of coadministration. We did not call it "self-government," which is the trap so many "children's towns" fall into. Children understand perfectly well that it would be sheer lunacy to hand over the management of an institution to them and utter deception to pretend that they are capable of running a system of education. What they are perfectly equipped to do is to participate in the administration of their own community affairs through their own elected Parliament and house committees.

Self-government is a pretense. Coadministration can be real. With us, it went to the heart and soul of what we were trying to do.

The best way to explain what we did is to describe what we did not do. We did not begin by setting rules, laying down restrictions or posting schedules. We began, instead, by asking for the children's cooperation. "We can't keep an eye on you all the time to make sure your house is in order," we told them. "We will leave it to you to keep order among yourselves."

In tasting freedom, they tested freedom; and in the testing they learned that freedom without order can be a pain in the neck. Within a few days, the occasion would arise where we could say, "Wouldn't you like to choose someone among you to see that there's no noise and disorder after lights-out?" And the children would agree.

Sports were always a very important part of their daily activities, both as an outlet for competitive instincts and for providing the physical exercise required by growing boys and girls. Since it was a leisure activity the adults kept out of it as much as possible. "Here is a soccer ball for you. You will find all the equipment you need outside." The ball and the rest of the equipment, they were advised, were to be looked upon as the common property of their house. "It would be a good idea, I think, to give somebody the responsibility of checking everything in and out so that nothing gets lost."

From keeping enough order so that they could get some sleep and protect their sports equipment, it was only a short step to: "We're planning a trip for tomorrow, and when we get home we'll probably be starved. So before we leave, sit down and peel the potatoes. If enough of you will stay with it you'll be surprised at how quickly you can get it done."

Soon enough, the spirit of cooperation and self-regulation was formalized through a written Constitution, which was submitted by us in rough form as a guide for general debate and discussion, and rewritten by a committee of children so that it would be in their own words. Our Home rules laid down broad principles with which we required compliance. Specific details were avoided since they would change to meet changing situations and different children.

As it was, the first reaction of the older, more sophisticated children was that all this talk about coadministration and democratic rights was just our clever little way of trying to manipulate them.

As they became convinced that there were no tricks up our sleeve, a remarkable thing happened, something that surprised and, perversely, pleased me. Precisely because "coadministration" gave them far more power than the word had perhaps implied to them, they began to call it "self-government." And when the fussy old director would correct them they would give me the look that says, "Why does he want to spoil all the fun by calling it by such a dull and unexciting name? Or is he only trying to make sure we know who's really the boss around here?"

The same thing happened with the Disciplinary Council. We deliberately refused to call it a Court because the jurisdiction of the Council was limited to matters that did not involve educational or administrative questions and, even more important, because we reserved the right to review all penalties. They liked to call it a Court anyway.

Whatever it was called, it was an enormous success. Within the general context of the Constitution, we had no trouble at all working out when the jurisdiction for an offense lay with us and when it lay with the Council.

For my own part, I preferred to have the children handle disciplinary cases wherever possible. With our children, even more than others, punishment by grownups usually called up all the old memories of being terrorized and, with them, the whole panoply of conscious and unconscious anger and resistance. Feeling the punishment to be unjustified, they were able to excuse or minimize their offense and shift the burden of guilt upon us. Kids cannot fool other kids, though, and knowing this, they can't fool themselves so easily, either. The very act of defending themselves before a panel of their peers absorbed them so completely that they didn't have time to think of anything else. In an atmosphere where the rules of the War of Generations could not be applied, they would, as often as not, come to understand the true nature of their offense from out of their own mouths.

I don't idealize children. The risk of having children's courts —and the reason we didn't have them—was that while kids can't be fooled on the basic question of innocence or guilt they don't have the ability to fit the penalty to the offense. And kids can be the toughest judges in the world. The penalties were usually so harsh that I would have to step in and reduce them. Which served a purpose too, in that it gave me a chance to discuss the reasons for both the verdict and the punishment with the offender at a time when he would presumably be feeling rather kindly toward me. It also gave me the opportunity to discuss the proper balance between crime and punishment with the members of the Council, who, in fact, felt much better about taking the responsibility of conducting trials and meting out punishment upon themselves when they knew that the ultimate responsibility lay elsewhere.

With us, the community was so important that any offense against it tended to become magnified out of all proportion:

> I remember most of all the community spirit. I can remember events when I felt this spirit was violated and they were always upsetting times for me I took it as such a violation of trust. My most precious possession was a fountain pen I had received as a birthday present several years before. During the time I was going to school in the village, I would sometimes leave my satchel, with the pen and some notebooks in it, in an open cubby hole in the general cloak room on my way to breakfast and pick it up again when I was through. One morning, I began to feel sick while I was eating. I went upstairs to the infirmary, and either Lene or Margot took my temperature and put me to bed. When I was released I found my fountain pen had been stolen. I was dreadfully upset because I couldn't imagine who would do such a thing in the Kinderheim. It was simply something that one did not do. I did report it, however. For it *was* my favorite possession. Nothing about it was ever found.
>
> —Girl who was living in Helvetia,
> thirteen at the time

The trial I remember most vividly occurred during the rehearsals for the circus, an exciting event in which every child participated. One of the comedy acts was to be a performing bear who would ride a bicycle up and down the aisles throughout the show doing whatever a bear on a bicycle does. The bear was to be played by Ernst Weil (Jumbo) and a bearskin. The bicycle belonged to Joey, a nine-year-old boy whose mother was one of our teachers. Joey was so unhappy at having been assigned the unglamorous job of showing our guests to their seats that as the week of the great event approached he demanded a performing role on the threat of withdrawing the use of his bicycle.

The director of the circus told him that if he was going to take that kind of attitude he couldn't be an usher either. At that point the case was first referred to me.

I didn't care whether we had a bear on a bicycle or, even, whether the show was good or bad. To me, all these festivals were purely educational. "If he insists, let him have his bicycle back," I said. "So we'll have a dancing bear instead of a bicycle-riding bear."

I had promised the director I would talk to Joey, though, and so I explained to him that however unglamorous the job seemed to him, ushers were needed. He had been assigned to the job. If he were now to be assigned to something else, another boy would have to take his place and he might not be happy about it either. "The bicycle is only being used for one day," I told him. "And you won't be using it, anyway."

Joey remained stubborn. If he didn't get the performing role, we didn't get the bicycle. Sour grapes, sure. On the other hand, Joey was undersized for his age and not very popular. If he felt that he was always the one being left out of things maybe he had a reason. Since I represented the authority in the community I told him I would have to give the matter more thought and waited hopefully to see what might develop.

The next day, it was right back in my lap. The director of the circus decided that Joey's attitude was so antisocial, an affront of such proportions to a community project, that it was a matter for the Disciplinary Council.

A vexing problem. We didn't want to encourage antisocial behavior, of course, but did the community have the right to deprive him of his right to be antisocial? The educational stakes were clear. In this little tug of war over a bicycle we were seeing the basic contradiction that arises out of community living. Where does justice lie when the rights of the individual (however selfish and cranky the assertion of those rights may appear to be) come into conflict with the perceived needs (however trivial and misguided they might appear to be) of the community.

With some apprehension, and only because I was so anxious to see how the Council would handle such a tricky problem, I gave the word to go ahead with the trial.

The trials at Tourelles were held in the big ballroom on the first floor, almost directly across from my office. Hundreds of children came to watch this one, that was how furious they were with him. I was in and out of the hearing room all morning, but even when I was not there I could hear what was going on by leaving my door open.

During the first part of the hearing, it came out that Joey had rented the bicycle to other children at times and had let others use it in return for the promise that they would fight with him against others. But when Joey was permitted to speak for himself, he sidestepped the main issue by claiming that at the time his mother gave him the bicycle she had told him he was not to lend it to anybody. Immediately, the chairman of the Council, an eleven-year-old girl, announced, "We want to discuss this with Ernst," and called a halt to the proceedings.

I can still see her as she led her committee into my office. Her name was Edith Roth. A redheaded girl. Her older brother, who was also a redhead (Roth means *red* in German), was one of the leaders of the Home, but it had been a surprise when she ran for chairman of what was in many respects the most important of our committees. Her victory had been a huge upset—which wasn't so much of an upset, if you follow me, because upsets were as much the rule as the exception in our elections. (We didn't have more than the normal percentage of redheads either. It just seems that every redhead we did have has been involved in one or another of these stories.)

"Why did you interrupt the hearing, Edith?" I asked her.

She pointed to the open door. "Didn't you hear what he said?"

Yes, I had heard.

"This is not a matter for our Court anymore," she intoned. "This involves a member of the staff now, and the Council does not have the authority to deal with staff members." A very nice mind for legal distinctions for an eleven-year-old girl. "In my opinion," she said, "you have to handle it, Ernst."

I can have a nice mind for legal distinctions too, when I have to. "It involves her as a mother, not as an educator." And that put it right back in their jurisdiction.

Edith argued back that the Court didn't have the right to question a staff member for any reason; that by simply putting the question to her they would be setting up the kind of conflict between teacher and child that we had all agreed would be unhealthy.

I couldn't see why that should be. All they had heard so far was Joey's testimony. At the very least, they had the right to ask her whether she had really given him those instructions. Maybe she had only said, the way mothers will, that she didn't want to see the bicycle ruined before the week was over.

The other members of the Council rallied behind their chairman. It would not only be unhealthy for the community, they argued, it would not be fair to either Joey or to his mother to put her in a position where she either had to lie for him or to brand him as a liar.

They were marvelous. They had told me, whether they knew it or not, that they recognized they were dealing with an unhappy boy. We all knew that he was lying. All right, I shrugged. Whether they chose to question her or not was entirely up to them. The trial was still in their hands.

Now I was more interested than ever in seeing how they were going to handle it. They handled it just beautifully. Without actually questioning Joey's mother, they succeeded in putting the question to her. The decision went like this: "If his mother gave him the bicycle and told him he should only use it himself we cannot dispute her wishes. But the Council requests that she take it back again because it should not be in the Home under such restrictions. If she did not give him those instructions, it is our verdict that he is to give it back tó her. If, after three months, he wants to change his attitude then he can have it back."

Solomon-like wisdom that was far more the exception than the rule.

As far as the punishment itself was concerned, I felt that three months was far too harsh. The idea was to encourage him to rejoin the community, not to make him feel more like an outcast than ever. I had a long talk with him, and the confiscation of his bicycle was cut down to one month.

The dangers attendant to having a mother and her child on the grounds among children who had no mothers is so obvious that only a fool would have failed to do everything within his power to avoid it. Having said that, I now have to confess that we had at least a dozen. A woman who had some kind of training she knew we could use would come to the Paris office and plead, "Take my child and I will work for nothing." We didn't want her to work for nothing. Nor did we want to turn away a child if the circumstances were really desperate. Still, most of the time I was able to say no. I didn't say no often enough.

The mothers and their children were kept apart as much as possible. They were always assigned to different living quarters, and we were very careful not to place the child in any of the mother's classes. And still I knew that I was asking for trouble. Some of the mothers were very bad teachers; some of them were very good. But each of them was a danger to us because they would support their child when they got into arguments with other youngsters, something that all the children resented deeply. And they were a danger to us as a total community because they would instinctively protect their child when he or she did something wrong.

The most disturbed—and disturbing—boy we had was the younger son of one of our most popular and most important women teachers. His father had been killed in Spain, and although I had known him only slightly the fallen comrades have a call on you. The older son was a very responsible young fellow of about fourteen. The younger boy was around nine and, as so frequently happens, was a little hellion. The terrible thing about him was that he tortured animals, behavior that went so totally

against everything we stood for as to be unheard of and unthinkable. Until I heard about it and had to think about it. He could
not have gotten away with it for as long as he did, of course,
unless his mother had protected him. I spoke to her about it. I
warned her that steps would have to be taken. And then I spoke
to the boy—and ended up protecting him too.

It is very easy to delude yourself that you are helping this type
of child, because he will radiate affection at you for showing such
an interest in him. He will also turn on you completely when he
has given himself some new reason to fear that you might want to
punish him.

Torturing animals can be called the courage of the coward. It
comes out of the child's need to prove to himself that there is not
a terror living inside him. Some of the other children at the Petite
Colonie must certainly have witnessed his handiwork because
there are times when the only way you can prove something
which is patently untrue to yourself is to prove it to your companions.

I had more fear for—and about—this boy than any of the
others. But, you know, you keep telling yourself that you are in a
position to do more for him than anybody else, and you know
you could never turn him over to anybody else—who else was
there?—without somehow feeling that you are betraying his
mother (and losing her in the bargain); and so you try not to fool
yourself too much on your motives and all the while you're
hoping for a miracle.

Miracles sometimes happen. I did everything wrong with my
bad boy, and he ended up in South America where he became a
cowboy—the perfect job for him—and was able to prove his
courage busting broncos and breaking steers.

Horst was Lene's bad boy, in the more maternal sense. Horst
was the sensitive, idealistic boy who was always off in the corner
brooding. The boy in whom the weakness and the wound were
always visible. The world had put the wound there. Germany; a
murdered brother; the *St. Louis;* the parents rotting away in
Gurs. "The only thing we can do now is to commit suicide," he
had shouted upon hearing that war had been declared. The

weakness was that he did not want to live in such a world. We would send him to Gurs to stay with his parents for two weeks, as we did with the others, and after a few days he would ask to be sent "home." Home. That was us. Lene could only try to comfort him and hope that in some way she was easing the pain.

How smart do you think you can be? How much do you think you can do? My bad boy found his salvation, no help from me, as a cowboy in South America. Lene's bad boy was taken by the Vichy gendarmerie and shipped to Auschwitz. The boy who could not live with the thought of an advancing army was there in the middle of the slaughterhouse. I can cry when I think of Horst. By the time he committed suicide—as of course he did—he must have been one great gaping wound.

11. We Called Them Educateurs

If I was unimpressed by Rachel on my initial inspection of the Petite Colonie, she was about as entranced with me as you might expect anybody to be who has just been told that someone is dropping by to decide whether he wants to replace her. As my lack of interest became increasingly evident you could almost see her annoyance turn into relief. "He isn't going to take it," I could see her thinking. "He thinks he's too good for us. I'm still going to be in charge around here."

Rachel was a Lithuanian Jew, and Lithuanian Jews have a reputation for being able to size up situations in a hurry. When the biggest room in the cottage was converted into an office for me she understood, without having to be told, that I would not be taking all that space for administrative purposes unless we were planning to expand. Or that if expansion was in the wind all she had to do was sit tight, wait for me to move on to bigger and better things and the big office would belong to her. After that, we enjoyed the loving relationship that can only come when someone discovers they are going to get something through you that they would never have been able to get without you.

It was important that we get along because it would have been almost impossible to keep any kind of order without Rachel. We were, after all, dealing with very young children who came from unassimilated Russian families, and Russian was the only language most of them spoke. Although Rachel had come to France

when she was only four or five years old she had always lived
within the Russian colony, and she spoke both French and Russian fluently. The children had to be kept busy, and she could
communicate with them far better than I could. Being as intelligent as she was, she recognized very quickly that if I said that I
had to control the administrative end of things, and Lene had to
control the treatment, I was also turning every other phase of the
children's lives over to her.

In case she didn't, I spelled it out for her after she had come in
to complain about some directive or other. "I don't understand a
word of Russian, you know," I said, looking at her across the
desk. "That can be a great advantage to both of us."

I really won her over, though, when the daily classes began.
Rachel was very eager for me to hire her sixteen-year-old sister to
help her, and since I was just as eager to keep her happy I insisted,
over the objections of the OSE people, that the girl be given a
chance. She was very good with the prekindergarten children;
excellent, in fact. It didn't matter that she couldn't handle the
older children because Rachel took care of them, and Rachel was
a jewel. An absolute genius. She'd had some training in teaching,
but that didn't have anything to do with it. Rachel's genius was
that she could always come up with new and exciting ideas that
weren't in any book. She was, for instance, able to make an
adventure out of the simple routine of washing up in the morning
by hanging the face towels on individual hooks, with each child's
hook identified by a personal symbol which he or she had selected for himself: a flower, a deer, a candle, a star, or something
similar.

By the time I moved over to Helvetia, I was able to leave the
Petite Colonie completely in her hands. Oh, I would drop in from
time to time, because there was nothing that could lift my spirits
more than to spend an hour or two among the little ones. Particularly in the late morning or afternoon. In all the Homes, the
children were expected to help out with the meals, and the Petite
Colonie was no exception. Each child took his regular turn at
setting up the chairs and tables, which were almost doll-size,
setting the table, serving and cleaning up afterward. It was a sheer

delight to see them bustling about in their labor, as somber and intense as only very small children can be when the smallest of accomplishments is filled with importance and the simplest of assignments is freighted with significance.

And very useful, too, in restoring a sense of perspective.

The other woman I found at the broken-down convalescent home was the cook, Margot Cohn. Two jewels out of two. When I moved my office to Helvetia she came with me. Not as a cook, but as the directress. Margot was married to a doctor who had a very bad heart; they had hoped to go to Palestine when it became necessary to flee Germany but they hadn't been able to make the connections in time.

Margot had been a social worker in Germany, which sounds far more impressive than it really was. A social worker in Europe before the war was not a social worker as we think of them in America. There was no decision-making responsibility attached to the job; it was simply a matter of interviewing people and filling out forms.

Never mind. You had only to talk to Margot to see that she had that special glow that is found only in a few very special people. There is no other way to put it except to say that the girls all fell in love with her. Without exception. The Robinsoner girls came strutting in full of vim, vigor and scorn for all middle-class values and within a week they were just as much in love with Margot as the Cubans.

Margot had a dedication that shone so brightly that I am going to jump through time and tell you now that when many of our children were sent to the Gurs concentration camp after the Nazis had taken over the previously unoccupied part of France in 1942, she insisted on going with them. She escaped with her life by a matter of hours when the OSE, which had organized a remarkable Underground network by then, got word that the prisoners were about to be shipped to Poland. One of the leaders of the network, an OSE director named Dr. Joseph Weill, had established connections among the Vichy police officials. By this I mean that he had spread enough money around to convince them that it would be well worth their while to pass the word to him when lives were in danger. (The Claude Rains character in the picture *Casablanca* was a marvelous portrayal of the Vichy police officer. They would not help the French Underground, let alone the Jewish Underground, but they would not go out of their way to turn them in, either. Unless there was something in it for them, they just followed orders except on those rare occasions when, if the risk was not too great, they would be moved to make a sentimental gesture.) One could not simply buy a prisoner out, you must understand. Margot, along with another of our teachers who had gone to Gurs with her, were marginal cases. They were living the lives of prisoners but they were also on the payroll of OSE as teachers. Weill was able to rush down from Paris with a packet of money in time to rescue Margot Cohn, her husband (who had no connection with OSE) and a handful of other women who were in the employ of the OSE. By pulling strings with the Swiss Red Cross, Weill was then able to get them across the border into Switzerland where Margot immediately organized a Red Cross home for other refugee children. I have a letter she sent to one of her former colleagues in which she wrote, "It is not the old life I can live anymore after I have lived in Montmorency."

The first person I actually hired at the Petite Colonie was Kaete Bodek. Like Margot, she had been a social worker in Germany. Like Margot, her husband had been a doctor. And that's where the similarity ended. Margot was completely nonpolitical. I had met Kaete and her husband while they were serving with the International Brigade in Spain, he as a doctor and she as a part-time nurse and full-time cook. Her husband had subsequently been killed, she was in need of a job and because we had separated the children into the two cottages by then I was able to hire her as a second cook.

Kaete came to Helvetia with me, too. Still as a cook. And not because I couldn't have used her talents as a teacher. In an institution full of children, the cook can be more important than half a dozen teachers. The children will come by during the day to coax an extra snack or a piece of cake out of her, and while they are sitting around in that relaxed and homely atmosphere they will offer up the kind of confidences they might not want to bring to their counselors.

At Helvetia, she became the *dünne* (thin) Kaete, and Kaete Hirsch, who was hired soon afterward as our second cook, was the *dicke* (fat) Kaete. Together, they became our Kitchen Administration, the soothers of all wounds; the comfortable, comforting mother figures.

Just as Tourelles was about to be opened our prospective director was ordered to report to the detention camp. I looked around to see who might be able to handle the job and knew exactly who it had to be. "As the senior nonexecutive employee," I told Kaete, "you're the new directress if you want it. If you don't want it, you're it anyway. We have a tradition of moving our cooks up the ladder around here."

We assembled our teaching staff in much the same way—by taking whom we could get and training them on the job. We told them that they were more than merely teachers, more than merely counselors, more than merely social workers—and more than the sum total of all three. We coined our own word to describe what they were, *educateurs,* a word that casts a far wider net than any word that can be found in the English language. It is a full-service word, and the way we used it—to switch to a completely American image—it touches every base and steals second along the way.

(Would you believe that today there is an organization of *educateurs* in Europe, and that it is a licensed profession in France. The credit belongs to a French Boy Scout leader named Doubrel, who was sent to Germany with the French army after the war to work with German juvenile delinquents—it has always amused me that Doubrel spoke German even worse than I spoke French—and who eventually opened schools in both France and Germany to train *educateurs* for work with maladjusted children. Doubrel took my methods and expanded upon them to suit his own purposes and theories, something I am aware of because we were in constant communication while I was running the Wiltwyck School for Boys in upper New York State, the only place where the *educateur* system has ever been used in the United States.)

Where did we get so many remarkable people? We took all the French teachers we could get, needless to say. Which means not very many. We couldn't come close to matching the French pay scale and our system of progressive education was too far removed from their training or temperament for them to be comfortable with us. Despite the very real sense of mission of those who did decide to give it a try, they were simply too steeped in the tradition of the authoritarian schoolmaster to work out very well.

The first people we hired were mostly refugees who had fought in Spain. They were idealists. They were adaptable. They were powerfully motivated. And they were unemployed. The next pool of talent came primarily from the Austrian Socialists. I have always said that there were 800,000 Socialists in Austria and I knew 900,000 of them. I went out and solicited those who had the qualities we were looking for, and if some of them solicited a job with us to keep from being deported I didn't inquire too much about their qualifications.

One of the first men I sought was Walter Gruen, a lawyer who had picked up a hammer and become a carpenter to help us in the remodeling of Helvetia. Walter was an old friend who was undergoing some kind of crisis of the spirit. He didn't want to teach, but he asked me if I would take him on as a gardener. All right. So we would have an intellectual doing gardening work. He could usually be found with a bunch of small children around him, instructing them on things both great and small. Or, if there were no youngsters around, he would get into long and not infrequently heated arguments with parents who came to visit their children. I would usually get a letter the next day telling me how grateful they were to know that their children were under the care and guidance of a man as brilliant as Dr. Gruen.

Life came back to him, really, not so much through his work with the children as through his relationship with a young, cheerful teacher from the Petite Colonie, Klari. Little Klari, no more than five feet tall, as cute as a button but solidly built and a powerful swimmer. An excellent teacher and a good person. She had written a book about life at the Petite Colonie which she called *126 Gosses,* which translates to *126 Kids.* She buried the manuscript in the garden when she went south with us, in the hope that she would be able to return for it one day.

Although Walter Gruen was able to leave France before we were, he had to intern himself in Gurs for a few weeks while he was waiting for his visa to Mexico to come through. While he was there, he wrote me the following letter:

"I could thank you for your material aid, for the pleasant work which helped me to forget much, very much. I could thank you for all the many things I was able to learn from you. But I know you well enough to spare myself the expression of such gratitude.

"What I do want to thank you for is a great *human* experience. An experience which unquestionably gave me back much of my strength and vitality and will.

"And finally I should like to speak of something that I first really became aware of only here, the magnificent 'atmosphere' you created in the Homes. I am able to appreciate this achievement only now, when I see with what satisfaction and ease of mind and confidence these parents sitting in this concentration camp speak of their children as 'so fortunately taken care of.' And by that the parents do not mean only food and shelter; I could almost envy you for this. . . ."

Klari was eventually able to join Walter in Mexico, where they got married. One fine afternoon she dove into the ocean to save a drowning man. He was saved, and little Klari drowned.

If the paucity of trained teachers was a handicap that had to be overcome, there was also a certain advantage in not having to break them away from their old ideas. The real problem with having to train so many people as we went along was that I found myself conducting far more classes than I had planned to. There was, after all, only so much that could be imparted by having them observe my classroom methods and techniques. In order to teach subjects like mathematics and physics, you have to know mathematics and physics.

The one complete teacher we did have was Karl, a very important member of the staff, and a very important man in my life. Karl was a Gentile whom I had first met in Vienna in the early thirties when I was chairman of the Socialist Youth. As the majority party in Vienna, we were running the school system and a lot of young teachers had been signing up only because they felt it would help their careers. To find out who among them were really dedicated I formed an elite group within the organization to be composed solely of those young teachers who were willing to spend their summer vacation, without pay, working on special projects. Karl was one of the first to volunteer. He spent the summer doing the hardest, dirtiest kind of work on a children's farm.

Karl was always a man for the dirty jobs. When Dollfuss came to power, and there was no work for any Socialist teacher anywhere in Austria except Vienna, I drew up a list of the people whom we would have to appoint to our schools the following year. When I then had to leave the country at a moment's notice, the last thing I did was to tell my friends to get that list out of my office before the government could get its hands on it. Karl was, of course, one of the men who broke into the office and made off with all my books and records. As a result, everybody did get their appointments. If the new government had tried to fire every teacher in Vienna who belonged to the Socialist party the entire school system would have collapsed. But Karl did not work for the Fascists gladly. As soon as he heard I was running a school in France, he flew to Paris to ask whether he could come to work for us. Salary was no object. "I know how dedicated you are, Karl," I told him. "I know that you mean what you are saying now. I also know how difficult it is to leave your country, because it is also my country and after five years I still dream of returning someday."

"I would rather dream of returning to a free Austria," replied Karl, "than work under the Fascists for one more day."

He was a godsend. A highly skilled teacher, completely versed in the Viennese system we had patterned ourselves after. He could teach any age group, any course, and, even with that full load, he was always ready to spend his free time training the others.

After the Nazis had swept down through what had been known as Unoccupied France, Karl joined the Underground and although he was married by then—he had married Lene's cousin Lori, who had taught poster art at Montmorency—took on the most dangerous of all assignments. He became part of a motorcycle brigade that ran supplies to the Underground hideouts. There being no way to disguise a squad of motorcycles racing down the road, the only protection they had was to travel in the open and, if they were stopped, claim that they were working for the Nazis. Unfortunately for Karl, there were other, older men in his brigade when it was stopped, men who were well known to the gendarmerie.

Once the Nazis had him, they had no trouble at all identifying him. A Gentile who had worked with the Jews and, even worse, married a Jewess. The word that came to us through the OSE was that Karl had been tortured and killed, and that Lori, who had just given birth, had been captured and sent to a concentration camp. The baby was smuggled back to Paris and for the next year and a half it was kept hidden in a hospital. That's right. For the first year and a half of that baby's life, it never moved outside a hospital room.

Karl had not been killed, though. They had merely beaten him to within an inch of his life and shipped him off to a concentration camp. As soon as he was released he joined the Communists because he was convinced that the Communists were the only revolutionary force willing to fight people like the Nazis on their own brutal terms.

I met with him once when I was in Vienna and found that he had been tortured so badly that he was a semi-invalid. His internal injuries were so severe that he had to follow a special diet.

Karl, my idealist, was no more. The sparkling, vivacious man who had believed so passionately that we would win the world through education and humanism had died at the hands of his torturers.

And then there was Mandel, who was not on the educational staff, and yet was one of the most important people we had. Leib Mandel was a small, compact man, dark and muscular. He had lived for a time in a kibbutz in Palestine, decided it wasn't for him and had come back to his native Paris and taken a job as a worker on a road gang. One day while Mandel was wiping the sweat off his brow he saw the words MAISON D'ENFANTS, OSE-UNION on the side of a passing truck. Having read about the Children's Home and having liked the whole idea of it, he put down his pick and walked over to the OSE offices on the Champs Elysées to apply for a job.

He could drive a truck, he said, he had done farm work in Palestine and he was game for anything.

Well, we did have a truck. So why not a driver? But Mandel became much more than that. After you have been an administrator for any length of time you discover that there are certain people who are so dedicated and so competent at whatever they do that they take on an importance far beyond anything indicated in their job title. It's not *what* they do that is so important in such people, it's how they do it. Mandel could take a group of older boys out into the woods and teach them all they would ever have to know about woodsmanship. They would sit in a tight circle around him and hear about those facets of life in the real world of toil and sweat that cannot be learned in any classroom. The children admired Mandel enormously. Every member of the staff looked upon him as a valued colleague. And I myself had found a friend for all seasons.

Eventually, he became my personal chauffeur for the frequent trips to Paris, and also my confidant and my sounding board. He knew Paris like the palm of his hand, and he talked about the city as if it were a living thing. "I built this street," he once said during a bone-rattling ride. "I know every cobblestone we are passing over by its first name."

Mandel also married one of the women staff members, and their baby was born only a few weeks before we left. All three of them died in the gas chambers. If Margot Cohn's information was correct—and it usually was—they had been caught by the

Swiss border guard while they were trying to get out of France. The Swiss were like that. As much as they love to talk about their "neutrality" they have always been neutral in favor of the winning side. Very early in the war, they had come to an agreement with Hitler. As long as Hitler left them alone, the Swiss would permit unrestricted passage of all traffic between Germany and Italy; troops, military supplies, everything. Which is a very strange kind of neutrality, especially since it was all Hitler wanted out of them, anyway.

Their policy with regard to refugees was to allow just enough of them in to assuage whatever guilt they might have felt. Usually, they would accept refugees with children—although not always—and turn back everybody else. Even there, though, they would break up the family completely, sending the wife to one camp, the husband to another and the children to separate Red Cross homes according to their ages. Lene had a patient, much later in life, who had undergone an operation for acute appendicitis in the Red Cross institution when he was eight years old. The government had permitted his parents to visit him. They had also sent two soldiers along with bared bayonets, a scene so traumatic that it had left him permanently scarred.

I had my own experiences with the Swiss not long after I had left Austria. Having just returned from an Underground meeting in Czechoslovakia, I was awakened by the police in my hotel room at six o'clock in the morning, arrested on the pretext (completely untrue) that I had listed a birthplace other than Vienna on my passport. I was taken to the police station and sent to Zurich (I wasn't chained to the seat only because I was willing to pay the round-trip fare to have a policeman accompany me), held incommunicado for six days (which is against their Constitution) and interrogated by the national police (which according to their Constitution they don't have). During the course of the interrogation, they let me know that they had been intercepting both my incoming and outgoing mail (censorship is forbidden in the Swiss Constitution) and then showed me a series of photographs of myself in the company of various visitors from Austria. Pictures which could only have been taken with long-range cameras and which they knew I would do almost anything to keep out of the hands of the Austrian police.

When it was over they said, "You are not being expelled from Switzerland. You can stay for as long as you want." The only condition was that once I had left the country I was not going to be allowed to return.

The Swiss, you see, are a nation of bankers, they always balance the books. To hurry me on my way, they informed my employers at the League of Nations that I was no longer going to be allowed to work in Switzerland because I was conspiring against a country with whom they had friendly relations.

After the war, however, I returned to Switzerland as a representative of UNRRA, a civilian with the approximate rank of general. And then, of course, there was nothing they would not do for me. I was still the same Ernst Papanek, only now I was on the winning side.

But Mandel was not. And still, I could never believe that anybody as vital as Mandel could be dead. When I got to the hall in Germany where the record of all those who had been killed in the gas chambers was kept, I found his name on the list. And still I couldn't believe it. One of the letters from the children had said that Mandel was in Vienna, an obvious misstatement; probably, I knew, an unconscious confusion of names. And yet, I have never been able to go to Vienna without making a new effort to find him.

It was, on the whole, a young group of *educateurs* that we had. A community of young men and women. The only grandmotherly type was Mrs. Deutsch, who was the divorced wife of Julius Deutsch, one of the great political figures of Europe. Julius Deutsch had been a leader of the 1918 Austrian Revolution, the Minister for Defense of the Austrian Republic and a general in the Spanish Civil War. Mrs. Deutsch, who was a kind of house mother for the big boys, was the only adult who was not addressed by her first name. Not by the children, not by the *educateurs,* not by me. In all their letters, the big boys remember Mrs. Deutsch most fondly for teaching them how to darn their

socks. Her daughter Annie—the girl who went to Gurs with
Margot—was one of the better teachers and also, quite obviously,
one of our better people.

Because of the heavy Socialist coloration of our staff, I laid
down a firm rule that there was to be no proselytizing among the
children, a rule that infuriated Walter Gruen, whose background
had been with the Red Falcons. The only staff member I ever
fired was an overzealous young man who went right back into
the classroom to preach his political gospel after I had warned
him not to do it again.

I was not so stupid, however, as not to recognize the Socialist
flavor of the place. Or, given my own beliefs, not to look upon it
as an educational asset. World history paraded before our children in the living flesh. Never has there been a group of children
who could learn so much about the Spanish Civil War from the
teachers they rubbed elbows with every day. Erich Ollenhauer,
the leader of the Social Democrats in Germany, was one of the
visitors who carried the history of the times with him. And so of
course, was Léon Blum, the deputy premier of France.

One of our leading figures was Lydia Dan, who was the sister
of Julius Martov. Martov had been Lenin's partner in organizing
the first Marxist organization in Petersburg. They had been sent
to Siberia and into exile together. In exile, they had founded an
international revolutionary periodical. The break between them
came during the famous Second Congress of 1903, held in a
London church, at which Lenin put forth his revisionist proposal
that membership in the party be limited to an elite corps of
"professional revolutionaries." Martov, who was more of a traditional Marxist, replied that a party that claimed to be representing laborers and peasants could hardly exclude all laborers
and peasants. The result was the split into the Bolshevik and
Menshevik factions, with Lenin becoming the Chairman of the
Bolsheviks, and Martov becoming the Chairman of the
Mensheviks. They joined together again in the Revolution of
1905, which forced the Czar to establish the Duma (parliament),
and remained two opposing factions within the same party until
the outbreak of World War One, at which time Lenin pro-

claimed his faction to be "the party" and broke off all relations between them.

Lydia Dan had been through it all. And not only because she was her brother's sister. Her husband, Theodor Dan, was Martov's chief lieutenant. He had been jailed with Martov after the 1917 Revolution, sent into exile with him, and, following Martov's death, became his successor as Menshevik Chairman and coleader of the Socialist International.

But Lydia Dan was a personage in her own right. Her connection with the OSE went back to the time when it was still in Russia, and she was one of the people who had set up the office in Berlin after it had been thrown out of Leningrad. Although she was not on the Board in Paris, she was recognized as a leader without portfolio and was always a willing go-between whenever we were in need of one. Madame Lydia spent a great deal of time at our Homes and was much beloved. When she came out to teach a class or would simply get involved in an informal discussion with the children, they knew they were in the presence of an extraordinary woman.

Whether it was Lydia Dan or Léon Blum or anyone else, the children were always encouraged to be completely open with adults. They were expected to conduct all visitors around the grounds, talking freely and making friends with them. And, if they wished, to take part in any conversation I might have with a visitor afterward. I was sitting under a shade tree with Léon Blum on one of his visits, surrounded by the usual cluster of children, when he happened to remark that we certainly did seem to have an insatiable appetite for castles. "It isn't the castles we like so much," I laughed. "It's those deep wine cellars. They make such marvelous bomb shelters."

Well, if that was all we were looking for, he said, then he had just seen one that would be perfect for us. "It's in Montintin, near Limoges."

An offhand observation that would have been forgotten immediately if the machine-gun rhythm of the name—which is pronounced *moe-ta-ta*—hadn't struck some pleasing chord of fantasy in the children. Instantly, they were racing around in circles, aiming imaginary machine guns and cutting down imaginary enemies. Léon Blum could not show his face after that without having machine guns pointed at him. His name could not even be mentioned without the answering echo of *moe-ta-ta* and an immediate renewal of the hostilities.

If I seem to be placing undue stress on what may seem to be little more than an anecdote, it is because the mythical castle of Montintin was what we headed for when the German panzers were only ten miles from Montmorency.

There was one policy which was not deliberate but purely intuitive. "I remember when Czechoslovakia was invaded," an Orthodox boy wrote at the time of my sixty-fifth birthday. "You were lecturing about it as the Topic of the Week, and we all had hateful comments about Hitler and Germany, and you admonished us, Ernst, in that gentle and reflective way of yours, that we must never hate. 'You should never hate anything or anybody no matter how great the evil, because hatred destroys the hater and is wholly ineffective against the object of your hatred.' But that we should bend all our energies, instead, toward doing what we could do to combat the evil constructively. I don't know how 11, 12 and 13-year-old children were able to absorb a concept as rarefied as that, I only know that we did. It could only have been that we could see how passionately you believed what you were telling us, and we were willing to acknowledge that you had our best interests at heart."

I believed it. Passionately. If you respond to persecution with thoughts of revenge, you can release a lot of hostility. But the release is temporary and you pay for it by taking on a freight of guilt. Most children are simply not equipped to absorb such guilt. "We are not Nazis," I would say whenever hate came boiling to the surface. "And we do not think like Nazis."

Let there be no misunderstanding here. Chanukah has always been my favorite holiday because it celebrates a time when the Jews did not sit back and wait for a miracle from God to save them. As far as I am concerned, the Warsaw uprising will always be one of the great epics of human courage. Resistance can be constructive. Hating can only be destructive.

I am no bleeding heart. I am sorry, but I am not. Just as I am a pacifist because I am convinced that the salvation of mankind is in the hands of the pacifists, I am not a conscientious objector because my reading of history has convinced me that the road to peace is not paved with nonresistance. There were times during the Austrian Civil War when I had to give the order to fire. And I gave it knowing that men were going to die. I gave it because guns were raised against us and the alternative was to surrender everything I believed in. But if you think I hated the men we were fighting, you are sadly mistaken. I gave the order and I raised my own gun knowing that I was losing something of myself by doing it and never abandoning the conviction that if I could have had the chance to talk to them I could have convinced them that they were my brothers and my comrades.

I am also perfectly aware that the dream of revenge was all that kept many prisoners alive in the concentration camps. And that many others went to their death with nothing to sustain them except the conviction that they would be avenged. But that is all revenge, or the dream thereof, can ever be. The weak man's response to frustration and defeat; the final emotional residue of helplessness. I do not scorn it as a useful device when there is nothing else to support you. I can only be happy that you survived. But I can still believe with all my heart that you would have survived as a better and freer man if you could have found some other way.

Our children were not in that situation. All our efforts were focused on showing them that they were not helpless, that time was on their side, that they would win. Our goal was to open the world to our children, not to close it. "We are not Nazis. We do not have Nazi thoughts."

On the evening of the great attack on Paris, May 30, 1940, while buildings were burning around us and ambulances were screaming up and down the streets, I called the leading people at Helvetia together and announced that as soon as the all-clear sounded we were going to bring all the children, except the little ones, to the assembly hall at Tourelles for a music concert. Immediately, there were objections: It took thirty minutes to walk to Tourelles from Helvetia, and twenty minutes from Eaubonne, and it was always possible that the bombers would return. No, most of the children were frightened enough as it was.

Exactly. What better way to overcome their fear—and my own—than to demonstrate that we were together and unharmed. What better way to show our contempt for the Nazi mentality than to demonstrate that we who pursue culture were superior to them and their terror.

And, finally, there was the most important reason of all. The concert was going to be dedicated exclusively to German and Austrian composers. On the worst day of our stay in Montmorency, in what could very well be the beginning of the end for us, I wanted the children to understand that Hitler, Goering and Himmler were not the only Germans and Austrians. There had been Germans and Austrians, I wanted them to remember, who had contributed great beauty to the world, and would do so again in the future.

The program, which consisted of pieces by Mozart, Schubert and Beethoven, came to an end with Margot singing Beethoven's *Ninth Symphony,* "Ode to Joy." Shortly after she began, the sirens began to wail again. Margot went on without missing a note, and she had never had a better voice. The bombers flew overhead, and nobody so much as shifted in his chair. The children sat there, contented and enthralled, not wanting it to end, the sound of bombers and antiaircraft nothing more now than distant noises in the night.

A month later, almost to the day, many of those same children laid their travel-weary bones down on the wooden floor of a bare, unheated castle to spend their first night in their new home. Above them, on the balcony, we adults settled in to watch over them. The only light came from a few flickering candles. The only sound came when a child, here and there, twisted and turned on the cold floor to work himself into a more comfortable position.

Through the darkness, the voice of one boy came loud and clear: "And I tell you, children, we will hear Beethoven's 'Ode to Joy' again. Only next time it will be without the accompaniment of bombs and antiaircraft guns."

Every adult told me the next morning that they were glad it was dark so that nobody could see the tears. I could believe them, for there had been tears in my eyes too. No matter what happened to us from that moment on, I knew that in this one thing we had won.

12. Flight From Paris

May 10, 1940, was a beautiful morning. We came out of the shelter after the all-clear just in time for breakfast. We turned on the radio to get some music and heard instead the grim announcement that the Nazi army had driven into Belgium, Holland and Luxembourg. The *Drole de Guerre* had ended. The real war had begun.

It is not the great historical event that sticks in your mind. Great historical events were marching so closely on each other's heels that they tended to become indistinguishable. The Great Bombing of Paris has become one of those curious nonevents of history. You can read long histories of those days that do not even mention it in a footnote. There is one thing in particular I remember when I think of the bombing. One child, one face that will always remain in my mind. Immediately after the attack we were asked to take in a number of suddenly homeless children, among them a boy of perhaps twelve and his younger sister.

At the sound of the air raid sirens, the mother and her children had headed for the shelter in the basement of their apartment house. The boy ran down the stairs, but for some inexplicable reason the mother and the girl took the elevator. There were very few elevators in Paris in those days, very few, and they moved with an excruciating slowness. By a thousand-to-one shot, a bomb dropped right down the chute of the elevator shaft, killing the mother instantly. By another thousand-to-one shot, the girl emerged uninjured, except that her face, neck, arms and legs had been singed by the exploding powder, which had enveloped her for the merest fraction of a second. Hundreds of tiny dots covered every square inch of exposed skin.

Few of our children had ever actually seen a child who had been injured in an air attack before, and the sight of her evoked all their worst fears. Worse, they showed it. Not so much by what they said, but in the way they shunned her. From every educational point of view, I should have rallied community spirit and asked for greater compassion and understanding. Instead, the administrator in me took over. After only the briefest discussion with Lene I persuaded myself that the best thing we could do for the girl would be to send her to the hospital in Paris where they had the facilities to perform whatever plastic surgery might be indicated. Her brother went south with us a few weeks later. The boy eventually came to the United States and became a chemist. He also became a Communist. The next time I saw his name he had been called before the McCarthy Committee, and when he was asked The Question became almost the only witness who not only eschewed the Fifth Amendment but insisted upon explaining why he was proud to be a Communist. McCarthy, who had been excoriating the other witnesses, was taken so completely aback that he told him that while he would not want him to be working for any company that handled classified material, he also wanted the record to show that he respected him for his honesty.

I had seen this girl for perhaps two days out of my entire life and yet even now I see her face more clearly than most of those I saw every day. I don't know whether the rejection of his sister had anything to do with turning the boy so bitter. I do know that plastic surgery was not what she needed at the moment. What she needed was exactly what we had to offer; acceptance and reassurance. She needed us, and she needed her brother.

How do I explain it except by saying that there are times when you stand and fight and other times when you cut and run and never quite know why you ran, or can forgive yourself for running.

The only defense I can offer for myself is that I had a hundred other things to worry about at that moment, almost all of them having to do with survival. With France itself under attack, the government was interning German and Austrian nationals. The bureaucrats of the concentration camps were taking over and bureaucrats have no sense, only lists. We were losing personnel every day, and Gurs was rapidly becoming a hellhole.

Ernst Weil, the boy who had been attending the Cordon Bleu, had just passed his sixteenth birthday (and many others were approaching sixteen), and that meant we were supposed to send him to Gurs. He had an affidavit from relatives in the United States, and we were working desperately to renew his visa and get him a quota number before they came for him. (We were finally able to clear his papers and book passage for him on the *Grace* for the morning of June 6. The *Grace* was the smallest ship on the French Line, and it also turned out to be the last passenger ship out of France before the collapse. Ernst Weil had left Germany on the *St. Louis,* the last refugee ship out of Germany, with the bands playing. He left France with the Stuka bombers attacking his ship as it cleared the harbor at St. Nazaire.)

The first thing we did after hearing about the attack on the Low Countries was to pull our children out of the French schools. In case of a bombing attack we wanted to have them all together. But more than that, we wanted to be ready to move out at a moment's notice. To keep the children abreast of the military situation the director, that grand strategist, would go from Home to Home every morning, station himself in front of a huge map and draw lines and arcs and perimeters to show exactly where the Germans' latest advance had brought them and how the Allied armies were being deployed to stop them.

Since like all military experts I was still fighting the last war, our contingency plans were based upon my firm belief that, if worse came to worst, the French were going to make their stand at the Marne. Every child had been given a little duffel bag containing emergency rations (chocolate bars), a pair of stockings, pajamas, toothbrush, toothpaste and a comb. A bag was kept on the chair next to each bed, alongside the clothing and gas

masks that had already been laid out for the night alerts. The
moment the Germans reached the Marne, we were going to
evacuate the Homes and head south.

"But where will we go, Ernst, if we have to evacuate?" the
children began to ask.

We would have a place, I assured them. The Undersecretary of
the Minister of Welfare, Chabaut, had been given the responsibility for our safety, and I had his guarantee that in the event of
emergency he would provide whatever housing facilities and
transportation were needed.

"Yes, Ernst. But where?"

"Why, to Montintin," I would say, knowing that it was always
good for a smile. "We can always go to Montintin, can't we?"

Actually, I had been asking for permission to leave as soon as it
became clear that the military situation was hopeless. The authorities, who had already clamped on a strict news censorship to
hide how badly things were going on all fronts, believed that any
mass evacuation of children would have a very bad effect on the
morale of the general population. The best I had been able to do
was get permission to evacuate the children under eight, and even
then we could only send them out in groups of fours and sixes.
Immediately, we began to send them to our two newest Homes in
the south. A castle in Haute Vienne, which was in central France,
and another at Haute Savoie, below Lake Geneva. At least two
groups a day would go out, and sometimes as many as four, and
you will understand that in such a time of crisis we could hardly
be blamed if we made an error in the translation and interpreted
eight to mean ten. The French were always willing to wink at that
kind of thing as long as we didn't insult them by trying to slip
through a child who was plainly in his teens.

I must say something in this regard about the kindness of the
ordinary French soldier. These were very small children who
were being jarred from the safety of their home for at least the
second time in their lives. Even though every group was accompanied by an adult, usually the mother of one of them, the drive
to the railroad station through streets that were choked with
roadblocks and heavy military equipment—antiaircraft guns,

antiparachutist nests, etc.—terrified them. Unfailingly, the soldiers at the checkpoints would joke with the kids, encourage them to touch their machine guns, put their soldier's hats on their heads and, having established such an intimate rapport, accept the candy the children offered them in return with exactly the right combination of gravity and delight.

The Marne contingency plan had to be abandoned on May 28 when the sudden surrender by King Leopold at a time when the Belgian army was doing what no other army had been able to do, fight the German army to a standstill, left France totally defenseless along the whole northern coast. (In Leopold's defense, he surrendered because the total collapse of the French army along his southern flank had left the Belgian army surrounded.)

With the Germans coming from the north, Paris was obviously going to have to be defended at the Seine. Situated as we were three miles north of the Seine, we would already have been overrun. The new contingency plan was this: Every counselor and *educateur* was assigned to a group and instructed to keep it together at all times. The larger groups had two adults assigned to them. Wherever they were, the moment they heard that the Germans had reached Beauvais, which was twenty to twenty-five miles to the north of us, they were to take their group to the Gare de Lyon, the railroad station at Montparnasse, and wait there for a reasonable length of time to find out whether we had transportation. If there was no word, or word came that there was no transportation, they were to cross the Seine at the back of the French army and strike out, on foot if necessary, down the main highway to Orléans. When they got to Orléans, they were to wait at the railroad station for three days from the time they had left Paris, join forces with whatever other groups they had met up with and move on down to Limoges.

Limoges is in the very center of France and would therefore be within reasonable distance of whatever location the OSE might have found for us. If nothing was heard from the OSE, we were still not too far from two of our southern Homes.

On June 4, we gathered around the radio to listen to Winston Churchill inform Parliament that the miraculous evacuation from Dunkirk had been completed. It was the "We Shall Never Surrender" speech in which he was able to turn a crushing military defeat into a victory of the human spirit. We discussed it. We gloried in it. A magnificent speech which did not alter the fact that with the British having escaped from the trap the full might of the German army would now be turned toward Paris.

At ten o'clock in the morning of June 6, I was at the Ministry of Welfare with the entire OSE Board. There could be no doubt any longer that the emergency was upon us. I had gone to the American Embassy the previous day to ask that my visa, which was expiring for the third time, be renewed again. Because I had excellent relations at the Embassy they had told me, after swearing me to secrecy, that Amiens, which was only sixty-five miles north of us, had fallen during the night. German parachutists had been dropped behind the bombers following a night attack to machine-gun the townspeople as they came out of the shelters and then put the whole town to the torch. The government had censored all news about it because it was calculated to strike such terror into the inhabitants of every town that lay in front of them that they would leave their homes and flee toward Paris. The roads leading into Paris from the east were already covered with fleeing Frenchmen, Belgians and Dutchmen. For what the Germans had done was to take France's beautifully symmetrical, marvelously organized transportation system, in which every highway and railroad line runs into Paris, and use it to their own advantage. In another day or two, an avalanche of tired and frightened people was going to hit Paris from all directions, flood the streets, disrupt the internal lines of communication and swamp the facilities of the city. Whatever chance there had been of defending Paris was gone. The American Embassy had it on good authority that the Reynaud government was planning to declare Paris an open city and move the government to Bordeaux.

Despite all of Chabaut's promises, it became evident very quickly that he had made no plans for us at all.

"Chabaut," I shouted. "You promised!"

So he had promised. . . . But he had never expected to be faced with such a complete breakdown of governmental control.

I looked to the leading figures of the OSE. "Gourwitch ... ? Brutzkus ... ? Minkovsky ... ?" The OSE had nothing either.

The whole morning and much of the afternoon was spent discussing alternatives and making phone calls. The Homes in the Riviera and the Creuse were out of the question. In addition to the two hundred younger children we had sent to them, the French government had asked them to take in as many of the children who were pouring out of Alsace-Lorraine as they could handle.

Not that it mattered. The situation had become so chaotic that it was unthinkable to scatter the children. There was no way we could hope to keep track of them. In this, at least, there was total agreement from Chabaut. The children of the OSE were his responsibility and the OSE had a powerful Board of Honor, made up of some of the most distinguished figures in France. Things were going to settle down one day, and Chabaut was not going to do anything unless everybody else in the room was willing to accept his share of the responsibility.

There was some talk of moving the children to Bordeaux. If the government was moving there, it would be safe. It took no more than a brief discussion to expose the false logic in that. If the government was going to Bordeaux, the government was also going to be snapping up all the available facilities.

We were well into the afternoon when out of the clear blue sky I heard myself saying what I had been telling the children for more than a month. "Maybe," I heard myself saying, "we will go to Montintin."

They stared at me. First with bewilderment, and then with something approaching hope.

"Where," asked Chabaut, "is Montintin?"

I could see that he had never heard of it before. Neither, I could see, had anybody else there.

"All I know," I said, "is that Léon Blum says there's a castle there. And that it's somewhere near Limoges."

Léon Blum's name was all the proof that we needed; officialdom is a disease we all suffer from. Léon Blum was a national hero at the moment, anyway. Among the Socialists he alone had been willing to put aside his pacifist philosophy and join the Right-wing Reynaud government in the name of national unity. (Just as Léon Blum alone among the members of the Parliament would soon be assuring his own doom by standing up and voting against the Pétain government's surrender.)

"Good," everybody said. "It's Montintin then."

Chabaut, of course, was for anything that would take the responsibility off his shoulders. And so, at that particular moment, were the OSE people. I say that, although the OSE people there were among the best people I have ever met in my life. The Homes were not just another institution for men like Gourwitch, Brutzkus and Minkovsky; they had become their life's work. Still, Montintin had to exist for them because if it didn't exist we were in very bad trouble.

And what about me? Out of the clear blue sky, I said. Perhaps not. Perhaps the idea of Montintin had been lying there in the back of my mind all the while, even while I was joking with the children, ready to be called up if we came to just such an impasse as this. When you thought about it, it did make a kind of crazy sense. Limoges, after all, was easy to get to; it was a major stop on the express railroad line. We were planning on meeting there if nothing else worked out anyway. Wasn't it better to go there, together, on a train than to break up and head out blindly? One other thing made it a logical choice: Limoges was such a solid Socialist district that it was commonly referred to as "the Red city" of France. If there wasn't any Montintin, we would at least be among friends.

I offered only one rather hesitant reservation. "But," I said, "I still don't really know where Montintin is."

"Exactly," Chabaut said, as if I had placed my finger, with my usual brilliance, on the one small problem that still remained. "You will have to leave right away to make the necessary arrangements and prepare the place for the children." We couldn't have two hundred children rattling around the countryside in search of a castle, could we?

Oh no! I wasn't going to leave without the children. "Don't worry," he said. "Go. We will send the children tomorrow, I promise you. I'll reserve a special car on the train for them."

A car? One car? "Chabaut, you told me a hundred times we would get more than one car. Three or four, you promised. I don't believe you anymore. I can't trust you."

Chabaut was hurt. "No, no. You will get what you need. I guarantee it."

The OSE people were solidly behind him. Chabaut was right; everything had to be done in a careful, orderly manner. With the Parliament in emergency session, Léon Blum would be impossible to reach, but Dr. Jacques Bloch, who was Gourwitch's assistant, would get all the necessary information from him before the day was over. "Go. Take the guarantee. If you do not go, we don't know where we're going to send the children." They themselves were preparing to move their offices to Vichy and would not leave Paris until the last child was on the train and they had seen the train pull out.

A special train? All right. "And tomorrow morning. Early." Sure, sure. Eight o'clock sharp. I had his word on it.

All right. But I was not going to leave until I knew that the stationmaster had been instructed to set aside all the space for us that was needed.

Chabaut immediately reached for the phone. "No," I said. I was going to go to the station and talk to the stationmaster myself.

The Ministry Building is on the Isle de la Cité, which sits like the hulk of a huge ship in the center of the narrow Seine. To get to the Gare d'Austerlitz, the station from which all trains traveling south originate, I had to walk only a short distance down the Isle and across the bridge. And what a ghostly, ghastly journey it was. Knowing that I would be leaving before the day was over, and that my own future was as uncertain as the future of the city, undoubtedly made it even more ghostly.

Because of the attack on Amiens, a smoke screen had been laid over Paris to make it as difficult as possible for the German bombardiers to pick out any landmarks. The smoke hung over the water like a heavy fog. As I walked along the cobbled, deserted street, the fog seemed to create a strange, crouching world all its own. The buildings I had known so well were like frightened animals, lurking in the bushes. Showing themselves and then scrambling back for cover. The great spires of Notre Dame alternately swimming into view and dissolving. There and gone; there and gone. Like Paris itself. Like France. There was the sense of something terrible and foreboding and inexpressibly sad. For was not Paris itself like a many-splendored bird fluttering its broken wings in the bushes?

The station manager informed me that the Ministry had indeed reserved two cars for us on the morning train. It would be leaving between ten and twelve o'clock.

But that was too late, I protested. "The Minister himself promised me the eight o'clock train."

The station manager shrugged that he would do the best he could, and just by the way he said it, the Gallic language with the eyebrows, told me that no real schedule existed anymore. All kinds of trains were pulling in and out, military and civilian—any trains that could be pressed into service. And still the government was refusing to admit that there was a general flight from Paris.

Nevertheless, I made my own reservation for the nine o'clock train that night. With luck, I'd be out by eleven. Between then and now there was a tremendous amount of work to be done. The Ministry of Welfare could reserve the train space but only the police could grant us travel permits. We were able to get a general permit for all the children under fifteen. We had twenty-three boys and girls who were fifteen or older, and each of them was going to need a special travel permit.

The children in the most immediate danger, however, were in a special category I haven't mentioned. We had, in our Homes, twenty-nine children whose parents were very high on the Nazi wanted list, either because they had been particularly active political opponents or, in one case, because they had defected. The two sons of Hermann Rauschnig, the ex-gauleiter of Danzig, had come to us only a few months earlier. They had come the way many of these children had, through a phone call from the Paris office asking if it would be possible to help the Underground out for a few days. It was always "for a few days," and we always knew that a few days meant the duration. If you were trying to hide a child what better place to hide him than among four hundred other children.

Rauschnig was no ally of ours. Rauschnig had been one of Hitler's closest friends during his rise to power. He had not broken with Hitler because of any ideological turnabout, but, like so many intellectuals who jump into politics, because he didn't feel he was being given enough power. He had, as a matter of fact, gone directly to Fascist Austria and remained there among friends until the Nazis came. But he was an enemy of Hitler, and what did the father's politics have to do with the children? Children are children and there were no two children on the face of the earth who were in greater danger. Hitler had a very effective way of dealing with defectors. He killed them and their entire families. The Rauschnig boys came with false papers, under false names. Except for the OSE Board and myself, I doubt if anybody knew their true identity. The boys themselves, and one of them was quite young, were very well aware of the danger they were in. They were tight-lipped, they were always together and they kept absolutely to themselves.

We asked the Quakers to take all twenty-nine of the children to Bordeaux. It was a major miscalculation. By the time we were settled in the South, the Nazi armies were occupying Bordeaux and we didn't breathe freely again until we had got them back. All but the Rauschnig boys. The Quakers kept them hidden in France for a time and finally, from what I understand, succeeded in getting them to the United States. I have since heard that the older boy became a professor. Whether under his real or an assumed name I never discovered.

Another problem took up the first part of my last night at Montmorency. We had a cute little fellow, Erik Thorn, who was in the Rothschild Hospital with diphtheria. A tremendous headache, especially for Lene. You can't imagine the self-searching and breast-beating. How can we leave a little boy all alone, sick and deserted? Yes, but how can we take anyone with such a communicable disease? But why can't we keep him with the children who have been immunized against diphtheria? Or, better yet, keep him surrounded by adults?

It was, of course, an exercise in futility. Diphtheria isn't anything to play around with. Children have died from it.

We left Erik in the hospital and asked the Quakers to take care of him as well. They did. He was one of the few children who had been in Montmorency who never did come south.

The reason the Quakers, and the Quakers alone, are able to do such things almost anywhere in the world is one of the fascinating chapters of human history. The great strength of the Quakers is that they are truly noncombatant and nonpartisan. They help everybody and, as a result, they have influence with everybody. In Spain, they helped both sides. They rescued the Franco children and sent them to Catholic homes; they rescued Loyalist children, some of whom eventually ended up in our French Homes. Their commitment is to the underdog; to any human being who is in trouble. And when the underdog becomes the overdog, as so frequently happens, they are able to exert an influence that cannot very easily be denied. They had helped the Nazis when the Nazis were first crawling out of their beer cellars. As a result, they were able to deal with Vichy—in the early days, at least—without too much interference from the Germans.

And then there were the Orthodox children. There was very little chance—and certainly no guarantee—that they would be able to maintain an Orthodox lifestyle under the conditions with which we would be faced. Earlier in the year we had opened up the Château Morelles, in Brout-Vernet, near Vichy. Except for Eaubonne, Morelles had the largest Orthodox contingent, and the director agreed to squeeze in another fifteen children. I went to Eaubonne, explained the situation and asked them to decide among themselves who those fifteen should be. After a poll had been taken, the president and vice-president of their council came back and informed me that only two of their number had "volunteered." But that wasn't all. Since naming the others was a bigger responsibility than the children felt they could handle, they had come to the decision that the administration would have to draw up the list. Many thoughts went through my head: they had simply wanted to make a final gesture of loyalty and support; they wanted me to decide for them whether an Orthodox life was more important than the solidarity of the total community; they were reluctant to assert their own wishes at the expense of others. But, mostly, it seemed to me that their decision had to be accepted at face value: The shock of leaving their Home at Eaubonne was so severe that in asking them to decide whether they wanted to leave the larger community as well, I had been asking too much of them.

Well, if you want to be an administrator, Rule Number 1 is: Make the decision, make it fast and accept the fact that you are going to make some mistakes. I added the names of the thirteen I considered the most Orthodox, resolving all doubts in favor of the child who was older.

Despite all the discussions and preparations, it came as a shock to everybody to hear that the time had finally come. For twelve months, the boys at Tourelles had been clearing a plot of land so they could have their own soccer field, and with our second "Olympics" tournament about to begin they had just about got it ready. When I came back from Paris and announced that they would be leaving in the morning, a truly astonishing thing happened. Singly, and in small groups, the boys of Tourelles drifted out to the field to finish the job. The goalposts were nailed together and put into place. The sidelines were laid down. The field that would never be used was given one final raking.

The soccer field was the one conspicuous piece of themselves they would be leaving behind and it was as if something in their total experience demanded that they leave it behind whole.

13. The Castle in Montintin

It was one of those European trains, such as you see in English motion pictures. Separate compartments with benches on both sides. I had taken care to reserve three compartments for us. To begin with, there were the four Papaneks. I had heard enough stories over the six years since I had left Austria to know how essential it was for families to remain together in times of chaos. Wives who had been separated from husbands and believed each other to be dead. Husbands who had lost touch with their families for months and, even, years discovered they had been living within a couple of blocks of each other at one time or another. My own mother and sister were on the same boat to Sweden after they had been separated following the takeover in Austria and never knew it. It was only through correspondence with a friend in the United States that they learned the other was alive and living in the same country. In our case, there was an even stronger consideration—we had only one set of papers. If anything happened to me, or if something should happen to prevent them from joining me, Lene and the boys would become nonpersons.

Altogether, our party consisted of nineteen or twenty persons. Kaete Bodek had prepared meals for large groups of people in Spain under the most adverse conditions, and she came along with her two young sons. With the likelihood that we would have to construct our own furniture we thought it wise to bring along both of our workshop instructors, Boris and Wallie. Also Margot, who was always so capable and resourceful. Also the three young women from the Petite Colonie, whose charges had already been sent to safety. Rachel, her sister and Klari. They had the youth and vigor to help clean up the place if it came to that, and the enthusiasm and brightness to make it pleasant. In addition to which, I had already sent out feelers to the Mexican Embassy for a visa for little Klari, so I thought it best to keep her with me.

Once we were able to push through the passengers who had piled up around the doorway, we found that the train really wasn't that crowded yet. Oh, a few people with tickets were already complaining that their seats had been taken but there was nothing so unusual about that in France. The same thing happened on almost any holiday weekend. Fifteen minutes later it was such a madhouse that when I heard my name being called, I didn't dare to leave the train. Instead, I leaned out the window and saw that it was Jacques Bloch and his wife. "Thank God," Bloch said. "We know there is a Montintin." It wasn't a village. It was an estate in the village of Château Chervix, about forty miles from Limoges, owned by a French Count.

While we were talking to Bloch, my eyes wandered down the platform and caught the sight of a familiar figure. Erich Ollenhauer. His wife and younger son were with him. Ollenhauer was standing rather disconsolately on the platform, briefcase in hand, trying, with absolutely no success, to get the passengers who were blocking the entrance to move. I shouted to him, and then stepped aside while stronger arms reached out to pull them in through the window to the cheers of the very same people who had just refused to let them by.

By the time the train pulled out, only a half hour late, people were draped all over it. Sitting on the roof. Hanging on the steps. Everywhere. It was terrible. We weren't traveling at any breakneck speed through the early part of the trip, but we were traveling through the night and there were blackout restrictions in effect. The rail hangers would get knocked off every time the train entered a tunnel. The roof riders would choke on the smoke from the train or, in lifting their heads up for a breath of air, crack their heads open against the top of the tunnel.

We reached Orléans at about midnight which, all things considered, was pretty good time. It was two hours before we got out. Just as we were pulling into the uncovered station, the first bomb exploded behind us. The train was diverted immediately into the yard, separated into three sections and placed on three different sidings. The worst part of it was that nobody was allowed to leave the train. I had been in bombings before and had seen some fighting, but sitting in a dark train, on a siding, unable to do a thing to protect yourself or your family is one of the most harrowing experiences it is possible to go through.

For Lene, who had never really been convinced of the logic in going south to begin with, it was even worse. If the Germans were going to capture Paris they were going to conquer the whole country, as far as she was concerned, and so what was the sense of running from one place to another? We had a visa to the United States, she said—as she had been saying all along—and we should have used it. "If we were going to stay, we'd have been better off staying in Paris. At least we had a shelter to go to when we were bombed."

What could I say?

"How are we going to get to Limoges now?" she wanted to know while the bombs fell and the sirens sounded.

"There'll be a miracle, and we'll get there."

Maybe it was a miracle, or maybe it was just the luck of war. Although the bombing destroyed the tracks leading into the station, neither the station nor the yard area was hit. The bombers left, the train was reassembled and we were on our way.

We arrived at Limoges at four in the morning, and with all the activity it might as well have been noon. Limoges is a large city with a good-sized terminal building, and there were hundreds and hundreds of refugees from the north there. Standing, sitting, sleeping on the floor. Wandering around aimlessly. Thousands of other people with no place to go were filling not only all the hotels and boardinghouses, but also all the other available space including the streets.

To get to Château Chervix, we were told to take the little local train to Magnon Bourg, a distance of about twenty miles. Châ-

teau Chervix was twenty miles from there. Luckily, our taxi
driver was able to tell us that although the Count didn't live at
Montintin, he did live close by. It took a bit of ringing at six
o'clock in the morning, but we finally were able to wake him up.
He was a thin, ascetic-looking man wearing an old bathrobe and
a nightcap. Looking like nothing quite so much as a Dickens
version of how a French Count is supposed to look.

I wanted to rent his castle, I told him, for 150 refugee children.

He liked the idea so much that he forget to be mad about being
woken up. And then he looked at me. "What kind of children?"

"All kinds of children," I said. "Mainly Jewish."

The thin, ascetic nose looked as if it had smelled something
bad. Absolutely not! There would be no Jewish children in his
castle.

Although the French aristocracy has been notably anti-Semitic
since the Dreyfus Affair it has never been known to permit its
anti-Semitism, or anything else, to interfere with the greater
pleasures that come from the pursuit of the franc. I offered him
forty thousand francs, practically all the money we had. A tremendous amount of money in those days. I was practically buying the castle and leaving the title in his hands. "In advance," I
said. "And in cash."

The thin, ascetic lips almost smiled.

We would be able to move in, he said, within the week.

"No, we have to move in today."

Out of the question. He'd need a day or two at the least to move
his things out of the castle.

"We'll help you."

It turned out to be a big medieval castle, completely broken
down and yet not without a certain charm. Three stories, and a
huge banquet room that brought to mind a picture of King
Arthur's Round Table.

We all pitched in and moved him out in a matter of hours. With
such haste, in fact, that Gustl brought on a momentary crisis by
dropping a bust of one of the Count's ancestors and shattering it
all over the floor. We held our breaths, collectively, and apologized profusely. The Count didn't say a word. No more than he

might have expected, his expression said, from a bunch of Jews. When the truck pulled away for the last time there wasn't a table, a chair or a bed in the whole castle. The only thing he left us with was a billiard table and that was only because it was attached very solidly to the floor. The electricity had been turned off, of course, and it took a couple of days before we were able to get it connected. The phone company's installation service was much faster, but when I tried to call Paris to find out what had been happening up there it was impossible to get through. (And remained impossible all the time I was there.) The railroad station at Limoges still had contact with Paris through its own communication system, though, and they were able to determine that the train had left with the children on it. The estimated time of arrival was placed at somewhere between four and eight o'clock.

> I don't remember how I got to the train that June 7, and so I suppose it was the usual way by Enghien. I remember at the station a very amusing thing. Kugel's father picked him up in his arms and carried him around calling him his baby and clucking and cooing. At the time, we were all terribly amused at this. . . .
> I remember very distinctly we were told there was a bureaucratic requirement by the French that the children who were more than 15 could not go without special travelling papers. Except for two of the girls who had come from Spain, all the girls in that age group were from the Cubans and I can remember standing on the platform just before I boarded the train and thinking that their age was finally working against them. . . .
> —Robinsoner girl

It was, by all accounts, a slow trip with stops—scheduled and nonscheduled—in every little town along the way. They had been given a special freight car for their baggage, and as more and more people clamored to come aboard, the children themselves went back and began to throw things out. It was very interesting. One of the boys had very carefully jotted down the exact location on a card: "Two kilometers from Etamps we threw all our bags out. . . . 2500 meters later we threw out our beds. . . . The station master at Orléans said he had 60 people who had to board the train so we took out everything that was left, keeping only our blankets and hand tools. He said we could come back later on and get them."

Orléans was being bombed constantly at that time, and while the children were there, waiting to get moving again, they found themselves under attack. The extent of the bombing—whether, in fact, it was the city or the railroad station that was under attack—differed widely with both the perception or imagination of each child. (In later years, it ranged all the way from no memory of any attack at all to a direct hit in which many of the passengers in the rear car were killed.)

I had left Lene and Kaete in the village to shop for food, and Wallie to rent a couple of trucks. Everybody else had remained back at the castle to clean up. There was a small bus—more like a taxi really—that went to the Limoges station, with a preliminary stop at Magnon Bourg. My intention had been to take the train at Magnon Bourg but when I got there I was told that no train had come up from the south all day, and none was expected.

Well, if nothing had come north on the trunk line, there was nothing at Limoges to send back. "I have 150 kids coming in," I told the beleaguered stationmaster. "How am I going to get them to Magnon Bourg?"

Couldn't they walk?

Twenty miles on top of an all-day railroad trip? Tired and hungry as they were?

So how about taking them on shifts by the bus-taxi.

Look, I said, that would be fifteen round trips. We'd be going back and forth for at least twenty-four hours. With all the people he already had there, he didn't really want a bunch of kids running around his station, did he? Well, I didn't want it either. All right. Since Limoges was the last stop on the trip anyway, why couldn't he just keep the kids on the train and send it on the trunk line to Magnon Bourg?

There's this about the French. People in authority respond to intelligent suggestions. They are not buck passers. They rather enjoy breaking with routine. That's what makes the French so unpredictable to foreigners; they are very realistic people with an artistic—and even romantic—flair. You may not understand why a Frenchman is doing what he does, but you can be sure that *he* does. (It is only when they try to be bureaucratic that they fail so dismally. They lost the war, in my opinion, when the decision was made to build the Maginot Line because it put them in a static, defensive position, something which is intolerable to the French.)

The police prefect, who had joined in the discussion by then, offered the only objection. The trunk line consisted of only a single track, and with the schedule having broken down so completely that nobody knew where anything was anymore, how—he asked—could we be sure we wouldn't run into a train coming the other way?

Easy. The station manager knew there was nothing coming because he had been calling around all day trying without success to get a train sent up so that he could clear some of the people out of his station.

By the time the children's train arrived, at six o'clock, he had already announced that anyone who wanted to go to Magnon Bourg with us could make the trip without charge.

It was important to me that I be on the platform when the train pulled in, because I knew that there would be some question about me in the children's minds, some nagging doubt about whether I had deserted them. Beyond even that, I wanted to be standing there, as if I were waiting for a normal train in normal times, to show them that although they had been uprooted they had no need to feel concerned about whether they were being taken care of.

But, you know, we tend to underestimate children and the sense of security they get from each other. A few years earlier, I had been sent to England to meet a trainful of Spanish refugee children. Everybody expected them to be numb and down-hearted, and they had come into Victoria Station shouting and waving and laughing. Although our children did not come in quite so noisy or high-spirited, they stuck their heads out of the window and shouted, "There's Ernst. There he is."

"We're here!"

"Boy, what a trip. Wait until I tell you."

And when they got off the train at Magnon Bourg half an hour later and saw Wallie waiting with the trucks they went wild.

> The train ride was an excitement, and at the little station where we finally arrived, we piled off this train and got into the trucks that were waiting for us. I remember I managed to get myself way up in front of the open truck body, it was planks all around, and I remember the fantastic excitement of standing in the front of the truck, and we were all singing at the top of our lungs. All the hiking songs, inspirational songs, that we could summon up, and we drove through the woods at breakneck speed with our hair streaming back in the mildness of the early evening of southern France. And then we arrived at this castle, and we were still high from the singing and we all went piling in and we saw there was no furniture there at all.
>
> —Twelve-year-old girl

Ernie Koppstein, who later became a doctor, couldn't have been more than nine years old when he got his first look at Montintin but he remembered it quite well, possibly because he always had a sketchpad in his hands. "Both the château and its surroundings were really lovely. Virtually idyllic, as I recall it. My drawings of Montintin show the thick mediaeval wooden doors in front, and barred lower windows, laced with vigorously growing vines and ivy, befitting a first-class French château. There was considerable ornate stonework, and dormer windows in the roof. Behind it was a smaller house, I believe a woodwork shop. [Note: There was also a farmhouse up on a hill which was turned into a Home for the Orthodox children.] I remember we had our meals and also our classes in the dining room to the left of the main entrance, using 'home made' tables and benches. We drank milk diluted with water and longed for ordinary sugar and sweets, which as you know, were nearly unobtainable then. To the right was a large interesting kitchen. Upstairs were our sleeping rooms with, of course, the dormer windows. All my clothes were marked with the number '255.' A lady dentist worked on my teeth in the same building, where I recall running up and down the quaint spiral staircases. Please excuse my saying so, but the toilet on the second floor landing left something to be desired. The heat came from wood-burning fireplaces, and though I didn't realize it then, it was picturesque and romantic. Not far from a plot of ground which we tilled ourselves. As I look at this picture I recall a nice elderly lady showing me how to knit a pair of socks. To this day I still know how to knit. . . ."

Dinner was cooked and waiting for us. And what a dinner. The only thing Lene had been able to get at the butcher shop was pork. Food was becoming scarce, pork was the staple product the farmers raised for market in that part of the country and Lene wasn't in any position to be choosy when buying on credit. Not that we had planned it that way. In addition to the cash that had already been handed over to the Count of Montintin, I had been given a JDC check for one thousand pounds drawn on the Westminster Bank of England. It wasn't, we discovered, worth the paper it was written on. With most of France already in the hands of the Germans everybody assumed that England would collapse very shortly too. Nobody was going to run the risk of getting stuck with that kind of money, not even the bank.

Fortunately, I had already prepared the Orthodox children for exactly this kind of situation. I explained once again that I knew the Bible well enough to know that they were permitted to eat pork in an emergency, and that I didn't think anybody was going to deny that this was an emergency. And then, to make it as easy as possible for them, I ordered them to eat it.

There were no arguments.

There were also no knives or forks. Despite all our preparations, we had, inexplicably, forgotten to pack them. Since we didn't have any dishes either—they had been thrown out of the train along with the pots and pans—we sat down on the floor and ate our first meal at Montintin off pieces of butcher's paper, with our fingers.

And, finally, it came time to go to bed. Although all the children had been assigned to one of the upstairs rooms by then, they all wanted to remain together in the huge room downstairs. Those who couldn't be squeezed in insisted upon bedding down in the adjoining halls.

> We all took our blankets that first night and lay down on the bare parquet floor of the big banquet room. We rolled ourselves in our blankets and lay down in great excitement, and we must have rolled around in our sleep because I remember waking up at the other end of the room. Must have been a turbulent night of dreaming. I know I felt such a spirit of quiet satisfaction that we had made it. It was fantastically exciting. Then the next day we explored the grounds of the castle. I remember almost immediately some of the girls, not the older ones but the girls of my age immediately became avid tree-climbers. We spent hours at the top of very high trees. It was tremendously exciting.
>
> —Hanna's diary

And then came the long, agonizing wait for the older boys and girls. I had come down Thursday. The main body of the children had come on Friday. On Saturday night, we had to leave. There had been talk in Paris of setting up governments-in-exile among the various refugee groups, and Ollenhauer had informed us that he was on his way to Agen, the appointed seat of the German government-in-exile. The Austrians were to meet in Montauban, and I was supposed to be there.

Fortunately for us, it turned out that Montauban was on the main railroad line, about 125 miles south of Limoges, and we were able to catch a train at Brive, a small city to the south of us.

Montauban, normally a city of 20,000, had been swelled by almost 200,000 refugees, most of them sleeping on straw, which had been spread across the main street. Local government had broken down almost completely, with only the mayor and the police, reinforced by a refugee police contingent which had left Holland en masse, continuing to function. We were still following the principle that all families had to remain together, and on our arrival our friends were able to find a very nice hotel room for us and the boys. For one night, anyway. Then a French major came by and commandeered it for himself, and we were sleeping out on the straw with everybody else.

It was a confusing situation. The mayor was with us. The police weren't sure who they were going to be with. When we finally got word that the meeting was going to be held in Fritz Adler's hotel room, it had already become clear that the only government-in-exile the French were going to be interested in anymore was, in all probability, their own.

Fritz Adler was the son of Viktor Adler, who had created the Socialist party of Austria. When World War I started, Fritz was the editor of both the official party newspaper and his own more militant magazine. Almost at once he found himself in sharp disagreement with his father, whom he admired tremendously, over what he took to be his father's compromising stance. When the premier, Count Stuergkh, announced that the entire nation was behind the Emperor in the war Fritz felt that he had to do something both to demonstrate the depth of the opposition that existed and to protest against the total censorship that had been imposed. What he did was to walk into Vienna's most fashionable restaurant and assassinate Count Stuergkh.

By resisting the government's attempt to portray him as a man who was not responsible for his actions, Fritz was able to turn his trial into a political forum on the right and duty of the individual to take action against a tyrannical government. I can offer myself as proof of his success. My father was a poor workingman who had always been a loyal subject of the old Emperor. I was sixteen years old at the time, and a great admirer of the Emperor myself. It was Fritz Adler who turned me, along with millions of others, into an ardent Socialist.

Although he was sentenced to be hanged, the government didn't dare to carry out the sentence. There were worldwide protest movements and petitions. It was quite probably the first worldwide political action in history. His sentence was commuted first to life imprisonment and then to eighteen years. When the Revolution came after the war, he was offered the chair in experimental physics at the University of Zurich, for along with his other talents Fritz Adler was one of the greatest mathematicians in Europe. Typically, he refused to take it because he thought it should go to his friend, Albert Einstein, who was rotting away as an assistant professor at what would amount to a junior college in America.

As we met in his hotel room in Montauban, Fritz Adler was easily the most wanted man in all of Europe. For years he had been the leader of the Socialist International, and Hitler had put a price on his head. To give him a place to hide while he was changing his appearance for a passport photo, I wrote a letter of introduction to the director of our Home at St. Raphael, identifying Fritz by a false name and recommending that he be hired as a math teacher.

June 10, the day the meeting took place, was also Lene's birthday. The Reynaud government celebrated it by leaving Paris, Mussolini celebrated it—now that he was certain there was no French army left to fight—by declaring war on France, and we celebrated it by having the worst argument of our lives. It began with me expressing my usual confidence that no matter how dark things might look Hitler was going to lose and we were going to win.

"Why do you always have to be such an optimist?" Lene snapped.

"Why do you always have to be such a pessimist?" I asked.

Why did she have to be a pessimist? We were sleeping out on the street and scrounging for food to feed two boys. The whole trip had been a wild-goose chase just as she had known it was going to be from the beginning, and we had just discovered that there were no trains running north anymore. Even if we got back to Montintin, the Italian army would probably be sweeping across southern France; why else had Mussolini declared war? We should have gone to America when we had the chance. And why didn't I get *mad* about something for once?

So I did. I got mad at her.

We were going to win, but first we had to get back to Montintin. I had borrowed ten thousand francs from Fritz in the name of the OSE, and the next day I was able to hire a taxi at an exorbitant price to drive us back. The driver earned every franc of it. Although I had seen the people in the railroad station at

Limoges and in the streets of Montauban I hadn't even begun to comprehend how vast the exodus had been. Five million people were on the roads of France. Five million! It wasn't only the trains that weren't going north. Everything and everybody on the highway was moving south. They were driving cars and riding bicycles. They were riding oxen and mules and horse-drawn wagons. They were, most of them, walking. Old people, young people, soldiers in uniform. On all that highway, during all that trip, the only thing moving north was us. As we inched our way against the tide, the people shouted at us in amazement or anger. Many of them assumed that we could only be going north to meet the German army and they would stick their head in the window and scream that we were traitors. Others thought we were going back to protect our home and property. "Whatever it is, let it go," they'd yell. "Let the Germans have it. Your life is more important." Most of them just stared at us. It was incomprehensible to the vast majority of that footsore army straining to put every possible kilometer between themselves and the Germans that anybody could be traveling north of their own free will.

The trip took almost twenty hours. We got back to the castle at two o'clock on the morning of June 12—Wednesday morning —and learned that the big children still hadn't arrived. I couldn't get Paris on the phone. I couldn't get the OSE office in Vichy. All we could do was worry . . . and wait.

I had instructed Mandel to drive the children over fifteen to the Paris station and, if the travel permits were there, load the truck with food and supplies and drive down himself. If the travel permits weren't there, he was to drive the girls down, and have the boys and their counselors walk.

For three straight days, the OSE was told that the travel permits would be issued the next morning. For three straight days, as the German army continued to sweep westward along the northern coast instead of south toward Paris, the OSE decided to wait one more day. On Sunday, with the advance elements of the German army at Creil, less than ten miles from our

Homes, the children were brought from Enghien to the central railroad station in Paris, Gare de Lyon. Still no travel permits. Gourwitch was given a flat guarantee that both the permits and the train space would be forthcoming on Monday. He instructed Mandel to wait one more day. The children spent all day and night at the station.

On Monday morning, as promised, the safe conducts and the reservation for a special car came through. By then, it didn't matter. Monday was June 10, the day the Reynaud government left Paris. Travel permits were no longer needed, nobody was bothering to check them. Reservations meant nothing either. The panic was on. Desperate people were rushing the trains at Gare d'Austerlitz and taking them over. Not only wasn't it possible for Gourwitch to claim the car that had been reserved for us, but the stations had become so mobbed that he literally was unable to get anywhere near the train.

The word was passed to Mandel to empty the truck and put the original plan into operation. The twelve girls were put into the truck, which was really more of a van—something like one of those milk delivery trucks except that there were huge windows all around the sides and back—along with Mandel, his wife and Annie Deutsch. The ten boys set out on foot with Karl.

The eleventh boy, Friedman, had become impatient by then. Friedman had a multispeed racing bicycle which he had been reluctant to leave behind anyway and, always the individualist, he had set out to bicycle down by himself.

Mandel's instructions were to double back from time to time to check on the boys, which sounds like an eminently workable arrangement to anyone completely out of touch with the real situation. The main flood of refugees from the east had already hit Paris and veered south along the Route d'Orléans, the main highway. There were so many people clogging the Route d'Orléans that it wouldn't have been possible for Mandel to have turned around even if there had been any reason to. There wasn't any. The boys weren't behind him. They were in front of him. The first stretch of the highway was a typically French boulevard with trees and greenery along the sides. It had taken the boys no more than three minutes to discover that by walking along the grass they would be able to move at about twice the speed of the highway traffic.

By the end of the first day, they had walked to Etamps, a distance of about fifteen miles and, by a happy coincidence, the first major stop on the railroad line. Once there, they left the highway and scouted around until they found a farmer who would let them sleep in his barn. In the morning, they went down to the station and managed to find a practically empty baggage car in a freight train that wasn't traveling very fast but was at least going their way.

Whenever the freight stopped at a little town, they would jump off and fan out. Some to find a bakery, some to the farmhouses to ask for milk, and the others to forage around for whatever food was to be found.

Mandel, holding to the road and getting occasional stretches of open road below Orléans, beat them to Limoges. He drove on to Château Chervix, arriving very late at night, and was driving along the narrow road through the forest when he came across a kind of courtyard and decided he had better pull in until daylight.

> Do you remember when we were evacuated from Villa Helvetia to Château Montintin, we older ones drove with Mandel in the caminoette all the way from Paris to Limoges. It took us many days and we lived through many air raids, but we couldn't find Château Montintin. We were only a few hundred yards away. But it was dark and in the middle of the forest so we decided to spend the night in the car. When we finally came to Montintin in the morning you were in the kitchen together with Lene and Kaete Bodek, worried because we were a few days overdue.
>
> —Yvonne

The freight car carrying the boys pulled into the yard at Limoges the next afternoon, five days after they had left Paris. It was June 14, the same day the German army marched into Paris. From Limoges, they took the bus to Château Chervix and walked the rest of the way to Montintin. Friedman, having taken his own sweet time about it, had arrived a few hours earlier.

With the arrival of the big boys, the axes began to swing. The logs piled up. We built chairs and tables and ate outside in shifts.

> Beds appeared from nowhere, and food came to be on the table from Dünne Kaete's kitchen. Lessons began again, and gymnastics in front of the castle every morning when the bell rang. A few went out every morning to the farm in the neighborhood for one or two bottles of milk. Milksoup, rejected by the fussy eaters, appeared on our tables. Rabbit stew, rejected by many more, began to be served. Midmorning bread with drippings, and afternoon applesauce and chestnut puree became the focus of our slightly hungry days.

—Hanna's diary

Because I knew I would have to leave soon I had gone around to the surrounding farmers to pay off what debts I could with the money I had borrowed from Fritz Adler. I asked them to bear with us in the future until we could either cash the check on the English bank or come up with some money from another source. I was asking them, you understand, to extend credit to us at a time when the food shortage was so severe that the citizens of some of the surrounding villages were setting up armed barricades along the highway to keep any more refugees from coming in. "Don't worry," the farmers said to a man. "As long as our children have bread to eat, your children will have bread to eat too."

Two days after the older children arrived, Reynaud resigned and was replaced by Pétain, who had been the leading French spokesman for "peace" even through the days of the *Drole de Guerre.*

That same night I was summoned to the police station and told by the police chief that he had been alerted to expect a list of the people within his jurisdiction who were considered to be politically undesirable. The message was perfectly clear. He didn't want to arrest me, he would do his best not to arrest me and so if I stayed around long enough so that he had no other choice but to arrest me the blame would be mine not his.

Sure enough. Almost immediately after Pétain asked the Germans for an armistice, the Socialist mayor of Limoges phoned to warn me that my name had already come in. "That's all right," I said. "Before you come to arrest me you will tip me off and I will run into the forest and hide."

The next day, the mayor called to tell me there was no sense in playing games about hiding in the forest anymore because a special task force from the national police had just arrived. "You have to get out right now," he said. And if I wanted to protect the "commune" at Montintin I had better take anyone else who might be on a German wanted list with me.

I told him I couldn't go even if I wanted to. We had run out of gasoline, and so had every gas station around.

An hour or so later, the mayor came driving in with three of his own gendarmes. Not to arrest me but to thrust a forty-liter can of gasoline at me. "Put this in the truck and go," he pleaded. "They'll be here in an hour."

There was one thing I had to do before I left.

Three days earlier, I had asked for a volunteer to try to get a message through to OSE headquarters in Vichy on Friedman's bicycle. I wanted the OSE to send back some money with him, and I also wanted them to appoint a director to replace me. There were three good reasons, to my way of thinking, why it was important for them to name my successor: 1) Because it was their right. 2) So that the responsibility would remain directly with them. 3) Because if the appointment came from "upstairs" instead of from me, there would be a minimum of jealousy and rancor.

The volunteer was Henri, a Swedish physical education instructor who had been hired by the Rothschild Home and sent to us for training. With everything falling apart, he had decided to come south with us. At first glance, he seemed to be the perfect man for the job. He was in great physical condition, a health nut really. He would have the boys out at 6:30 in the morning for their calisthenics and then run them for two miles. The boys would come back panting, and Henri wouldn't even look as if he had worked up a good sweat. For in all things, great and small, Henri was a man with a certain flair. He was a tall fellow, quite blond, and always seemed to have a deep, well-tended tan. He dressed in the fashion of the boulevardiers of Montparnasse, even to the ascot under his sport jacket. Altogether, he had cut such a swath among the young women *educateurs* that they oohed-and-aahed over him as he made ready to leave and pleaded with him not to go.

I took one look at him and groaned. For reasons that must have seemed good to him, Henri had camouflaged the bicycle by tying leaves and branches all around it. No, no, I said. I wasn't asking him to ride through any forests. All I wanted him to do was bicycle up to the civilian barricades, looking as Swedish as possible, show them the letter and convince them that he didn't want to stay in their village, all he wanted was to pass through. By camouflaging the bicycle all he was doing was casting suspicion upon himself.

But Henri was not a man to let a dramatic moment go by unnoticed. Not with all those women around him, anyway. Frankly, I was sure he was going to get rid of all that junk just as soon as he was out of sight. How wrong I was. Henri had returned that very morning with scratches all over him and blood all over his legs to report that he had been unable to get through.

I now had to call a meeting to appoint the new director. And it couldn't be Margot. Or Kaete. Or Karl. We were no longer in the happy position of dealing with the government through benevolent channels as we had been in Montmorency. The director had to be the person best equipped to deal with an arbitrary authority at a provincial and not necessarily sympathetic level. The political situation wasn't merely the paramount consideration, it was the only consideration. My candidate for the job was Lucia. She was French. She was Gentile. Her brother and father had both been captured while fighting in the French army. She was completely nonpolitical.

It didn't matter that as a teacher, Lucia had not been particularly outstanding. Like most French teachers, she was a rather aloof, formal figure, who felt that children should know their place. Nor had she ever demonstrated any particular talent, or even desire, for the leadership I was thrusting upon her. But if she was rigid, I knew that she was also conscientious. And if she had her reservations about our method of education she had nevertheless chosen to cast her lot with us. In addition to which she had become a very good friend of Kaete, and I was hoping that Lucia would lean heavily upon her. (It didn't work out that way. She came to lean heavily upon Kaete's brother-in-law Heinz. So heavily that they moved into the same room. Kaete, who didn't like her brother-in-law at all, became quite cool to her.)

Now, you can't call a night meeting right after the mayor has come around in a police car without the children suspecting that something is going on. When the meeting broke up, John Windmuller came up to me, as a delegation of one, to find out what was happening. While I was breaking the news to him I could see in his eyes something that looked not so much like an accusation of betrayal as a sixteen-year-old boy fighting very hard not to believe that he was being betrayed.

The same uncertain attitude prevailed while we were loading the baggage into the truck. Nobody wanted to say, "What is going to happen to us now?" But that was the question behind everything that was being said. For while the children knew I might very well be killed if I stayed they could not help but wonder whether they weren't going to be killed because I wasn't staying. They couldn't say, "You're running out on us, Ernst, aren't you?" and I couldn't say, "There's a chance for you to be safe here this way. There's no chance if I stay." So I said, "I will try to get to the United States." And they said, "Yes, you'll get there."

I said: "As soon as I'm in the United States I will begin to work to get you over."

They said: "Sure, we will meet you in America."

And all the while I could feel the barrier rising between us in the night air. For the first time I felt that they distrusted me.

There had never been any doubt where we would be going. Back to Montauban. Mandel was therefore taking us to the nearest station to the south of us, which was at Brive. Holding to our rule that nobody traveled any distance without his family, Mrs. Mandel was in the front seat beside him. (We even put what was left of the gasoline in the trunk, just in case.) It was a full truck. We were taking the other political activists who were in danger with us, along with their children, and by the time we were ready to leave, some of them were sitting on the top of the car. It was one of those circular dirt driveways, with a garden in the middle and the forest stretching out on both sides. As we began to move out, the children moved with us. I was sitting by the window in the front seat. The members of the executive committee of the Children's Parliament were right alongside the car. Just outside my window were John Windmuller, Michael Stiassny and Guenther Heilbron. I put out my hand to them. Michael, a tall, blond boy whose parents I had known in Vienna, grasped my hand on one side of me; Guenther, our tall handsome athlete, grasped it on the other. Their hands were grasped in turn by the child alongside them, and so on down the line. We turned onto the road, and still they held on, a human chain conducting us into the void. We drove along like that for what seemed like a long, long time. In absolute darkness except for the headlights of the truck. In total silence.

And then, one by one, they dropped off into the night until, at last, there were only Michael and Guenther. And then only Michael. And then nobody at all.

> Ernst left one day with the whole family. We stayed back, abandoned, cynical, and for the first time in real fear. There was perhaps a reason for leaving, a sharp danger—but we did not, could not, believe it. A new directress began to take over, and her boy friend taught us the glories of Goethe by having us read *Egmont* aloud that summer. We built a sandpit for the broadjump and high jump under the trees in front of the castle, on a little slope where one could jump higher and farther than ever before. We collected stamps even harder, fled into the treetops, and began to argue among ourselves even slapping each other's faces sometimes. Vera drew more pictures and hung them on more walls. Someone heard about the possibilities of going to South America.
>
> —Hanna's diary

In 1945, I came back to Europe as the executive director of

Child Welfare Projects of the Unitarian Service Committee, attached to UNRRA. While I was in Paris, I heard that many of our children who had survived were in a Boy Scout home in the little town of Moissac. The driver who had been assigned to me was a Yugoslavian photographer who had just been discharged from the British army and didn't want to go home. At the first opportunity, we drove to Moissac. The director, who had heard about me in a vague sort of way, handed me the list of his entire roster. "Let's give them a surprise," he said. "You pick out the ones who were with you and I'll send for them without telling them why."

There weren't as many there as I had hoped. Only eight, plus Boris Ginodman. We talked about them while we were waiting. Finally, the door swung open and there stood Michael Stiassny. Just standing there, looking at me. Michael Stiassny, the last figure I had seen on the narrow dirt road out of Montintin. And then very quietly, he said, "I knew you would be back one day."

14. Soldiers on a Train

No trains had been running south from Limoges for a week, but there were rumors that there was still a daily train running south from Brive. We joined the ranks of refugees on the main road until suddenly everything came to a halt. When we walked up front to find out what was happening, civilians with armbands and guns informed us that the whole county had been cut off to everybody except soldiers. And then the army began to come through. In small groups, and large groups. With big guns, and small guns. Straggling and in no kind of military step or formation. Sometimes with long stretches of space in between. One little patch of a defeated army was all it was, but from where we sat it looked like Napoleon's retreat from Moscow.

After two hours I said, "Mandel, do you have a road map?"

According to the map, there seemed to be a little road farther on back and, sure enough, nobody was guarding it. We traveled in a circle along a series of narrow dirt roads. It began to pour. Those on the top of the truck were soaked to the skin. How we got to the station I'll never know.

The train was sitting there at the station, loaded down with troops and already taking on steam. The roofs, as usual, were completely covered with civilians. I asked the railroad official who was standing there when the next train would be leaving.

"There won't be any more trains," he shrugged.

No, I didn't mean today. I meant what time would the train be leaving tomorrow?

"There won't be any train tomorrow. This is the last one."

"How do we get south, then?"

He shrugged again, and let his eyes run toward the train. "Get on that one."

When Lene asked where we could buy tickets everybody roared. Tickets? What tickets? Tickets hadn't been sold for days.

The train was already beginning to move anyway, and as we ran for it the roof sitters cheered us on. The soldiers held their hands out and pulled us in. They vacated seats for us. These were peasants on their way home, alive, uninjured and happy that the war was over. And quite willing to talk about it, even to a stranger with a conspicuous German accent. "So we lost the war," they kept saying. "In 1871, the Germans won and they got Alsace-Lorraine. In 1918, we won and we got it back. Now Alsace-Lorraine will go back to the Germans, they'll get one or two of our colonies maybe too, and we will go home and harvest the fields."

It was impossible to get them to understand that Hitler had not been fighting for Alsace-Lorraine, that he had been waging an all-out war for total dominance. They could not believe that they were going to remain under German control whether that control was exercised directly from Berlin or through the totally subservient Pétain regime. "Pétain is right," they kept saying. They could not accept the fact that their country had become a prison.

I had made a very bad mistake in not stopping in at the American Embassy the day I left to pick up my new visa. The Embassy had sent the visa on to the "safe" city of Bordeaux, and the safe city of Bordeaux was now occupied by the German army.

Not that it mattered that much for the moment. The armistice had closed off all the exits. Under the armistice agreement, southern France was supposed to remain under the control of France, meaning Vichy; in practice, German officers were in every port regulating and checking all movement. The control was so tight that not even the might of the British navy could help. The British attempted to rescue two German Socialists who had been Cabinet members in the Weimar regime, Hilferding, the Minister of Finance, and Breitscheid, the Minister of Foreign Affairs. The Germans were waiting. Hilferding and Breitscheid were captured and killed.

The whole visa situation brightened considerably after two months when William Green, the head of the American Federation of Labor, obtained fifty visitor's visas from Roosevelt for the Socialist leaders who were deemed to be in the greatest danger and arranged with Sumner Welles, the Undersecretary of State, to have the visas waiting at the Marseilles consulate. Why William Green? Well, that's what the Social Democratic party is, the labor movement of Europe. Although the American labor movement has always been unique in that it has no direct connection with the Socialists, it has always had close ties with the international labor movement and, when it has chosen to, powerful influence in the Socialist International.

The Underground had been working all the while to set up an escape route through France and Spain, into Portugal, and since I had been making it known how important it was for me to get to the United States and make arrangements for bringing the children over, the Papaneks were given the somewhat dubious honor of being the first family to attempt to get through. The first step, of course, was to get to Marseilles. The mayor of Montauban gave me a letter granting us permission to leave France, a letter which had all the legal force of a letter from my son Georgie. Its real purpose was to test the prefect of police in Montauban, the man who did have the authority to grant me a travel permit. He told me I could pick it up the next day, but when I came back for it informed me that he would first have to clear my application with the Armistice Conference Board. Since he knew I was on the list of anti-Nazi refugees who were supposed to be turned over to the Board, he was in effect telling me that he was not going to stick his neck out one way or the other.

There was one train running south to Marseilles daily. We were instructed by the Underground to appear at the station in the morning without any luggage. "Don't wear or carry so much as an overcoat," we were told. "And don't tell even your closest friends that you are leaving."

Gendarmes were stationed all around the station. As we approached the gate, they all turned their backs or looked right through us. We were air. When I tried to show my ticket at the checkpoint that had been set up, the railroad official also turned his back. When the conductor came around to pick up the tickets during the trip, he and the two gendarmes who accompanied him passed us by as if we weren't there.

Just before the train reached Marseilles, though, the conductor came hurrying over to us, accompanied by the gendarmes. "Listen," he said. "We don't know if our friends are on duty today. If they don't let you pass, go to the engineer in the front of the train and he will hide you in the enginehouse until we can get you out."

There was no trouble at all. When we got to the gate, we saw an old friend from Vienna waiting on the other side. The gendarme who was very noisily checking everybody else's permits let us through without a glance.

The Underground's plan was to send two families a day through the escape route. Our traveling companions were going to be our old friends, Oscar and Marianne Pollack.

The Pollacks already had a visa for England. We, of course, still had to go to the American consulate at Marseilles to pick up ours. It was not going to be that easy, though. The American consul was an American aristocrat—a Cabot or a Lodge, I forget which. He had received no orders to issue any visas, he told our Underground guides, and he didn't believe a word they were saying. He was the only man who had the authority to issue visas, he wanted them to know, and they could be very sure that he wasn't going to issue one on any cock-and-bull story such as ours. At last, he did agree to check our story by cabling Sumner Welles in Washington. Good. That would settle the matter once and for all. The next day he informed us that he had indeed received a cable signed by Sumner Welles and that it did indeed say that he should give us the visas. "But I know how you people in the Underground work," he smiled. "You have a man in the State Department working with you. Anybody could have put Sumner Welles's name on a cable."

Fortunately, Lene had come with us—anything to get out of

that hotel. "That should be easy enough to find out," she said. "Pick up the phone and ask him."

The consul returned an entirely different man. Not only did he give us the visas, but he sent word to the Portuguese consul in Marseilles that he was to grant us transit visas. He also asked the Portuguese consul to let the Spanish consulate know that we would be passing through Spain on our way to the United States. He even went so far as to invite us to remain in the consulate as his guests until we were ready to leave. It was an invitation we would have leaped to accept if the Underground people hadn't let him know how offended they were at the suggestion that they couldn't protect us.

The trip took longer than anybody had anticipated. The first trip in this kind of an operation has also got to be something of a trial run, and it was a rare stop where something didn't go wrong.

We were, for instance, supposed to cross the border near Cerbère, down at the western corner of the Mediterranean where France and Spain meet. The commandant of the small police contingent at the Cerbère station stopped us and asked to see our papers. I did the only thing I could think of. I reached into my pocket and pulled out the letter from the mayor of Montauban. No good, he said. He could not let us through without an exit visa. The next two mornings, we went back again and each time the commandant turned us away.

We had a very nice hotel room overlooking the beach, and Georgie, who had little patience with our security measures, had been pestering us to let him go in the water. Now that we had been turned back a third time, he began to scream that he wanted to go swimming. As Lene and I were trying to quiet him, Marianne Pollack hissed, "Don't stop him. Don't stop him. Get him to cry louder." She lifted her fist and scowled at him ferociously. "*Hit* him if you have to." Now that she had Georgie really screaming she went running to the commandant. "See what you're doing. This poor little boy knows his father will be killed if you don't let him through. What kind of a Frenchman are you?"

The kind of a Frenchman who didn't let anybody pass without an exit visa.

We were completely baffled. We had run into trouble before, sure, but never this kind of a stone wall. Here, it seemed, at the most crucial leg of all, the exit from France, the Underground had broken down. We were already five days behind schedule. Not only weren't we getting through, but eight or ten other families were undoubtedly piled up behind us at Perpignan.

Upset as we were, we took the long way back to the hotel. I happened to look up as we were passing a school building. L'Ecole Jean Jaurès, I saw. I looked at Pollack. Pollack looked at me. In we went. Jaurès had been the great Socialist leader of France before World War I, and so it took no genius to conclude that the principal of any school named after him would have to be a Socialist too. Not only a Socialist, as it turned out, but also one of the organizers of the Underground in Cerbère. He had, in fact, known we were coming and assumed we had already passed through. "This is impossible," he said, reaching for his hat. "The commandant of police is one of us. He knew you were coming too."

When he came back he was laughing. "You won't believe it," he said, shaking his head. "Absolutely everybody on our police force is in the Underground except for one miserable Vichy fanatic. Just your luck, the swine has been on duty the past three days, and the commandant was afraid he'd give the whole game away if he let you through." The Vichy man was going off duty the next day, he assured us, and we'd be passed right through.

He was right. The Vichy man wasn't there, but everybody else was. The story had gone all over town and the good people of Cerbère had turned out, en masse, to give us a rousing sendoff. Very heartwarming. Very amusing. But not, we had to say, very Undergroundish.

In some ways, I had been more worried about Spain than France. Our route was taking us through cities I had visited frequently during the Civil War, and I was afraid I might still be on Franco's wanted list. Our first stop was the little border town of Port Bou, and the only hotel in town was the small, badly damaged one that I had used as headquarters when I was bringing children out of Republican Spain or carrying in milk and other supplies.

I told the lady at the desk we had only francs and no papers, and when she replied that she preferred francs I knew that the place was still being run by anti-Falangists.

"I would rather not register," I told her.

"Oh," she said, understanding perfectly. "You have been here during the Civil War?" In Spain, as in many other European countries, you are supposed to leave your papers at the desk, and the police come around every day to check the register. "All right," she said, putting the register away. "The police don't come around until eleven o'clock. You can register after then."

At the railroad station the next day, the Spanish police made us take off all our clothes. They went through our little valises and found only pajamas and toothbrushes. The customs officers went over all kinds of books and although they apparently did not find my name, they were able to hold us there long enough to make us miss the train. We had to spend another very nervous day hoping they didn't come up with anything overnight.

I was even more worried about Barcelona. Our instructions from the Underground had been to ask for Porter 13 when we finally arrived at the station. Porter 13 was a refined-looking man who had obviously never lifted a suitcase in his life. He couldn't get us to Madrid that day, he told us. We were going to have to spend the night in Barcelona. He sent us to a very nice hotel where we were whisked right up to our rooms. We were there about an hour when Georgie began to complain of a stomachache. And it kept getting worse. Lene's diagnosis was that he had all the early symptoms of appendicitis, but since it was impossible to be absolutely sure yet she didn't want to have to be the one to make the final decision. "If I say we have to send him to the hospital and you get caught and delivered over to Hitler, I'll feel I killed you. If I say we can go on and his appendix bursts, I'll feel I killed him."

There was nothing else to do. We looked through the telephone book for a doctor with a Jewish name, took a deep breath and called Dr. Abraham Levy. His diagnosis was the same as Lene's. Namely, that it was going to take another day for the symptoms to develop one way or the other.

"Doctor," I said, "I wouldn't like to have to stay in Barcelona for another day."

Oh, why not? Barcelona was a very nice city. And then he looked at me. "You had better tell me. What is your name?"

"Ernst Papanek."

"Oh," he said. "Are you related to the Papanek who runs the children's institutions for the OSE in France?"

"I am that Papanek," I said.

"Wait here," he said. "You gave hope to so many Jewish families that whatever we can do for you we will do."

Two hours later, he was back with four other members of the Jewish Community, one of them wearing *peis* and a long caftan. "What," they asked me, "do the children in the Homes need most?"

That was easy. "They need to get out of France."

And sitting there, we discussed how they could go about setting up a little Underground of their own for the exclusive purpose of rescuing children. There are men and women in the United States and other countries today who did indeed get out of France as a result of that accidental meeting.

The next morning, Georgie woke up feeling just fine. We caught the train for Madrid immediately, and three days later—twelve days after we had left Montauban—we were safely in Portugal.

The Pollacks left almost immediately for England. (After the war they returned to Vienna where Oscar became editor of the *Arbeiter Zeitung* and Marianne was elected to the Austrian Parliament.) We left for New York a couple of weeks later on a Greek ship, *Nea Hellas,* together with some of the others who had come to Lisbon behind us. Just to make us feel at home we were stopped the second night out by an English submarine.

We arrived at the port of New York on September 12, at five o'clock in the morning. In the police boat which met us outside the harbor was Minkoff, one of the leaders of the council of the

Jewish Labor Committee, the organization which had inter-
ceded with Green for the fifty visas. Minkoff was there to cau-
tion us not to give any interviews when we landed and to say
as little as possible thereafter about how we had got out of
France.

For a few months, the Underground continued to operate
faultlessly. One of the more celebrated figures who came
through was Lion Feuchtwanger, the great German novelist.
Feuchtwanger then wrote a magazine article describing the Underground operation in detail, and that was the end of that.
Some brave men and women undoubtedly met their death as a
direct result of what he had written, and hundreds upon
hundreds who might have been saved died.

The foolish act of a literary man unversed in the ways of the
world, you may be thinking. Not at all. Lion Feuchtwanger knew
exactly what he was doing because it seemed to me inescapable
that he was doing it on orders. Feuchtwanger was a Communist,
and it is Communist policy to take credit for all revolutionary
activity that proves to be effective and, where they cannot take
credit, to destroy it.

BOOK II

Some of Them Died in the Rain

After World War I, there was an American Red Cross worker assigned to a little camp just outside one of the more desolated villages in Yugoslavia who kept sending urgent reports back to the States on the desperate condition of the children in her jurisdiction. Of how the mothers were coming in daily to plead for food and clothing. Particularly shoes. For in all wars, at all times, food is the first thing to run out and shoes are the first thing to wear out.

As time went by and the weather turned cold and rainy, the mothers' complaints became more shrill; the stories of the children's needs more pitiful. The letters of the Red Cross worker became increasingly angry, increasingly critical of bureaucratic delay and governmental indifference.

At last, after many weeks, the supplies arrived. Food. Clothing. Shoes. A whole freight car. The Red Cross worker posted a notice on her bulletin board advising the mothers of the town that they had only to bring the children in and they would be given everything they needed.

Nobody came. She sent a worker into the village. The worker did not return. Filled with righteous anger, convinced that her efforts were unappreciated and that she had been made a fool, the Red Cross worker pulled on her galoshes, put on her coat and went into the village herself.

At first, it seemed to her that the whole village was deserted, but then, as her eyes scanned the expanse of snow, she saw one figure seated listlessly on the steps of the town hall. An old woman whom she recognized as a former worker at the camp.

"The supplies have arrived," she told the woman. "And now nobody seems to be interested anymore. I want you to go around to all the mothers and tell them that if they do not bring their children in I will send the food and clothing somewhere where they will perhaps be appreciated."

"There are no more children," the old woman said.

No more children? How could that be? "What happened to all the children who were here only last week?"

Some of them had starved. Some had been given to soldiers who had come through with food, others had been taken to another village where, it was rumored, there might be something to eat. "And," said the old woman, looking up at her through pale, washed-out eyes, "some of them died in the rain."

It never changes, you know.

It never really changes.

1. A Confusion of Organizations

I had thought that once I reached the United States it would be only a matter of time before the children started coming over. Even the political climate seemed to be with us. Because the immigration laws were even more restrictive regarding unaccompanied children than regarding adults, an organization called the U.S. Committee for the Care of European Children had been formed, privately funded and headed by Marshall Field, to cut through the quota system for children whose lives were in danger.

I was wrong. The U.S. Committee had managed to obtain visas for English children, but they had little success, in the end, in cutting the red tape for Jewish children from the continent. But there was more to it than that. Political pressure was not applied because there was no sense of urgency among the leaders of the American Jewish organizations. Nothing remotely resembling a feeling of *Emergency!* Under the armistice agreement, I was reminded again and again that unoccupied France was going to remain under the rule of the Vichy government. "The children are safe there," I was told. "Safer than they'd be here."

They would not, and could not, bring themselves to believe that the children were in mortal danger, because once they did it became incumbent upon them to move heaven on earth to rescue them. And in a time of increasing anti-Semitism in the United

States, they did not want to take the risk of fanning the flames by bringing Jewish children over by the boatload.

A few children came. One hundred and forty of ours out of a total of 320. The boatloads stayed in Europe and died.

From the outset, I found myself confronted by a maze of organizations. And if it was difficult to tell them apart without a scorecard, it was even harder, in the first few weeks, to tell whose side they were on.

The OSE: It had been my understanding that the OSE had an American office, presided over by the former chairman of the Polish OSE, Dr. Leon Wulman.

There was no OSE office in the United States, I discovered, and there continued to be no office for three and a half more months. The address I had been given was the hotel where Wulman was living. My first phone calls to him were not returned, which indicated to me that he wasn't exactly overjoyed to learn of my arrival.

After the war was over and we began to count up those who had died in the rain, it was Wulman who was selected to be the scapegoat. Rabbi Lange, the Chief Rabbi of France—the same Rabbi Lange who had brought on the Revolt of the Orthodox— treated Wulman with such contempt when he was here after the war that even I, who had no great regard for him, was hurt.

The Joint Distribution Committee: The chairman of the European operation and therefore the top man was Morris Troper, the man who had made the arrangements to permit the *St. Louis* to land in Antwerp. His office was in Paris, he had visited us in Montmorency and he gave me no reason to believe that he was anything except solidly behind my efforts when I met him in New York. By degrees, his attitude seemed to change from enthusiastic to less enthusiastic to less than enthusiastic. My suspicions were confirmed soon enough by the directors of the newly formed American committee of the OSE, Drs. J. J. Rongy and A. J. Golub. Rongy and Golub were both very distinguished physicians. As native-born Americans they were subject to the vague guilt feelings of people who have always been outside the combat zone. "Look," Rongy said when I kept pressing for more positive action. "Joint is against it."

I said: "Talk to Troper and you'll find out that isn't so."

"No," they replied. "You talk to Troper and you'll find out what we are saying is the absolute truth."

The U.S. Committee for the Care of European Children: The executive director was Elsa Castendyke, who had come to the committee directly from her job as head of the Children's Bureau of the Department of Labor. (If you wonder what the Children's Bureau was doing in the Department of Labor, it had to do with the original law forbidding child labor.) Miss Castendyke had also visited us at Montmorency and sent me a most flattering letter. She supported me completely. The president of the committee was Marshall Field, one of nature's noble men. In all those first hard months, Marshall Field, the millionaire, was the only person who ever bothered to ask me what I was doing for a living. An excellent question. When we first arrived, I had decided that the best thing to do was to get a job as a custodian of a public school. I would be around children, where I could perhaps be helpful and, more to the point, I could do most of my work in the early morning hours and have much of the day left to pursue my main interest. One lives and one learns. In Europe, a custodian is a menial, and therefore noncompetitive, job. In New York City, as I discovered to my astonishment, the custodian was paid on a scale that made him a high-paid employee. So I had become a dishwasher in an all-night restaurant with the understanding that I could work a few hours here and a few hours there. Lene could not practice medicine until she passed the state exams, which were given in English, a language she was just beginning to learn. Lene, as I didn't bother to tell Field, was working as a night nurse. When the OSE office opened at the end of the year I was put on a temporary three-month arrangement. The salary was only a little more than I had been making as a dishwasher but at least it allowed me to get some sleep.

The only problem where the U.S. Committee was concerned was that their ability to accomplish anything was severely restricted. In the United States, as Elsa Castendyke informed me, all matters involving the welfare of children had to be dealt with according to religious affiliation.

National Refugee Service: This was the organization concerned with helping *all* Jewish refugee children. The director was Cecilia Roczovsky, whom I had already corresponded with. Miss Roczovsky was an old battler in the field. Unfortunately, she had battled so long and so unsuccessfully under the restrictions of the quota system that she put forth a very realistic—i.e., pessimistic—view of our chances. Miss Roczovsky informed me that she was in touch with the Baroness Eduard de Rothschild regarding the evacuation of the children from her home in France to the Philippine Islands and that this was a solution that might be undertaken for our children as well. I could only say that with the United States and Japan so clearly on a collision course we would be running too great a risk of sending the children from one war-torn country to another.

German-Jewish Children's Aid: A subdivision of the European-Jewish Aid which was a subdivision of the National Refugee Service. It was the German-Jewish Children's Aid which owned the franchise, in a manner of speaking, on the disposition of our children. More specifically, we were under the jurisdiction and at the mercy of Lotte Marcuse, the placement director. The day before my first meeting with Mrs. Marcuse, Elsa Castendyke came up from Washington to warn me about her. "She is very shifty," Castendyke said. "She will give you a lot of talk and nothing will happen. You will think she agrees with everything you have said, and then you will think back on it and realize that she hasn't committed herself to a thing."

I found that Mrs. Marcuse did not differ to any great degree from the officials of other Jewish agencies. I had come from Europe lamenting that the children were in mortal danger. The leaders of the Jewish agencies agreed that something had to be done for them and then did nothing. Mrs. Marcuse said, in effect: "This is not the impression we have received from other sources. But now that I have heard how dangerous you believe their situation to be I will most certainly look into it more carefully."

As time went on, we had another basic disagreement. Mrs. Marcuse was a social worker, and she had no patience whatsoever with my argument that the children should be kept together as a community until the fate of their parents became known. It was her intention, she made clear, to do with them exactly what she had been doing with the other children who came under her care. Place them in individual foster homes around the country.

In fairness to Mrs. Marcuse it should be said that she was following the conventional practices of social work in the United States. As I discovered before the year had come to an end when I was invited to deliver a lecture about the Montmorency Homes at the New York School of Social Work. Now, these were people with whom I had some credentials. The auditorium was filled to overflowing with students and with professionals in the field. The Commissioner of Welfare for New York City was there, as was the Commissioner of Welfare for the U.S. Government. The lecture was well received, but in the question-and-answer period that followed I was attacked savagely on my thesis that the Homes could be transposed to the United States. In that entire auditorium there were only two people who supported me. One was Elsa Castendyke. The other was Nora Johnson, the director of the Children's Aid Society. (Miss Johnson was so impressed that she offered me a position as consultant—a position which, of course, I was in no position to accept at that time.)

One of the difficulties was language. I wasn't aware that the word *institution* had such an unfortunate connotation in this country—probably because it brought to mind the word *institutionalized,* a word which had no counterpart in Europe. "This is not the American way!" they shouted at me. In America, children were sent to institutions only as a punishment or because of a conspicuous inability to cope with life on the outside.

It was one of those annihilating experiences—annihilating because it was so unexpected—where you think of all the things you should have said two hours later. Like: Oh? I wasn't aware that children were sent to boarding schools in the United States as a punishment. Or, since what we were involved in was really a play on words: Of course. The home is the only sacred institution in America. I should have understood that.

All I could do, really, was admit that it had not occurred to me before that a home—any home—was better than an institution —any institution—and then suggest that the one thing I did understand, even better perhaps than they, was the problems of refugee children.

The most revealing comment came after an argument had broken out on the floor as to whether there would be enough foster homes to take care of all the children, Jewish and otherwise, who might be coming into the country. Dorothy Hutchinson, one of the leading professors of the New York School of Social Work, arose to announce that even if there weren't enough foster homes—and she, for one, didn't believe there were—she would still be against anything relating in any way to an "institution."

A few years later, when Dorothy Hutchinson and I were working for OFFRA (which became UNRRA when the war ended), we were sent to the University of Maryland together to train social workers who would follow the Allied armies into Europe. On the way down I told her I would like to sit in on a few of her classes so that we wouldn't be contradicting each other.

"Oh," she laughed. "You're still thinking about that first meeting, aren't you?" Well, I didn't have to worry anymore; my initiation was over. "You are a fully accredited graduate of the New York School of Social Work yourself. You're a member of the clique now." As such, I was apparently free to put forth any theories I wanted and expect some measure of agreement from the other members of the clique. Or, at the very least, the courtesy of a discreet silence. And, you know, it was only then that I understood that much of the opposition had stemmed from their natural resentment toward an outsider who had come barging into their sacred bailiwick to tell them that their theories were wrong.

All right. Having made my obeisance to both the mainstream of professional thinking and the politics of academia, I now have to say something else where Mrs. Marcuse and the Joint are concerned. There is nothing more satisfying than a theory of education and child welfare which allows you to do exactly what you wanted to do in the first place. Keep the children hidden and out of sight. Drs. Rongy and Golub as much as told me at one point that the Joint didn't want them in the United States at all. What I had to understand, Rongy said, was that the Joint wasn't in the business of supporting people within this country. Its function was to disburse funds overseas. The Joint had contributed money toward the children's upkeep before, he reminded me. And it would again. In France. If I wanted to establish a Home in the United States, he said, I should be trying to get the money from the Federation of Jewish Philanthropies, the umbrella organization that raises all the money for Jewish causes within the country.

The Federation of Jewish Philanthropies: Through Dr. Rongy, an appointment was set up with an official of the Federation, Dr. Hexter. This interview I will never forget. Dr. Hexter listened to everything I had to say and, choosing his words with great care, told me: "I don't see how we can do anything to help you but I'll promise you one thing. You won't face any opposition from us if the OSE is able to get the children over here and find a place for them."

I thought that was very generous of him.

There was one official of the Joint who had been a firm ally from the beginning, Paul Fagen. Fagen was a lawyer with excellent connections in Washington, and after two months of the runaround he decided that the best way to move the Joint off dead-center would be to get the visas ourselves.

I remember very distinctly that we missed our train to Washington because the appointment with Hexter materialized very suddenly for that same day; Friday, October 25. Rather than call off the appointment Fagen had made with Adolf Berle, the Assistant Secretary of State, we jumped into Fagen's car, drove down to Washington and were closeted with Berle through Saturday and Sunday. Berle was anxious to pick my mind about the political situation in Middle Europe, which was perfectly understandable, but he had an absolutely insane idea for restoring the Hapsburgs to the throne of Hungary. Berle kept telling me that he was an Austrian himself. He wasn't; his forebears had come from Hungary. If he had known anything at all about the relations between Hungary and Austria he would have understood that to impose an Austrian king upon Hungary would have been the one sure way of inciting a revolution.

As far as our kids were concerned, Berle was perfectly willing to guarantee us the five hundred visas we were asking for, and, although events were to prove us overoptimistic, we left Washington convinced that we had them.

That was the last time I ever saw Fagen. All I could learn when I made inquiries was that he was on some kind of special assignment overseas. I heard his name mentioned occasionally in later years; I heard he was working with the Justice Department in Europe at one time. But I never saw him again.

When Fagen dropped out of sight, I began to spend most of my time with the Grand Old Man of the Joint Distribution Committee, Dr. Emanuel Rosen. Rosen had been the Director of European Affairs before he was superseded by Troper, and if he was no longer the strong man of the organization he still had a certain amount of power and he knew how the organization worked.

I had seen Rosen often in France. And heard from him even more frequently. Rosen had excellent relations with the Trujillo government in the Dominican Republic and he was always sending cables to Gourwitch suggesting that Papanek set up "a farm-school settlement" there for the older boys and girls. He had even sent me a visa; the last thing I had done before leaving Portugal was return it to the Dominican consulate in Lisbon on the chance that it could be used by someone else. Considering that his good relations with the Trujillo people had survived the debacle of the *St. Louis,* I couldn't help but wonder what in the world could have gone wrong there. Though I was never able to get a categorical explanation from him I was left with the very clear impression that there had been two opposing factions within the Joint—one with connections in Santo Domingo, the other with connections in Havana—competing to see who could get the better deal. Instead, the dictators of Cuba and the Dominican Republic had turned the game around on them and begun to bid them up. Until finally the publicity became so great that both Federico Laredo Bru and Trujillo were faced with the choice of backing away completely or letting the whole world know that they were engaged in their humanitarian rescue work at so much per head.

Although I still didn't find the prospect of bringing our children to a dictatorship particularly appealing, it had begun to look like a practical alternative and—at any rate—worth investigating for any other children who might be able to go there.

Rosen himself didn't feel there was any sense in opening negotiations unless we had three hundred dollars in hand for every child we planned to send there. Two hundred for their transportation and one hundred dollars in settlement costs.

"If you really want to shake the Joint up," he advised me, "show them you can raise the money yourself." Once I was able to do that, Rosen assured me, we had only to threaten that I would go to the public and ask for contributions on my own. "Whether it's to bring the children here or to Santo Domingo or anywhere else, doesn't matter. Just somewhere where they'll be safe." I had to laugh. All I had to do was prove that I could raise a lot of money, huh? I was a foreigner. I could barely speak the language.

I had been walking Rosen to his apartment on Riverside Drive while we were talking and we were practically at his door. "Nothing to it," he said. "I'll show you." He ran his finger down the doorbells and pressed. The buzzer sounded. "You want ten thousand dollars?" He snapped his fingers. "Ten thousand dollars you'll have by morning." Up the stairs we went. Two somewhat elderly ladies were waiting there in their nightgowns.

At Rosen's urging I told the whole story. The children, the danger, the necessity of alerting the Jewish people. And then, as if the thought had just occurred to him, Rosen said, "Why, Mady, you could give ten thousand dollars yourself."

Of course she could. Without blinking an eye. She was willing to write a check to the United Jewish Appeal, the Joint's fund-raising arm, anytime Rosen wanted her to. And that was how I began my career as a fund-raiser for the UJA.

I protested at first that not everybody was going to be as easy as Rosen's two ladies. It didn't matter, the UJA people told me. All I had to do was tell my story and leave the rest of it up to them.

They had it down to an absolute science. A roomful of people would be collected in the apartment of someone sympathetic to the cause, and I would get up and make my speech. When I was finished, an official from UJA would get up and say, "You have heard how the children are suffering! You have heard how necessary it is for us to help them! How much will you pledge?"

"A thousand dollars," a man would say.

"A thousand dollars! What are you trying to do, kid me? I know the kind of year you had last year. I have you down for five thousand."

A little arguing back and forth, and the man would say, "All right, all right. Three thousand and stop *hocking* me already."

It never failed. I would tell them about Emil Geisler. The first time or two I felt a little uneasy about using him to pluck at the heartstrings and wring out the tears, but in no time at all I got used to it. And, I must say, very good at it. Tell your story, Rosen had said, and the money will come. I told my story, the money came rolling in and I got so I rather enjoyed it.

Now I will tell you how my career as a fund-raiser came to an end. From the very beginning I had been in constant communication with Gourwitch. If *communication* is the word for it. On November 5, I would get a letter from Gourwitch which began, "Your letter of September 15 reached me on October 10." In the intervening time I had probably written ten other letters and his answer would bear about as much relevance to the current situation as you might expect.

At any rate, a letter finally arrived in which Gourwitch instructed me that I was to leave all fund-raising in the hands of the Joint. Rosen had been right. Too right. The Joint was so worried that I would be able to raise the money by myself that they had taken care to see that it would never happen. I had raised a lot of money for them, and there still was not the slightest indication that anything was being done to move any of the children out of France.

There was one other organization I was dealing with. The Quakers. At Gourwitch's direction, I was meeting with the representatives of the Quakers, both in New York and at their headquarters in Philadelphia, to solicit their aid in dealing with the Vichy officials in France for the exit visas. As always, they were anxious to do everything possible to help.

From the first day, I had been drawing up lists of names. Relatives in this country wrote me. Imploring letters came from the children in Montintin and from their parents in Gurs. I had managed to acquire a stack of affidavits by either writing to relatives or by looking through the telephone books for people who had the same last name as those children who were sixteen or approaching sixteen. I would simply call them up cold, ask if they were related to the family in question and, upon being told that they weren't, ask if they would sign an affidavit for us anyway on my personal guarantee that we would pick up the child upon his or her arrival and never ask or expect anything else of them.

I was able to give the Quakers the names of 176 children for whom I had obtained affidavits, and we agreed that we would work toward an original shipment of three hundred. Fine. And then, the situation changed. Before I knew quite what was happening, the Quakers weren't merely acting as a go-between for us, they were also making it clear they had the exclusive rights to deal with the Vichy government in the evacuation of all children from France. Both in regard to the exit visas and, of equal importance, transportation.

Month after month passed, and nothing happened.

In January, a Red Cross ship was going to make the crossing, and when that fell through too Gourwitch absolutely infuriated me by informing the parents who questioned him about it that there was "no chance" of getting the children over, and then infuriated me further by cabling me to stop making unrealistic promises. "I can understand your difficulties in all of this," I wrote back, "although I cannot operate on the basis of them. You were lacking in faith that action might succeed after you were disappointed by the Quakers. But it was you who had been of the opinion that by some miracle the Quakers might evince an interest in the children, after all. I, because I saw nothing to be gained by writing of my own work, did not give you all the details on the ups and downs of the discussions, the resistance and rampant jealousies. It took a lot of optimism, endurance and resistance to continue the work, especially when no one believed in it any longer, nor volunteered to help. But during those times I could not afford to say there is 'no chance' because, then, there would not have been any."

On May 12, 1941, Gourwitch wrote:

> As to the lists [of the names of the children who had been cleared for emigration] sent to you too late, we have already explained to you that from the very beginning we have been misled by the Quakers, who desired to direct this action all by themselves, jealously safeguarding their prerogatives and refusing to cooperate on this ground with any other competent organization. Desiring to cooperate with them we could not send to you the lists in time. On the other hand, we have to say that the Quakers are cooperating very loyally with us now and that they are giving us almost the total number of places out of the hundred visas granted. In spite of our energetic interventions and all the attempts of the Quakers to settle the question of the passage, this very important problem has not yet been solved. The Joint, who is very much interested in the immigration of children, hopes to retain 50 places on a boat leaving from Lisbon at the beginning of June. . . . We are ready, but the American Consul in Marseille has stated last week that he received no special instructions from the State Department in Washington, and therefore he will have to consider the 100 visas as quota visas. Since a number of nationalities, such as the German and Polish, have no free numbers on the quotas one will have to wait till such numbers are available, this would mean months and months of delay.

On May 22, we received word that forty of our children were—at last—leaving for Lisbon. To celebrate the occasion, the American office of the OSE fired me.

2. The Children of Montintin

"The famous check," Gourwitch would write from time to time, "is still uncashed." I had mailed it back to him before I left. They never did cash it. The OSE and the JDC had also moved their accounts to the bank in Bordeaux. Those funds remained frozen too. Gourwitch was almost totally dependent on money sent over by the American Joint, and as things went from bad to worse in Unoccupied France the need for cash became greater and greater.

The farmers around Limoges kept their promise to feed our children as best they could considering that it was well over a year before they got paid. Some of them didn't get paid until after the war was over. The trouble was that there just wasn't enough food to go around.

> For some of us Montintin was a continual search for food. My friend Dorli and I spent our time devising schemes for getting more to eat than we were getting because what there was was also very good. We developed elaborate schemes for cheating to get extra food. You know, like suddenly excusing ourselves in the middle of some class in order to go and get a heel of bread that was being given to some other age group, all sorts of schemes. I was going through a period of very rapid growth at that time and was terribly underweight and I ate everybody's leftovers.
>
> —Hanna's diary

The big boys would be on morning wood-chopping duty. (We got an extra egg a day for that.) The Vichy gendarmes were as miserable as the Nazis; we could see their limousines in front of the house and would not go back. We would stay out all day if necessary. There was an incredible shortage of food. Two times a week we would get one square of meat. Some of us would stuff our stomach with wild berries and get diarrhea. There was a rootlike turnip indigenous to the area called *topinambour*. Kaete used it in every conceivable way, all inedible. I was sometimes sent around to get milk from the farmers and might be able to get two quarts for the whole place. One night coming back I was going down a little hill, fell and lost control. They found me crying there at the bottom of the hill, and everybody asked, "Where are you hurt?" I wasn't hurt. I had broken the two bottles of milk in my knapsack.

—Ernst Valfer

Everybody was hungry all the time. Once in a great while we might have a slice of bread and a touch of butter. Once I saved mine all day thinking how good it was going to be. I met one of the girls who I happened to like very much.

"What a wonderful piece of bread," she said.

I asked her if she would like a bite.

"No."

"Oh, go ahead. I've had a lot of it already."

"Well . . . if you're not hungry."

"Sure, take a big bite."

Believe me, it was the biggest present I've ever given anybody.

—Orthodox boy

Of course it would be an Orthodox boy who would save a piece of bread all day and then share it. The great strength of an Orthodox upbringing is that they are taught to do without. They learn to do without as a service to God and, having learned it, they discover that the satisfaction of self-denial is permanent and the pleasures of self-indulgence fleeting. Viewing the Orthodox children solely through the eyes of an educator, I had come to appreciate the value of self-denial in the building of character.

I say all that because Lydia Dan, whose ties to religion were as nonexistent as mine, had taken over as a kind of high-level troubleshooter out of the main Vichy office, and the Orthodox drove her crazy. (She was supposed to come to the United States later to use her enormous influence to help me handle the Joint. Just as she was ready to leave, Feuchtwanger shut down the Underground route for us.)

The first dietary crisis at Montintin had occurred very early over the serving of rabbit stew, with most of the Conservative children deciding to get into the spirit of the thing and join the Orthodox in a boycott—a sacrifice made easier by the apparent inedibility of the final product.

Poor Lydia. "My first trip," she wrote me, in describing her new job to me, "will be to Montintin where the question of the dietary laws has to be settled."

> It is all pretty bleak, there is nothing left for us but to be amazed at how far human stupidity can be carried. Today, for example, I got an urgent telephone call from Brout-Vernet (we have local telephone service now, and I wish it would go away): I must find Rabbi Schneerson and ask him what they should do at Brout-Vernet: while they were eating duck they discovered that there was something abnormal in the poor creature's intestines. They did not eat the duck, that goes without saying, but apparently they will have to take further precautions in the purification procedures from now on. France is suffering her greatest catastrophe and they are concerned only with the digestive tract of a duck which we were able to obtain for them only by mortgaging our soul, our honor and our prospects for entering into the Kingdom of Heaven.

As for the children themselves, the first thing they had to do was to work out their relationship with their new directress.

> I don't wish to embarrass you, Ernst, but I must say that Lucia would not have been so disliked if she would have been closer to what had happened before. But when Lucia took over, coming from an entire different philosophy of education, which on its own may be just as good—I don't want to make value judgments here—the effect was a shattering one. She had been brought up in an environment where children even at our age were expected to fit into the decisions that the adults made for them. Under more

normal circumstances this might have worked, but this was really a stress situation; first, because we were people without any rights in a dangerous situation in a strange country, and secondly because she took over so suddenly when you left. So the relationship with Lucia was under an ill-star from the very outset. I think it got better as time went on, it got more business-like, but it never straightened itself out completely.

—Cuban boy

A French woman became directress. A distance was kept. Not the cold feeling that still existed for Mme. Koffsky at the Orthodox home. Neither a warm feeling nor cold. The Directress had a friend, who taught German and also became involved in Administration policy, and we got into a hot argument with him and there was another big revolt. By the end, there were boys 18, 17, 16. The Administration was concerned with preventive problems. Proprietory habits were drummed into us. We would walk in the forest with the girls and wouldn't hold hands. We would bump into each other and would apologize. John Windmuller was supposed to be seen kissing a girl. This was enough for the Administration. "Incidents have been observed to lead us to believe that certain things happen, and if anything further is seen boys and girls will have to be separated."

Ernst Valfer had a big fight with him. It was something to do with a dispute between the Prince Consort and Boris, the shop instructor. Boris, who was always anti-administration, wanted to hold the weekly dances again. Many took sides. Ernst Valfer sided strongly with Boris, and the guy wanted him kicked out of the home. We went out into the forest and had one of our old-time conferences. An on-the-spot retrial. The verdict was that Ernst would stay and the Prince Consort would be kicked out of the house. The solution was that we had the dances after all—and Boris began to hold classes again in ballroom dancing as well.

—Orthodox boy

John Windmuller has a clearer memory of what the big fight was all about, and it was just about what you would imagine: "I think we were in some respects a rather puritanical little group. We thought this was simply not proper, that these two people were sleeping in the same room. As a matter of fact, that room was right next to the big boys' room, at least it was on the same floor, and at that point we made quite an issue of it; so much so that Heinz felt the need to justify it. Now formerly there was no need to do that, but after all we were a community that had to get along with itself and there was trouble that had to be straightened out. So the explanation which we received at the time was that the relationship was a platonic one. This was my first acquaintance with the word platonic in that context, and we thought this was ridiculous. But in another way perhaps it wasn't. I suspect that it was at least a partial truth. Anyway, from this point on the expression 'platonic relationship' became one of those winged words that you will use at every opportunity, appropriate and inappropriate. It obviously did not make Lucia's position as directress any easier because the little authority that we saw in her vanished under these circumstances."

The mosquitoes were terrible. We would get pussy willows and rub it on the places where we had been bitten and you can laugh if you want but it worked. We were beginning to smoke potato leaves, by drying them out and grinding them into a mash. I am sure we did not have the full approval of the authorities but what could they do? We began by smoking them out in the forest, gradually approaching the house over the months until we were lighting up inside.

It was a curious situation because tobacco was extremely scarce and it was rationed. The local authorities decided we boys who were 16 were entitled to our ration, and we would buy a few cigarettes or else a little square packet of tobacco with which you could roll your own. We would buy these packets but because they were in such great demand and since we were not yet professional smokers we would trade them in for other luxuries, such as candy. We had our own self-imposed ration for the potato-leaf cigarettes, incidentally, no more than one or two a day. I believe we even had a vote on it.

—Cuban boy

Slowly the Robinsoner left, one by one, called back by their families, by the promise of a visa to America. We were all in danger—but there were not enough visas. And so we left, one by one, quietly, like traitors, on the small truck, to meet the train, alone again, going to our parents, and on . . . and stood weeping by windows looking into rainstorms for days, crying perhaps for the Olympics taking place there, crying perhaps for the others in the castle. But we could not yet cry about the days to come. We were, so far, home free.

—Hanna's diary

August 30. We have already burned all the papers that have to do with the Red Falcons, and I have torn all the pages out of this diary that have to do with politics. The distinction between Robinsoner and Cubans has completely disappeared these past few weeks. There are no longer any fights. The name of Touretia has been developed for Montintin, combining the name of Tourelles and Helvetia as a gesture of solidarity. As the kids leave, they write little notes in each other's books, and many of them write that we should forget the Robinsoner and Cuban distinctions because that is not the good part.

—Diary and Remembrances of a Robinsoner girl

The French fascists were as miserable as the Germans. The secret, national black-shirted police took great pleasure in toying with us. They would come up in the night, grab two or three of the oldest and take them away. The others would wake up and find some of us missing.

—Ernst Valfer

Letter from Yvonne Goldberg and Eva Unikower:
"Yesterday again, a group of children left Montintin for the United States. We were waving goodby, wishing them good luck, but we were sad and worried that we were left back and would have no chance to leave France before the Nazis might come. We have no relatives and friends in the United States: nobody will give us an affidavit to apply for a visa. Couldn't you try to get one of your friends to make out an affidavit for us. Maybe this would give us a chance to be saved.
"P.S. Do you remember Emil Geisler? He too has no relatives or friends in the United States. He was sixteen a few days ago

and he will have to go to a concentration camp as all boys over sixteen have to do. Maybe you could also get an affidavit for him so that he can immigrate to the United States."

> From April 1941 to May 1941 I was at Château de Magillier. From there we headed first to Marseilles, and finally to Lisbon, by way of Madrid. In Portugal we got our first taste of plenty. I must have eaten enough for 3 people! We were even treated to a movie at Estoril, Walt Disney's "Pinocchio."
>
> Our ship, the *Mouzinho,* left Lisbon on June 10, 1941, and I arrived in New York with 100 other children 10 days later. Among my souvenirs is the identification tag from the American Friends Service Committee, which we all wore around our necks. It has a big no. 50 on it, and also: "In case of emergency . . .", etc. In my souvenir book I see the handwriting of some of the boys I came over with. I sure would like to know where at least some of these boys are.
>
> —Ernst Koppstein

The first group was brought to Marseilles, where they were assembled in a Catholic home for two weeks while arrangements were being completed for a special order from Pétain granting them unrestricted passage through France. The train pulled out of Marseilles late at night. There was a ten-minute stopover at the railway station near Gurs for a brief final visit with the parents who were interned there. When they made the final stop at the customs station in Cerbère, the French police embraced them. On the other side of the border, they were given a complete shakedown and frisking and then put on a train which the Spanish must have been saving for the occasion; an old, dirty, slow-moving train without any toilet facilities.

After spending the night in Madrid they were put on an old American express train which took them into Lisbon.

Morris Troper, the European director, was waiting in Lisbon to take the bows for the Joint. Among other things, the Joint had produced a commemorative brochure that featured an open letter from Troper to Mrs. Eleanor Roosevelt, who was the honorary chairman of Marshall Field's U.S. Committee. The main purpose of the letter seemed to be to tell everybody about the terrible condition the children were in. "When they came here," Troper wrote, "they looked like tired, wan, broken little old men and women. None dared to laugh aloud and few smiled—even the younger of seven and eight. Their clothes were in tatters. The more fortunate of them clumped around in wooden-soled shoes. One of the most pathetic sights I have ever seen was that of these children, freed of restraints, trying to learn to play again. They played grimly as though fearing that at any moment the sun, the beach, the food and the new unaccustomed liberty would be snatched from them and they would be thrown back into the misery and distress from which they had just escaped. . . ."

An exercise in imagination. Pure fantasy. From the time the train crossed the border into Portugal, the children had been greeted as heroes. When they arrived in Lisbon, they were met by representatives of *O Seculo*, the leading Portuguese daily, whose publisher, Joa o Perieira da Rosa, had been conducting an energetic campaign to save the starving children of Europe. They were brought to a home that the newspaper maintained for the poor children of Lisbon, and da Rosa himself came out every day to see that all their needs were taken care of, including special kosher food and dishes for the Orthodox. Individual Portuguese made special trips to visit them, bearing gifts. The workmen at the home and, later, the workmen at the dock, refused to accept any payment for helping them.

I am all for propaganda where propaganda can be helpful. Unhappily Troper's letter was the worst kind of propaganda to be spreading at that particular time.

Pétain was only the figurehead of the Vichy government. Pierre Laval was the man who was running things. It was remarked of him often in those days that his name read the same backward or forward, which suggested quite accurately that Laval could go in any direction without having to move. Like most of the politicians of Europe, Laval had entered politics as a Socialist and he had always maintained his contacts in the Socialist camp. In the first days after the armistice, Theodor Dan had several meetings with him, and he had given Dan his solemn promise that there would be five thousand exit visas for children.

"World history," he had said, "would never forgive us if we handed them over to the Nazis."

Sooner or later, Laval broke every promise he made to Dan. In an interview in *Aufbau,* the German-language newspaper, he explained why he had reneged on the exit visas for the children: "You want to parade these children down Fifth Avenue and show everybody what the terrible French people have done to them."

And that was exactly what Troper was doing.

3. The Children Arrive; the Children Disappear

Actually, the American OSE had fired me twice. Originally, I had been hired on a temporary basis to find out whether it would be practical to establish a Montmorency-type Home in this country. Two weeks before the deadline, I asked Leon Wulman to hold a full-scale meeting at the offices of the American OSE. I had the support of Marshall Field and his U.S. Committee. I had the support of the Quakers, who favor community living as a general principle. I had two independent backers, Mme. Gunzbourg, who was now living in New York, and Rosen's two ladies in the upstairs apartment. And I had just received word from the State Department that we had been granted our first one hundred visas.

Instead of holding the meeting, Wulman informed me that since the National Refugee Service's opposition to institutions couldn't possibly be overcome my employment was being terminated. The whole thing, in short, had been a charade.

Through the intervention of Gourwitch, I was rehired a month later on the same basis with the understanding that my employment would become permanent—i.e., on a professional, contractual basis—as soon as it became certain that there would be children coming into the United States from France.

And so as soon as it became definite that the first shipment of children was indeed on its way I was informed that Gourwitch had agreed that my work with the OSE should come to an end if there was no possibility of setting up the Home. Mme. Gunzbourg promptly resigned from the OSE with a blistering statement that she no longer believed the OSE desired to carry on its work in the interests of the children.

For me, it was a little more difficult. It is not easy to keep demanding that you be put on the payroll, with adequate compensation, without opening yourself up to the charge that the only survival you are interested in is your own. Let me explain it this way: When I was being held in a Danzig prison by the Nazis just before the plebiscite in that city, I went on a hunger strike to demonstrate that I did not recognize their right to hold me—having taken the elementary precaution of hiding bits and pieces of bread around the cell. To make a symbolic stand is very important; to starve to death is ridiculous.

I had no choice, then, but to demand that I be treated with all the respect that would normally be accorded to a professional because if I allowed them to treat me as a temporary, not very important employee, I was allowing them to treat the children as a temporary, not very important problem. Just as by firing me, at the time I was fired, they were serving notice, as I saw it, that as far as they were concerned the emigration was over.

Poor Gourwitch. I wrote him an angry letter and when his answer finally came it seemed that Wulman had misrepresented his position completely. By the time the letter arrived, of course, the children had been in the country for a full month.

The day before they landed, there had been a stormy meeting in Mrs. Marcuse's office. Elsa Castendyke, who had resigned in disgust and gone back to her job with the Children's Bureau, was there much in the same capacity that I was. As an interested party. Representing the U.S. Committee were Mrs. Eleanor Roosevelt, who as honorary chairman had been taking an increased interest as the time of the first transport drew near; and Marshall Field, who became increasingly incensed as the meeting wore on.

For the first time, Marshall Field was realizing what the argument had been all about. That it was not just a dispute between social workers as to whether the children would be better off if they remained together or were assigned to foster homes. What Mrs. Marcuse had in mind was a complete resettlement plan based on the incredible theory that the children must make a complete break with their past—as if she really believed it were possible to wipe the slate clean and begin all over again.

Those with affidavits from relatives who wanted to take care of them would, of course, be turned over to them. The others were to be sent to agencies that would place them with foster families, and neither I nor anyone else outside the National Refugee Service were to know where they were.

The agencies were to give out absolutely no information about them. The children were not to receive any unsettling news of their families; were, in fact, to be discouraged from corresponding with anyone overseas. Presumably, they would never wonder whether their parents were dead or alive—let alone wonder, either then or later, under what circumstances they might have met their deaths.

They would become assimilated into their new country, according to the Marcuse plan, by becoming lost in it. Everything we had worked to accomplish at Montmorency was being destroyed. Everything.

After the meeting, we repaired in dispirit and disarray to the Gramercy Hotel, where Elsa Castendyke always stayed when she was in New York. Marshall Field was in shock. "They don't want them here," he kept saying. "They don't want them here, and if they do come they want to hide them."

All the difficulties the U.S. Committee had been encountering at the State Department were suddenly clear to him. Perhaps too clear. If the hard-liners at the State Department were always getting their way, he could now see, it was because there was no pressure being applied from above. And if there was no pressure coming from either Congress or the President's office it could only be because no meaningful pressure had come from the Jewish agencies who were occupying the grounds.

I was a disappointment to Marshall Field too before we were

through. As the meeting in Mrs. Marcuse's office had been about to break up Field had infuriated her by suggesting that I meet him at the Battery at 8 A.M. so that I could go out to the *Mouzinho* with him in the customs boat to greet the children. As far as Mrs. Marcuse was concerned, it was her prerogative to go out with him to extend the official welcome. As far as Field was concerned, the sight of my familiar face would be far more reassuring to them than any words that might come from a stranger.

"All right," she snapped. "If Papanek greets them, let Papanek take care of them! We will no longer be responsible." That's how petty it got.

"Remember, Ernst," Field said, as we were taking leave of each other in front of the Gramercy Hotel, "I'll see you at the Battery at eight."

I told him I'd be there, and then took very good care not to arrive until the boat was docking. That's how sure I was that, given the opportunity, she would have washed her hands of all responsibility and canceled the rest of the agreement with the Quakers.

It was just as well we were there, I must say, and not only because the children were so happy to see us. While they were undergoing physical exams at the Jewish Academy Orphanage on Amsterdam Avenue, Elsa Castendyke came running out, terribly upset. Every one of them had shown a positive TB reaction. They were all going to have to be placed in quarantine, she moaned, and all future transports were going to have to be called off.

Lene told her not to worry. Lene had vaccinated them all just before we evacuated Montmorency, and so naturally they had all shown a positive reaction.

The largest group, comprising eighteen children, was being sent to Chicago, and I made it my business to go with them. Two were going to relatives in the Chicago area. Six others were going on to Detroit and St. Louis. The remaining ten were being sent to Woodlawn Hall, an orphanage run by the Jewish Children's Bureau of Chicago, for immediate placement in foster homes.

I had my own special reason for accompanying them. Traumata from out of the past. When the Spanish refugee children had been sent to England, they too had been offered to foster parents. The Spanish children had been lined up on the stage at the Kent Academy, and it had turned into something like a slave market. The bright, active children were snatched up and fought over, and you could just see the leftover children, those who were not taken until the very end, shrivel up and die inside themselves.

I remained at Woodlawn for five days preparing the children while a social worker was preparing the families. The prospective foster parents were allowed to stipulate whether they wanted a boy or a girl. Beyond that, they were given a history of the child who was assigned to them and a report on his emotional and—if they asked—intellectual development. There was no lineup, no competitive bidding, no leftovers.

The second group of forty-five children came two months later. I learned they were coming when the National Refugee Service sent two passes that entitled Lene and me to be admitted to the dock. Dr. Brutzkus, the man who had gotten the Homes started, was in the United States by then—a tired, old man—and so was Gourwitch's sister. I requested a pair of tickets for them and was informed, very brusquely, that only two tickets had been reserved for the OSE. "One for Dr. Papanek and one for Mrs. Papanek."

When I told them they could give those tickets to Brutzkus and Mme. Gourwitch because we already had official passes, I was informed that in that case the tickets would have to be turned back to the Quakers. So I turned our own passes over to Brutzkus, and when they arrived at the dock they were completely ignored. They had not been invited, I was told when I called to protest such an obvious snub, and they—meaning the French OSE—were not welcome.

I should have been at the dock myself, of course. If I had not known that all along, it was impressed upon me quite forcefully by the letters that came from the children wanting to know why Lene and I had deserted them.

The third transport was supposed to follow in a couple of weeks. In point of fact, it took a month. I was forced to write to Castendyke's successor at the U.S. Committee to find out when the ship would be in, and Lene and I were at the dock to greet it.

Nothing, however, could change the policy of the German-Jewish Aid—as I learned soon enough from a heartbreaking letter that came from Gourwitch:

"It is difficult for me to convey to you my sadness over the breaking of all ties between our children and our Committee after arrival in New York. These children have been under our care for a long time, some of them for nearly four years, and we were interested in their fate and well-being. It is painful for us not to receive letters from them. We are told here that it is not a proof of children's forgetfulness but is a result of the policy of the United States Committee who forbid correspondence between children and their relatives and friends in Europe in order not to break up their assimilation and upbringing. This seems ever so strange to us. It was not our viewpoint at Montmorency. We never allowed parents to interfere with our methods of education but we never forbade the children to write to their parents and friends! ... Other children, who did not leave and were promised long letters and reports from their little friends who emigrated, are very disappointed and have the impression that they are already forgotten."

The policy of breaking all ties with the past was often carried to ludicrous lengths. When the OSE asked me to inform the son of a well-known Yiddish writer that his father had been shot as a hostage and had met his death heroically, Mrs. Marcuse refused to tell me where the boy was. I wrote to every agency and office that might conceivably have information about him. Some of them said they had been instructed not to give out such information, some said they knew nothing about the boy and couldn't have told me even if they had known, and some didn't answer at all. It took two or three months of letter writing before I found someone in an agency in St. Louis who was willing to give me the address on his own authority.

Nothing demonstrates Mrs. Marcuse's attitude quite so well as

the situation that developed around Erik Thorn, the boy who had
been left behind with diphtheria. Having taken care of Erik for a
full year, the Quakers sent him back to us as one of the original
forty on the *Mouzinho*. Erik's father was in a concentration camp
but, as it happened, Erik had an aunt in this country, his father's
sister. Because his records had gone with him to the Quakers I
hadn't known about her in time to ask her for an affidavit. Both
she and his father were notified by us of the boy's arrival, of
course, and both of them were understandably eager to have Erik
live with her. Not Marcuse, though. Marcuse remained as ada-
mant as ever in her belief that nothing could be worse for these
children than to be with their own blood relatives. Even when it
was a married aunt who had been in the country for years. All I
could do was suggest that she have her brother write a letter
granting her legal custody of his son and, in order to make sure
that the letter wasn't filed and forgotten, send it to me rather than
directly to Mrs. Marcuse.

In his opening paragraph, Mr. Thorn took the precaution of
explaining that he was writing at the request of his sister, and that
was all Mrs. Marcuse needed:

> As for the letter from Mr. Thorn, I want to say that it is indeed
> exceedingly interesting because it shows me what I suspected,
> namely, that Mrs. Beer has been lying to us all along, saying that
> her brother conferred to her guardianship rights over the boy and
> wanted her to have him in her home. According to Mr. Thorn's
> letter, she was the one who asked him.
>
> Erik is, of course, a child who needs a great deal of individual
> understanding and I believe that the child welfare agency, who is
> working with him, has at least as good an understanding as the
> father, who hasn't seen him in several years. I am translating his
> letter to you to the agency so that they can gain an understanding
> of certain elements in the present situation which have been
> puzzling all of us.
>
> You can, of course, use any kind of document or letter in
> support of a theory in which you have such a strong belief.

And it was so pointless. In the short run, it was possible to
cause a lot of mischief in individual cases and bring on a certain

amount of hardship. But in the long run, it was impossible to keep the children from contacting each other and contacting me. I knew where those first children I had accompanied to Chicago had gone. I also knew that eight others had been sent to institutions in San Francisco and Los Angeles which were run, separately, by a pair of remarkable brothers with an unforgettable name. The Bonaparte brothers. To them, Mrs. Marcuse's instructions were so ridiculous that they simply ignored them. As a matter of fact, they agreed with me that these particular children were far better off remaining together in their institutions.

And then there were the kids in and around New York. Although everybody without an affidavit had been hustled out of New York as quickly as possible, there were twenty of our kids living with relatives around the area. Shortly after the third transport came in, we made plans to get together at the Trude Frankel Kindergarten, where I had been engaged as a consultant, for a picnic. A heavy snowstorm interfered and so our first reunion was held, believe it or not, on Sunday morning, December 7. All twenty of the children showed up—plus an extra added attraction. One of the girls walked in with a sailor on her arm. He was Joe Moses, a boy who had come over on the *Mouzinho* and gone to live with an uncle in San Francisco. Joe had talked his uncle into allowing him to join the navy as soon as he turned sixteen, and his ship had docked in New York the previous day.

There was a little radio perched on the windowsill, and we automatically turned it on to catch the news, just as we had always done in Montmorency. The very first thing we heard, of course, was that Pearl Harbor had been bombed.

The second thing we heard was that all servicemen were to report immediately to their camp or ship. A few minutes later Joe Moses was gone and the whole spirit of our first reunion had suddenly changed.

That wasn't all that changed. The next day, the United States and Germany were at war. The German "military observers" tightened their control over Unoccupied France and although the Quakers continued their negotiations for another transport nothing ever came of them. A few sixteen-year-olds and, by now, seventeen-year-olds were able to trickle in under the regular quota now that the normal immigration from Germany was cut off. But that was all.

By summer, there were rumors that Pierre Laval had agreed to hand over the Jews in the Unoccupied Zone, an ominous piece of news which was followed by an even more ominous official announcement that Vichy was about to undertake a census of all foreign Jews in France. The Nazis had been shipping Jews to concentration camps in Poland for a full year under the euphemism of "resettlement"; when the Jewish children in the Unoccupied Zone were gathered up it was under the equally euphemistic term "family regrouping."

The arrests and deportations had already begun in the Occupied Zone, and the reports in the Swiss newspaper, *La Sentinelle,* which were even more graphic than the accounts provided by OSE, left no doubt that family regrouping was not exactly what they had in mind: "Children from three years up were taken away from their mothers. Merciful police agents entrusted them to neighbors, while others—and they are in the majority—shut up the apartments, leaving the children in the street, or piling them into trucks packed with hundreds of tiny tots. Their pitiful cries, their desperate calling of 'mother,' resounded through the dark and deserted streets. About 5000 children were lodged in three school buildings. The Welfare Department and the General Union of French Jews were charged with the care of some of them. There were numerous cases of measles and scarlet fever among the children. Four of them died twelve hours after their arrest.

"The delivery of national relief rushed by the Government was forbidden by the German authorities. The Quakers, the Salvation Army, and the General Union of French Jews tried to feed this starving crowd. Their situation in the camps—devoid of the most elementary provisions for shelter and sanitation, without dressings for wounds, without cooking facilities—is even worse than in the Parc des Princes.

"A large number of children have lost their identification tags and cannot for the present be identified.

"In Paris, the great majority of those arrested were aliens; in the provinces, both French and foreign Jews, men and women, were seized, this time by the German police. Surrounded by soldiers with fixed bayonets, they were hustled into trucks, men and women separately, and provisionally interned, many of them at the camp of Pithiviers. The children were left in the streets, the apartments sealed up, and the neighbors forbidden to take care of the children. Even in the most isolated localities, where only a single Jew was living, the police came to make arrests.

"A large number of Jews succeeded in escaping to the free zone. Men, women and children crossed the boundary line at various points, after walking many miles and paying large sums of money to agents who smuggled them across."

They didn't remain free for long.

August 26, 1942, became the Night of the Broken Crystal for the children in the Unoccupied Zone.

Joseph Millner, the secretary of the French OSE, had been visiting the Château du Mesgellier in the Creuse and he was awakened by a call from the director of a Home that had been only recently opened in Limoges. A raid was underway. The gendarmerie had struck in the middle of the night and were taking all the children whose parents had arrived in France after 1936.

Wrote Millner:

> When the telephone call from Limoges had hardly ended, I learned that Mesgellier was surrounded by the police. Four policemen, a captain in front of them, penetrated into my room.
>
> ——Do you have the child so-and-so?
>
> That child was 5 years old and five policemen had come to look for him; one policeman for every year of his life. His mother had just been arrested at Brandbourg, near Guéret. They had come for him in order to "make his family complete." His father, of Czech origin, fighting as a volunteer, had been declared missing at the front; that meant he had died for France. I tell that to the

captain who starts crying and is telling me that he himself is father of five children.

——You have a nice job!

——What do you want, said the captain. We have lost the war....

The Chief of Police of Limoges whom I saw that day told me triumphantly: The Germans have been asking for children from two years on up, but the Vichy government had received a concession. They would not touch children under 6 years of age! From Vichy telephone calls went to all police stations to hurry up. As a matter of fact, the "selection" was nothing but a farce. Soon trains started from everywhere toward Rivesaltes. In the Camp at Rivesaltes 14,000 Jews have been interned.

All the Homes had been raided, including Montintin. We knew it. But for almost a month, there was no solid news. And then, finally, a letter came to me from Karl. The most terrible letter I have ever received:

"Last week we lived through a kind of a St. Bartholomew Night. At five o'clock in the morning we had guests who arrived with trucks. They took a lot of people away with them. Then it was said that the boys under eighteen would be released again, but in the meantime they were already sent further on. Allegedly to Poland but we don't really know anything definite. Among those taken were Emil Geisler, Benno Singer, Hans Martin. Guenther and Horst, who were on vacation [at Gurs] with their parents, were also taken; also girls from the other houses. In the days that followed there was a hunt for those who had escaped, but the forests are large. There were tragi-comic scenes too. For instance, Friedman, whom you know well, slipped out of their hands twice. The second time he went to the toilet under guard, but he managed to escape from there too. Yesterday, the little ones were taken from our houses, allegedly to be sent to their parents in the concentration camps. They took even two-year-olds from the nursery and let them sleep at the railway station. What they intend to do with them we don't know. In any case it would be very nice if we could still come over to you, but it doesn't look as though we can."

To compound the tragedy I had sent an affidavit for every one of the boys who was named. Only one of them, the indestructible Emil Geisler—of whom we shall speak again later—survived. As for Friedman, he had escaped the second time by jumping out of the bathroom window but ... the forests weren't quite large enough. We never heard another word about him. His name appears nowhere in the concentration camp records. Perhaps he was hunted down in the forest and shot. Perhaps he perished, unidentified, in an accident. Perhaps he died somewhere in the rain.

What the records do show is that sixty-nine of the children who were taken from our Homes that night died in a rain of gas at Auschwitz. That the number didn't reach into the hundreds was due solely to the action of the Maquis, the French Underground, who blew a bridge, attacked the train and rescued a vast majority of the children before they were driven off.

After the events of August 26, I heard no more talk about how safe it was in Unoccupied France. Marshall Field and the Quakers renewed their pressure on the State Department, President Roosevelt was finally moved to contribute something more than empty words of sympathy and the State Department agreed to issue five thousand emergency visas.

If the children could have been saved, then Marshall Field would have deserved the credit. By the time the State Department capitulated, Marshall Field had already converted a Portuguese freighter into a passenger ship and was prepared to send it to Marseilles to take out the first one thousand children. An enormous private undertaking involving medical personnel, supplies and everything else that goes into a rescue operation of that magnitude.

The children had been gathered in Marseilles and were waiting. On the morning of November 7, the refitted freighter steamed out of Baltimore with its carefully screened staff of doctors, nurses and social workers. No more than an hour after it had cleared the harbor, word came that the American army under Eisenhower had landed in North Africa. The German army immediately swept down through the Unoccupied Zone to occupy the Mediterranean ports. All France was sealed tight.

The freighter changed its course in midsea and headed for Portugal. It returned two months later with no more than a handful of children who had been waiting in Lisbon for their papers to be cleared.

The OSE's work in France turned almost exclusively to Underground rescue work. The man in charge of field operations was a French patriot, Georges Garel, an active anti-Nazi who had a reputation as a daring commando-type raider, not unlike the Paul Lukas character in *Watch on the Rhine*. Most of the boys were hidden with farmers or collected in fairly large groups in the deep forest where they lived a highly regulated life under the command of a Boy Scout leader. The girls were hidden primarily in convents until, armed with false papers, they could be placed in private homes. Some were treated very well by the families they lived with; some were treated as unpaid servants.

The following two letters, written immediately after the war to friends in the United States, are fairly representative of what happened to the girls. By coincidence, the letters were written by Yvonne and Eva, the same two girls who had written to me from Montintin to ask whether I could get them affidavits.

It was in the letter from Yvonne that I learned that some of our children were at Moissac and also—as you will see—received the erroneous information about Mandel being in Vienna:

> Now I want to tell you how I survived the war time. When the big "razzias" started in August 1942, I was fortunately not at the children's home; otherwise I would have had the same fate as all the others. I stayed with my relatives at that time and heard about it on time to be able to hide. Then I travelled on the French railroads for a few weeks ending up in a convent, finally. There I remained almost a year; when I left it in July, 1945 I went to Toulouse as a servant. I did not like it there and was sent to Albi, always under a fictitious name. I called myself Yvonne Globe, had a wrong certificate and was always ready to lie when I was

asked any question. I got into a Christian family and stayed there until the liberation of France. Then I used my correct name again and worked for a dentist until July 1945. Since I was dependent on a Committee I left Albi one day and went to Moissac. I don't know whether you knew Miss Bernheim [successor of Lucia]; meanwhile she got married to Boris Ginodman, and she takes care of me. Here in the children's home I met many children from Montintin again. Boris is here with his wife, and he is still a carpenter, has not changed at all. Mickey Stiassny is in our home too now, Eva Unikower got converted in a convent, lives in Versailles now but writes to me in spite of that. Henny Bienstock is in Switzerland, Oskar is in Palestine and Werner Hausman is a soldier in Munich. I never thought that Oskar would go to Palestine. Maybe you know too that Guenther and Horst died in a camp; we have never heard any more from Hannelore, Karla, Inge Heilbron, Ruth Drucker, Sonia Kieslowitz, Margot Koenig, etc. But imagine, Geisler came back, also Jean Martin, Mandel and Karl. They are in Vienna. Annie Deutsch and Gustl Papanek are supposed to be in Vienna too. All the older people are scattered all over the world and many are dead.

My parents and my brother died in one of the camps too. . . .

Eva's letter, which mentions her conversion only by indirection, was actually written a couple of months before Yvonne's:

Yes, we were lucky enough to pass, to be able to stay and not to leave. I want to tell you frankly that the news is not good; there are very few people who came back. As for me, I'll try to tell you what I have done during these years. I stayed in the Children's Home until September 1942 and during four months we were hiding, traveled here and there, from the center to the south, but we had no stable location. In January 1943, a hotel school was found (by OSE) where we were able to hide and under a false name, of course, which I'll keep for a few weeks, because I am just getting papers for myself. At this school we took courses and were taken for people from Alsace and Lorraine. In November 1944 the school was closed and, by chance, we found an apartment and there the little "Alsatians" were placed together with two girls whom we called "aunts." In July 1945 we went back to Paris and started working for the Mothers Aid Society [Aide aux Mères].

This is an association to which mothers turn who need help. Then we are sent to different families to help the mother for a few hours. Some, the majority of those who work, live with their families; those who have no family live two in one room. I work seven hours plus the time of the subway. Twice a week I take classes of dressmaking. I'd like to thank you in advance for the package which, at this moment, is on its way; it is very kind of you and makes me very happy. It proves too how much we "old ones" stick together.

Georges Garel and his people were well paid. They had to be. In work as dangerous as theirs, money was their main weapon. For their own safety as well as the safety of the children, they were always armed well enough to enable them to operate independently, on the spot. But if it was an enormously expensive operation in terms of money, it was even more expensive in terms of life. At a bare minimum, thirty-two of Garel's men were killed.

The leaders of the Underground operation for the OSE in the Occupied Zone were Minkovsky, who remained in Paris throughout the war, and a remarkable woman named Jenny Masour. Jenny Masour was a very pleasant, very modest woman who traveled around the country getting false papers and finding places where individual children could be hidden. The records of these children had to be kept intact somewhere, of course, in order that their real identities might be restored to them after the war, and Jenny kept everybody in a constant state of fear by keeping them on her person. If she had ever been captured, the whole operation would have collapsed overnight.

Because of his dual reputation as a war hero and a celebrated man of science, Minkovsky was the logical man to stay in Paris. As incredible as it would seem to be that the Nazis would allow a Jewish organization dedicated to the care of the Jewish community to operate openly on the Champs Elysées, they still didn't touch Minkovsky. What restrictions were placed on him, if any, what compromises he had to make, I was never able to find out because Minkovsky—like Masour—would not talk about it. Neither about his own role nor about any other phase of the Underground.

And not only because of the emotional freight that subject so obviously carried. Those who took the greatest risks had very mixed feelings about the performance of the American Jews. On the one hand, the Joint Distribution Committee had supplied most of their money. And it was an enormous sum. For that, they could not help but be grateful. On the other hand, they were not able to forgive them for not doing more to get the children to America while there had still been a chance. I always felt that Minkovsky wasn't so much incensed about the attitude of the Americans as embarrassed about it. The one thing he did tell me, significantly, was that immediately after the war the Joint ordered that all Gentiles to whom money was owed be paid off. Whatever they said was due them—and no questions asked. Six million dollars was paid out retroactively, mostly to people who had lent the money or performed the services with no real expectation, or even desire, of ever being reimbursed.

Before my last trip to Paris, in 1970, I wrote to Minkovsky to tell him I was thinking of writing a book and would like, at long last, to really sit down and talk about the work of the Underground. Upon my arrival, he sent his calling card to my hotel naming the time and place we were to meet. Inside the flap, he had written: "You know I would do anything for you, Ernst. But this one thing I cannot do even for you."

When I was with the Unitarian Service Committee, Jenny Masour became my liaison with the French OSE and we worked together closely. I wrote to her too, pointing out that she and Minkovsky were the only ones who knew the whole story. I asked whether she wouldn't change her mind and talk about it for the sake of the historical record before we were all dead and gone. The answer that came back was: "You, dear Ernst, are a better friend to me than the historical record ever was. What I would not do for you, why would I do for your client, history? Leave it be. P.S. Who would have thought we should have lived to grow this old?"

I have talked about Minkovsky and Masour. I have not said

anything about Falk Walk. Falk Walk was always a very easy man not to say anything about. A mousy-looking man, with a mousy little moustache. A funny little man with a funny rhyming name. Falk Walk had always been the general factotum, the man who put the policies into effect after others had made the decisions. Alone among the directors of the OSE, he was neither a medical doctor nor a scientist and he had that wholly unnecessary sense of unease that people without formal educations so frequently show toward those who have earned all the degrees and gathered all the honors. Almost alone among them he was a practicing Orthodox Jew. I can remember him trying to explain to me, with uncharacteristic heat, that Chanukah wasn't celebrated because the Maccabees had won a great military victory over impossible odds but because of the miracle of the candles continuing to burn for eight days.

And yet, as innocuous and nondescript as he appeared, the children had always recognized him for the decent, solid man that he was. Whenever they wanted anything from the Paris office, Falk Walk was the man they would go to. They knew he was always available to them. They knew he would treat them with respect. And they knew that if he said he was going to do something it was as good as done. After the Germans marched into Paris, Falk Walk, the general factotum, became the secretary-general of the Occupied Zone. What that means is that he was the man who stayed in the Paris office with Minkovsky.

Falk Walk did not have the protection of a great name or reputation like Minkovsky. If Falk Walk disappeared, hardly anybody would notice that he was gone. But there was a job that had to be done, and so he stayed. For three years, Falk Walk went to that office in Paris every day, knowing that the day would come when he would not return. Until the day came when he walked into the office and was never heard of again.

BOOK III

The Spiral of Guilt

The children who were rescued by the Maquis from that train to Auschwitz were hidden all through France. Individually and in groups. About two dozen of the boys were holed up in a deserted farmhouse in central France under the command of a Boy Scout leader named Gamson, who ran the place like a military camp. Sentries manned field telephones at every possible approach, and at the slightest sign of anything suspicious a warning would be called back so that everybody could scatter into the woods.

All of the boys had forged identification papers, but falsified bread- and sugar-ration cards were much harder to come by. Bread and sugar were in such short supply anyway, that it wasn't always possible to get them even when you did have a ration card.

Food was always so scarce that when bread and sugar began to disappear from the meager stockpiles during the night everybody was outraged. With their very survival depending upon their ability to live together and share together, the presence of a thief in their midst—they all agreed—could not be tolerated.

After every attempt to trap the thief had failed, Gamson decided to try a new approach. He would speak to each of them in private, he said, right down the line from beginning to end, and give his word that if the culprit would confess to him, his identity would never be revealed to the other members of the group. For it was his belief, he told them earnestly, that once the culprit was able to unburden himself, the stealing would come to an end.

One by one, he spoke to all of them. And one by one, they all confessed. Every last one of them. *Everybody* had been stealing, and everybody was riddled with shame and guilt.

Gamson was then faced with the question of whether to call them back together and let each of them know that everybody else had been stealing too or whether to keep his word and remain silent. He decided to remain silent, which I thought to be a terrible mistake.

1. One Walked Away—Emil Geisler—II

In the early days at Montintin when the craftsman was king, Emil Geisler was in his glory. All the boys had received some training in the construction trades but nobody, except the workshop teachers themselves, could hold a candle to Emil. Even the old irritating habit of disappearing into the woods had become a community asset. When we found ourselves in need of some especially heavy planks for our tables, Emil would say: "I saw a tree three kilometers from here that will be just right."

No longer did I say, "But the tree does not belong to us." Instead, I asked, "How soon can we get it here?"

"Don't worry," Emil would say. "Leave everything up to me."

He would take a couple of other boys into the woods and in a few hours they'd be back dragging a huge tree trunk behind them. Exactly the kind of lumber we needed.

When I heard that he had been taken in the raid on Montintin I put it down to his usual bad luck. Twenty-six years went by before I found out how bad his luck had really been that night.

When the Maquis attacked the freight train taking the children to Auschwitz, Emil was one of the seventy who had been trapped in the wrong freight car. Sixty-nine of those seventy died in the gas ovens. One boy, Emil Geisler, managed to save himself by escaping from the camp itself.

Once outside the camp, he had automatically pointed himself toward the only place he could think of, by any stretch of the imagination, as home. Montintin. In the middle of the war, this very Jewish-looking boy walked across most of Poland, walked across the length of Germany, and across most of Occupied France. Hiding by day and traveling only by night he made it across 950 miles. All along the way, he was helped and hidden and fed by sympathetic people. He was even hidden for periods of time by people who turned out to be nominal members of the Nazi party, something that happened more than you would imagine. When the individual is suddenly confronted with a situation which calls out to him as a human being rather than as a member of the pack he finds that his humanity has not so easily been cut out of him.

When, at last, Emil reached Limoges he was taken in by the French farmers with whom he had sometimes worked during his days at Montintin. (Thousands of children were similarly hidden all over France, including most of those rescued from the train to Auschwitz.) When the tide of battle turned and the British army liberated Limoges, Emil tried to enlist. All our older boys enlisted in whichever army reached them first—British, American or Free French. Poor Emil was not granted even this last opportunity to strike a direct blow at the enemy. His physical examination turned up an active case of tuberculosis, and he ended the war not as a British soldier but as a patient in a Swiss sanitarium.

As anyone who knew him might have guessed, he was a terrible patient. Before the sanitarium was ready to release him he disappeared from his bed, skipped across the border and hitchhiked to Paris to look for a job. Within a year he collapsed, and the French OSE had to ship him back to the sanitarium in Switzerland.

The next I heard of him came when he did something completely out of character. On August 26, 1947, the fifth anniversary of the raid on Montintin, he sat down and wrote two letters. The first one was sent to a Cuban boy named Rudy Singer, whose address he had. Along with it came a letter that he was asking Rudy to send on to John Windmuller, whose address he did not have.

The letter to Rudy read:

> Since 3 weeks I am again in Switzerland, this time in Moratana. What is new with you? I will tell you a little bit about me. My health is completely restored and in 3 months I will again have the right to work. I will be able to work in Paris, I do not yet know at what. In Paris there are the Adlers, Mickey, Yvonne, Freido, Stutnizer. I believe you will still recall August 26th when they caught us and brought us to the camp. It is exactly 5 years today that 8 boys from Montintin were put into the concentration camp and from there only Jojo and I returned. Jojo is in Palestine now. I do not know more about him. There is nothing else to write, so I will close.

In point of fact, Jojo had not returned from Auschwitz. He had died there.

The letter to John Windmuller covers much the same general ground except for one request which I paid no attention to at the time.

> I have been convalescing for 3 months in Switzerland in Moratana, which is near Davos, a very famous spa for tuberculosis. What are you doing? How is Ernst Papanek, Gustl, Ernst Weil, Ruth. I heard that your brother Rudy is very sick. What is the trouble with him? I wish him a speedy recovery. Please write to me the address of Oskar. I want to write to him. Today it is exactly 5 years that we were brought to the camp to go to Germany and work there. From there only Jojo and I came back. Guenther and Horst died. Now I have to take my walking cure. Therefore enough for today.

The irony of a walking cure for Emil Geisler was almost too much to bear. What wasn't so obvious, there being no reason why it should be, was that with his mind having been brought back so forcefully to the events of that August 26 by the fifth anniversary, the real reason for his writing, the one thing he was asking for, was the address of Oskar.

A few months later, I got word that Emil was in Paris again and, finally, toward the end of 1949, that he had gone to Israel to join the fishing kibbutz of Stod Jam, the famous kibbutz which had served as the port into which Jews had been smuggled during the days of the British-Israeli fighting. At the time, I was happy to hear it. It seemed to me that if Israel were to be the homeland for The Wandering Jew, nobody could offer better credentials than Emil Geisler.

I wrote to him, but our correspondence through the succeeding years was severely limited by Emil's own derelictions as a writer. Lene and I have always sent New Year's cards to all the children we have been able to reestablish contact with. To the handful who are in Israel, we have always mailed the cards at Chanukah, along with coffee, chocolates and candy. Occasionally, once every two or three years, we would get back a card from Emil with the briefest possible acknowledgment.

In the summer of 1956 Lene and I went to Istanbul to attend an international conference on mental health. I had been in correspondence with two experimental homes in Israel, and after we had visited them we were taken in hand by Elisheva Yaron of the Hebrew University, an old friend from the States, for a weekend tour through Tel Aviv, Haifa and Galilee. Given this sudden opportunity we made a slight addition of our own to the agenda.

To get to Stod Jam we traveled the one paved highway between Tel Aviv and Haifa, swung off through one of the few wooded areas in the country and on past the excavation work being done in the old Roman city of Caesarea.

At the entrance of the kibbutz, just before the roads began to fork out in all directions, were a string of long, flat wooden buildings. By this time, Lene and I were so wilted by the long ride in the summer heat that Ellie instructed the driver to park the car in a shady spot up the road while she went into the first of the buildings, an auto-repair shop, to ask where we could find Emil Geisler.

The foreman pointed to a red-haired man working on one of the cars in the corner. "That's him," he said, "right over there."

Ellie, quite pleased at the chance to be a bearer of glad tidings, went over to tell Emil he had visitors outside.

Without saying a word, he washed his hands and dried them.

"Aren't you even going to ask who the visitors are?" she asked him in amazement.

He looked at her without batting an eyelid. "It is the Papaneks," he said.

Since we had been berating ourselves all the way down for not letting him know we might come, she was completely taken aback. "But," she stuttered, "I was under the impression they hadn't written you."

"No," he said. "They did not write me. But who in the world would come to visit me? There are only the Papaneks."

We had not seen him since we left Montintin, you understand, sixteen years earlier.

It was an emotional moment for us when we saw Emil coming toward us. He embraced us both, kissing us on our cheeks, and beamed at us in the old, shy way. I would have recognized him anywhere. His hair was still bright red and only slightly thinned; his complexion was still very ruddy and his freckles had barely faded. He was taller than he had been at fifteen, of course, and, even in his loose coveralls, he seemed to be skinnier than ever. We drove immediately to the village to pay a courtesy call on the manager of the kibbutz. Emil was eager to show us off to him—to demonstrate that he was not a man without connections—and he was just as eager to show off the manager, a wonderful character, to us.

The manager, a stocky, white-bearded man of perhaps sixty-five, was a typical Jewish scholar, by which I mean there was that roughness of character, directness of speech and natural authority. He spoke to us in a mixture of German and Yiddish with an occasional English word thrown in for good luck. To Ellie and everyone else he spoke pure Hebrew. Except Emil. In all Emil's years in the country he had not bothered, it became obvious, to learn the language.

The old man talked to us about the Homes in France in a way that clearly indicated that Emil had told him a great deal about those days. "This is such a nice boy," he said, almost as if Emil were not standing right beside us. "But he has no friends. You must see what you can do about getting him to loosen up a little."

While we had been driving up from the shop, Emil had pointed out the dormitory where he and all the other single men lived, taking great pains to let us know that each man's right to a private life was scrupulously respected. Fine. Immediately we had invited him to have supper with us at a small roadside restaurant we had noticed just before we turned off the main road from Tel Aviv—one of the few roadside restaurants we had seen anywhere in Israel.

The old man couldn't have been more pleased. "Listen," he told Emil, "take the day off. Take tomorrow off too. Take off as long as you want."

With that kind of cue, I immediately invited Emil to make the trip with us to Haifa and Galilee. But Emil shook his head abruptly and snapped, "No. No, no, no." And there was nothing we or the manager could say to make him change his mind.

We still had the rest of the day, though. As always, Emil knew the surrounding area like the back of his hand. At the excavation site in Caesarea, he was greeted so warmly by the workers that we could see he spent a good deal of his spare time there. We could also see why. The workers were from French Africa and, like Emil, they spoke almost no Hebrew.

Theoretically, visitors were not supposed to take pictures, since the kibbutz itself sold picture postcards as a minor source of income. But once the workers discovered that we spoke French, they posed handsomely beside the statues they were in the process of digging out and kept insisting, "Come on, take a picture of me over here."

When we left the excavation site, Emil took us on a conducted tour through a destroyed Arab village, lecturing from the car as we drove along the old dirt roads. We were eager to get out, though, so we could prowl through the remains and take some pictures.

With much the same abruptness with which he had turned down our invitation to Galilee, he told us we would be wasting our time. "I can tell you everything you want to know," he said, "from right here."

Our disappointment must have shown on our faces because he quickly capitulated, guided us through some of the buildings and even posed with Lene as if they were coming out of the ruins.

Afterward we started to drive toward the restaurant. We were a good three or four miles away from the camp when Emil suddenly slapped the driver on the shoulder and ordered him to stop. Before we quite realized what was happening, he had got out of the car and, leaning back through the open door, patted my wife on the cheek and patted me on the shoulder. "Goodbye," he said, "and good luck. I hope I will hear from you again."

"But, Emil," I said. "What are you doing? Why are you leaving us now?"

In all my life I had never heard him raise his voice. Now, all at once, he was shouting in a kind of frenzy. "Do you believe I can stay out the whole day? I have to work, you know. I've got a lot of things to do yet today!"

I was completely bewildered. "We know you have a lot to do, but I thought you took the day off. We thought you were going to have supper with us."

"No, no," he shouted, not so much to us now as to the open air. "I cannot leave my work."

I was about to ask him to at least let us drive him back to the kibbutz when I saw the tears. He was crying the way a small child cries, with the tears running down his cheeks and into his mouth. And this was no boy. This was a man of thirty. This was a man who had undergone enough terror and upheaval to have put most men into their graves.

The four of us were stunned. We just sat there, watching after him as he walked away down the long ribbon of road, with nothing between him and the horizon but a great expanse of sand and an occasional solitary tree. Even the driver, a Yemenite Jew who had not understood a word we had said all day, was aware that something extraordinary had happened.

"Let's follow him," Lene said. But we all knew that would only make matters worse. We hoped desperately that he would at least turn around and wave, as if that would somehow release us.

He did not so much as turn his head. We watched him as he got smaller and smaller and all but disappeared from sight.

It was while we were sitting there, staring after him, that Ellie told us what he had said back in the workshop about having nobody but the Papaneks to visit him. It was one of the most shattering things I had ever heard in my life. We understood then—or thought we did—that he simply could not stand it any longer. He had to release his emotions; he had to shout, to get out and walk, to get back to work.

One thing had been said that we sorely regretted. As I have already mentioned, very few of our children were in Israel. While we were speaking with Emil about those who had come and gone he had brought up the name of one of the girls who had married in Jerusalem and remained to raise a family.

"When will *you* get married, Emil?" Lene had asked, the way women will.

He blushed, red as blood. "Give me time, give me time. I will also get married yet."

Something else had impressed me. After we left the excavation, he asked if we would send him some newspapers and magazines written in German and French.

"Aha," I said, remembering how difficult it had been to get him into a classroom. "Don't tell me you have become a reader?"

"French and German, I read not only for the content," he replied, telling me perhaps more than he thought. "I read them to hear the language again."

I asked him if he had ever thought about returning to Paris. Or even to Saarbrücken, which had become a part of France again.

"No," he said. "I have here a place where I live. I have friends here and I have work here."

But apparently he had no real friends. Apparently he will never get married. Apparently he feels safe nowhere on earth but in Israel. He wanted to be assimilated, I was sure of that; there was nothing in life for him, I felt, unless he was assimilated. And yet, it seemed to me, Israel had not been able to assimilate him.

It was only much later that I realized my experience with him had come full circle; the first and the last time I saw him he cried.

And I do not believe he is a man who has cried often in his life. He is, I believe, a courageous man. Courageous in the sense of the Good Soldier Schweik. Not the wild courage of the bared chest and the open fight, but the inner courage of sheer perseverance, of being able to lose face without ever losing sight of ultimate goals. This is a Jewish characteristic, this inner courage. Particularly of the long persecuted Jews of Middle Europe. They try to avoid the open blow, they do not surrender.

That first day, in front of the Villa Helvetia, I slammed a door in his face. I said, *No, you cannot come in.* And that was an open blow from which there seemed no escape. In Israel—I hope I am wrong about this but I believe it is the truth—in Israel, I slammed another door in his face. I showed him we could do nothing further for him.

I believe he expected us to do something for him that we were unable to do and, worse, were not even aware he expected us to do. Emil Geisler, like Michael Stiassny, knew we would be back one day and that somehow we would be able to turn his life around; to assure him, at the very least, that the future was still on his side.

Obviously, we were a bitter disappointment to him. After a few hours, he saw that we were just two middle-aged people, snapping our pictures like any other tourists. We had come, after all those years, not to open any doors for him again but only on a single day's stopover between Tel Aviv and Haifa.

I wonder if it did not finally come to him on that road from the camp, that he would walk past no more borders to new opportunities. I wonder if he did not suddenly recognize that his chances had run out. That he had spent too much of himself on too many dark roads between Saarbrücken and Stod Jam.

There is still one more thing I must bring up before I leave Emil Geisler, something that colors everything else about him and keeps him, perhaps, in Israel. I am speaking now about the escape from Auschwitz.

Let me say first that after the war was over we had nothing like the psychological and psychiatric problems we had anticipated back in Montmorency. Of all our children who came to the United States, I know of only three cases of juvenile delinquency. We were all struck, however, by a psychological problem we had barely anticipated—that there would be among the survivors an overwhelming sense of guilt at nothing more than the fact of their survival.

I heard it articulated for the first time within a group of children I accompanied to Chicago on the Pullman. This was a luxury such as these children had never experienced or hoped to experience, for in those days there were no such things as sleeper trains in Europe. One boy sat back expansively, spread his hands across the back of the chair and said: "Well, there had to be a world war and millions of Jews killed so that I could be sitting here in this Pullman car today."

The misery of his people had somehow been turned to his advantage, he was saying. And what a measly advantage it had turned out to be.

But, you say, what has this to do with Emil Geisler? The children who came to the United States were, after all, the lucky ones. Some mild feeling of guilt toward their friends who had either perished or been left behind was perfectly understandable. Unfortunate perhaps but understandable.

Emil was one of those who *had* been left behind. It seemed to be Emil's fate that he was always one of those who were left behind. You would imagine that anyone who had suffered as he had suffered and yet endured as he had endured would—far from feeling guilty about his survival—permit himself to feel like something of a hero.

But it does not work that way. The ones who saw the most and suffered the most and *still* survived are the ones who feel the guiltiest. Emil, let us not forget, is the sole survivor of his family and the lone survivor of the seventy children who were not rescued from that train to Auschwitz. Is it possible to conceive what a burden it is to be a lone survivor?

When I tried to find out about the Maquis' attack on the train, he had almost nothing to say. When I asked him about his miraculous escape from Auschwitz, he would only say that he had not been the only one. "Three or four of the others escaped too," he insisted. He could not recall their names, however, and—with all our checking—it was impossible that any of the others could have survived without our learning about it.

Emil's reluctance to discuss anything except the long walk back to Limoges—and little enough about that—had come as no great surprise to me. All the survivors of concentration camps retreat into that same shell. Long before my visit to Stod Jam, I had discovered that you can question and question, poke and probe, and never get back anything beyond a kind of vague disclaimer calculated to minimize the accident of their survival, to close the gap between themselves and the dead.

For behind every innocent question they hear the voice of the Inquisitor snap:

Why are you alive, and the others dead?

What did you do?

Whom did you know?

And behind all that: *Whom did you betray?*

We ask no such questions, of course. We have no right to ask them. I would stake my life that Emil betrayed no one. How did he escape? I think his history provides all the necessary clues. It is possible that Emil, a useful boy anywhere, made himself useful in the camp to the point where some guard became fond enough of him to open a gate. It is even more possible that while he was making himself useful, he was given just enough freedom so that with his genius for fading into the shadows he found an opportunity to escape without any help at all.

Imagine Emil, in later years, remembering every job he ever did for the guards, remembering every little word of ingratiation, every favor given and taken, and you can easily see how this seedling guilt can grow and grow until each act becomes not a necessary accommodation but something closer to an act of cowardice; yes, something like betrayal.

Imagine this guilt growing and growing, then, until five years after his escape he is driven to leave Paris and go to Israel to pay penance to his people. To find, perhaps, someone to forgive him for being alive.

When we got to Haifa we sent Emil a card. We referred to our visit only to tell him how sorry we were that we could not have spent more time together. We continued to send cards all along our route.

In Istanbul, we were visited by my son Gustav and his wife Hanna—the Hanna of Hanna's diary. Each of them added a postscript of his own.

We mailed him French and German magazines and newspapers from almost every stop.

We received no answer.

At Chanukah, six months later, we played a little trick on him. We sent our usual package through a private agency which, as part of its service, brings back an acknowledgment from the recipient. Emil's acknowledgment came back in the form of a Chanukah card on which he scribbled, "Enjoyed especially the coffee because this we cannot get here. I hope you are having a nice time."

2. Why Me?

The guilt of the survivor. I saw it unfold before my eyes in classic form soon after the war had ended. By that time, I was the executive director of American Youth for World Youth, an organization which eventually involved ten million students in this country. (The program called for young people to make direct contact with their counterparts abroad; i.e., adopt schools, organize their own money-raising events, grow and can food, assemble kits and generally find their own ways to be helpful.)

One of the men working with us was Paul Goldberg, a Polish refugee who had been delegated to us by the World Jewish Congress, one of the many agencies cooperating with us. Like so many refugees, Goldberg had his own tragedy to live with. The war had broken out while he was in Switzerland attending an international congress and he had been forced to go to London, leaving behind a wife, an eleven-year-old daughter named Sue and a seven-year-old daughter with the unforgettable name of Aurora. At his request we made constant inquiries to every agency in the field, private and governmental. What little information we were able to get clearly indicated that they had been wiped out during the uprising in the Warsaw ghetto.

And then, one morning while I was leafing through the mail I flipped over a routine thank-you letter from an orphanage in Russian-occupied Poland—and felt my heart skip a beat. The letter had been signed by five of the children representatives, and one of the signatures leaped right off the paper at me. Aurora Goldberg. Immediately, I called Paul. How many Aurora Goldbergs, after all, could there be in the world?

Any number, as far as the Polish authorities were concerned. The countries of Europe, bled white by the war, were fighting to hold onto every unattached child they could lay their hands on. Since Paul had no papers, the authorities maintained over a period of months that he could offer no real proof that he was the girl's father. At length, with great difficulty, we were able to arrange for Aurora to be sent to a recuperation camp in Sweden, and once she was there it became an easy matter to whisk her onto a ship for England and on to the United States.

By that time, we knew that her mother and sister had indeed been killed during the Warsaw Uprising. Aurora had survived only because she had been among the rather large group of younger children who had been smuggled out of the ghetto and placed with Polish farmers.

After all that waiting, Paul was almost destroyed by the reunion. For by this time Aurora was thirteen years old and not at all reluctant to accuse her father of saving himself and leaving her mother and sister to die. They would come to the office, first one and then the other, to complain about each other. The relationship between them deteriorated so badly that she would insult him in the presence of others.

For five or six months I took those accusations of hers at face value. Until . . . well, I had been invited to their apartment for dinner, and after we had eaten I was out in the kitchen helping Aurora with the dishes. Exactly what was it, I asked her, that she thought her father could have done. "He didn't know where any of you were. How could he? Even you—did you know where your mother and sister were?"

The dish fell from her hand and shattered against the floor. "You don't like me anymore," she cried.

Of course I liked her. Why shouldn't I like her?

"No, you think it should have been them that were saved. Them, not me! You think Sue was better than me, don't you? He told you how good she was."

She was trembling worse than I had ever seen anybody tremble in my life. "It should have been me that was killed," she moaned. "It should have been me." Over and over. "It should have been me."

And there it was. It wasn't anything that had to be interpreted. She had said it all.

I had survived too, I reminded her. So had millions of others. And most of them hadn't suffered the losses or undergone the hardships she had. "What right do we have to hate millions of people because they stayed alive while others died?" I asked her. No more right, as she should have been able to see, than they had to hate us.

Intellectually, she could accept that. Emotionally, she couldn't.

For Aurora, it has been a long walk down an endless road. She came to work with American Youth for World Youth, doing contact work with Polish children, particularly with her former friends at the orphanage. Since she spoke very limited English, she entered a private school where she could get special help. Three years later, she was graduated as valedictorian of her class.

She had also become a leader of a Zionist youth group in high school. Upon graduation she went to Israel to live in a kibbutz, discovered very quickly that it wasn't the life for her and returned to America to enter college. Gradually, her attitude toward her father improved, although their relationship didn't become cordial until she moved into her own apartment and consulted a psychiatrist.

The sense of guilt was never completely eradicated. She found she was able to function best while she was helping other people, and so she went back to college to get her degree in social work. She manages. She copes. She functions. But to this day, she finds it necessary to pay an occasional visit to a psychiatrist.

I am not suggesting that everybody emerged with this sense of guilt or, even, that it so completely overpowered those who did. Most of them understood, emotionally as well as intellectually, that survival was a matter of luck. And had a story they could tell to prove it. I had an aunt who was at Ravensbrueck, the notorious concentration camp for women in which the inmates were used as guinea pigs for medical experiments. One night, shortly after she arrived, there was an alarm. "Everybody out of bed and out into the yard!"

The count came up one short. Unbelievable! While the SS commander was raging and threatening and bullying, out walked my aunt, a handsome, tiny lady of about sixty.

Where had she been? screamed the SS leader. How dare she come out late!

"I do not go out to meet people, no matter how late," said my aunt, regally, "until after I have washed myself and put up my hair."

The SS man's mouth fell open. Nobody had ever dared to speak up like that before. Or, need it be said, to confront him with a logic so far removed from the logic of a concentration camp. In the long, trembling silence that followed, everybody in the yard was aware that her life was on a razor's edge. And then the SS commander scowled ferociously. Not at my aunt. At the other prisoners. "I want you all to follow this little lady's example," he shouted. "*She* knows how to behave properly. I don't want to see any of you people fall in again unless you have washed up and combed your hair and made yourself presentable."

It made absolutely no sense. It was grotesque. Any woman who had dared to *ask* for permission to put up her hair would not have lived to ask another question. How do you explain it? Maybe the SS commander had hesitated too long; maybe she reminded him of somebody in his own family. Maybe he had yelled himself out in those last few seconds before the decision had to be made. Or maybe it had just been a long day for him, too. Who knows?

Having allowed her to get away with it, he had to go all the way. My aunt was made the capo of her barracks charged, presumably, with keeping everybody else in line. Once the SS commander had shown such respect for her, the guards were afraid not to. And so it was that one old Jewish woman survived.

There were also those who set out to survive, refused to consider the possibility of not surviving and therefore accepted survival as no more than their due. A friend of mine named Hugo Price would boast how he had worked like a buffalo in the concentration camps. Hugo, who was very Jewish-looking, would labor until his hands were bloody, and then work even harder while he made jokes about his bloody hands. "This impressed the Nazis very much," he would laugh. "I was their star performer." For people such as Hugo, survival became exactly that, a personal triumph.

Abraham, a Polish Jewish boy I met at a camp for displaced persons, had come home one afternoon to find that the Nazis had taken away his whole family; his father, mother, three brothers and sister. For two months he was hidden by a Christian family who shared their meager provisions with him. At the end of those two months, he came to the decision that he had no right to allow them to risk their lives for him. So he walked out of the house and went to the Karzyso Work Camp, which was run by the Nazis. "I am a Jew," he announced at the gate. "I have come to report for work."

At first, they didn't know what to make of him. "You are volunteering to work here?" And then they began to laugh. "Sure, we have plenty of work for an ambitious young man. Come on in, we can use you."

He became the camp joke, and when the joke began to pall they shipped him around from one camp to another, always billed as The Volunteer. By the time he landed in Mauthausen, a work quarry which was also used as an extermination camp, the war was almost over.

In his own eyes, Abraham—unlike Hugo—was no hero. He had merely calculated the odds for prolonging his own life, he said, without risking the lives of his friends. If he was discovered in hiding, he would be treated as an enemy; if he surrendered, he might be viewed more like a prisoner of war.

In my eyes, this boy had a powerful instinct for survival although I'm aware that others might disagree. A contrary case could be made that his act revealed a distinct ambivalence about survival. That perhaps he had simply decided to get it over with, one way or another, and was able to console himself that if he was indeed rushing to his death he was at least holding his fate in his own hands.

Because our children were in a protected position their fate, by and large, was not in their own hands. And if that wasn't true of all of them it was certainly true of those who were brought to the United States.

The question asked of me again and again as these children married, settled down and began to raise families of their own was: "Why did you bring me over and not someone else?"

Many years after I had come to New York I received a call from a girl who identified herself as Sarah Cohen and wanted to know if I remembered her?

Of course I did. "I'll be over in half an hour," she said. She didn't ask whether I wanted to see her; she didn't even ask whether I was free. She would be over. Period. As it turned out, she was married, had four children and was teaching school in Canada. It also turned out that although she had identified herself by the name by which I knew her, she now called herself Nora. Quite a few of the girls changed their first name, a phenomenon I wouldn't want to overinterpret. In some cases, it was no more than a free-style anglicizing of their German names; in other cases, they preferred the name they had been given on their false passports. With most of them, I suppose, starting a new life in a new country had offered them a chance to drop a name they didn't like and adopt one they did.

The first thing she said after our greeting was: "Why was I chosen to come over, and what happened to those who were not?"

That was easy. She had come over, because she had been among the first to be processed in Marseilles. The only criteria for that, as far as I knew, were "good health" and random chance. Of those who had not been brought over, about a hundred had been killed.

That wasn't good enough for her. "You did not save me because I was such a good student?"

"I did not know whether you were a good student or a bad one."

"Did you save me because my uncle was a professor and told you I was an intelligent girl?"

"I did not know you had an uncle. As far as I know neither did anybody else."

She jumped up and kissed me. "Thank you! Oh, thank you! I was afraid you might have become one of those snobs who only wanted to save the intelligent children who would have the best chance of making good."

The question persists. Twenty-seven years after the children had reached the shores of this country it came up again in a letter from a Cuban girl who had married one of the Cuban boys. "Both Hank and I think of our arrival in the U.S. as coming into the promised land in spite of Congress's earlier refusal. We still feel that way. We also feel an obligation to justify our survival somehow because of the recurring question, 'Why us?' This obligation calls for service to others, but it will never really answer the question."

It is not an obligation, I must hasten to add, which was felt by everybody. There are, for instance, two brothers. The older one went into business for himself, worked very hard and has done very well. The younger one has always sponged off him. "I'm worried about my brother," the successful one told me during a visit. "He simply refuses to apply himself to anything long enough to hold a decent job." It wasn't that he begrudged him the money. "I'm only glad I'm able to give it to him. But I'm afraid for him. I'm afraid that something was destroyed in him over there. He thinks his experiences in the war entitle him to ask the world for anything. I can't even talk to him about it. Everything irritates him, and the hell of it is that he believes he's entitled to be irritated, too."

3. The Unforgotten

I never met Suzy. I spoke to her over the phone only once. If it hadn't been for an article I wrote about Emil Geisler for the *Saturday Evening Post,* I never would have heard of her. Shortly after the article appeared, I attended a conference in Boys Town, Nebraska. Just as I was about to leave a phone call came from a man in Omaha whose wife, Beatrice, had been in Montintin with her younger sister Suzy shortly after I left and had spent most of the war in a convent in Marseilles.

"I'm terribly worried about my wife," was the way he first put it. Her parents had been in Gurs and had later been sent to Auschwitz where they had been killed. Many of the mother's letters, written over a period of two years and undelivered in France, had followed Beatrice and Suzy to the United States. Twenty years later, these letters were still a part of their lives. "Actually," he said, "my wife isn't too bad." The only trouble with Beatrice was that she insisted upon depressing herself by reading them over and over. It was her sister Suzy who really worried him. Twenty years later, Suzy still had not opened any of her letters. From time to time, she would withdraw to her room, place all the envelopes in front of her and cry. For days afterward she would lie in bed, refusing to talk to anybody.

Would it be all right, he wanted to know, if he asked his wife to write to me. "In other words, if I can get my wife to write to you, will you answer her?"

After I had corresponded with them for a few months—first Beatrice, then Suzy—Beatrice sent her letters to me. Routine, not very interesting letters written first in German and then in French—the prisoner trying to curry favor by using the jailer's language—and then in German again after she had been sent to Auschwitz.

The one thing that came through most clearly was that Beatrice had been quite content to let her counselor do the writing for a long time and that Suzy hadn't written at all.

Now, I am quite aware that you cannot judge any correspondence away from the people and the time. But, all in all, they were pretty banal.

> Please, what shoes do you have now? Please pay attention to the heels and repair work so that you can wear them longer. Maybe later, dear Beatrice, I can sew a dress for you. There is no opportunity for me to do that yet. Did you light a candle? How was Channukah?

A letter from Aunt Trudy informs Beatrice that her little sister has arrived in Marseilles. "But your letter is so short, I know you are unhappy about there being so little time to write. But Mama is not well. We all have to do the best that we can, and we are fortunate that we are able to write which I believe for a long time you didn't do."

In the last letters from Auschwitz, the mother has begun to lose touch with reality. "I have good news from Trudy and from dear father," she writes. "When I get underwear for you I will send it to you." It had already been established that Trudy and their father were both dead, and I don't have to tell you that there would be no underwear mailed out from Auschwitz.

And finally:

> The children are all gone. They were in Ravensbrueck together. Aunt Clara works the whole day in the kitchen. Your letter I will give to her. Did you get the 30 francs which I sent you. You did not write about it. I am looking forward to the package you will send. Can you buy anything in the place where you are? How is school? What do you learn? That you are always at the top of your class gives me pleasure. When I can do it, I will send you the underwear. Beatrice, you should always keep yourself clean. Write a little letter to Auntie Clara. I will send it to her. But you have to write it, not anyone else.

The fact that she was able to send the letters to me—and to give me permission afterward to print them—was proof in itself that Beatrice was not sick. It was only because her sister had made such a fetish of the letters that they had taken on such importance for her.

Suzy is sick. She is riven with guilt. She did not write and therefore does not deserve the letters and therefore cannot be permitted to read them. I did not tell her that, of course. I simply wrote that it was wrong to place such importance upon them. My advice to her was: Open the letters. Read them. Burn them.

"How can I burn the last letters ever written by my parents?" she wrote back.

All right. "Do not burn them. Read them, put them away and take them out again whenever you want to. But I am convinced that once you have opened them and put an end to your fears and expectations you will not want to keep them."

She cannot bring herself to do it. She sits there, paralyzed, and cries. The tune that goes around in her head—guilt followed by hostility followed by more guilt—goes something like this:

I did not write to my mother and my father and my aunt. I'm sorry about that.
I don't have to write letters if I don't want to.
I do not want to know what is in them.
The letters did not arrive in time. If they had come while my mother and father were still alive I would have read them right away.
I do not know how my own mother and father died.
I did not write to my mother and my father and my aunt. I'm sorry about that. . . .

Isn't there more to it than that? Quite probably. We never know more than we are permitted to know. What happened, for instance, in those two and a half years in the convent? Did she court favor with the nuns? Did she attempt to bring an end to her troubles by thinking about converting? By *wishing* to convert? Did she go so far as to receive instruction? Was *not* writing to her parents one of her ways of disassociating herself from them and thereby from her Jewishness?

It happened, you know. The nuns in those convents performed

great acts of heroism in protecting these children. Most of them —the vast majority—wanted nothing more than the privilege of helping. There were others who would have helped the children more and served their own vocation better if they could have resisted the temptation to fish for converts.

The letters, as letters, are meaningless. They have nothing to do with the life of a middle-aged woman in the United States. But the guilt of surviving, as unworthy as she feels herself to be, has so consumed Suzy that she has retreated from life. She lives with her sister in her sister's husband's home. She has constructed her own jail. Suzy is still a little girl in hiding, only now she is hiding from herself.

Madeleine was a child I knew very well. One of the Robinsoner. A very beautiful and very troubled little girl; a girl who was split in many ways. Her father was a banker and a Socialist leader, an odd combination. Her mother, who had given her a strong Jewish upbringing, committed suicide in Paris. As far as her relationship with her father went, she wasn't particularly close to him but she wasn't particularly distant either. If she did hold him responsible for her mother's death she was not the kind of girl who could have said so.

It was impossible, however, not to see how deeply Madeleine felt her mother's loss. Margot Cohn, who recognized how much she needed an older woman she could confide in, would take long, long walks with her during which they could be seen in deep and intimate conversation. So did Lene. Madeleine idolized Lene, followed her around the dispensary and let everyone know that she was going to be a doctor just like her.

While she was being hidden in a convent she undoubtedly wanted to show the Mother Superior that she wanted to be just like her, too. And so, naturally, she converted to Catholicism. Another split.

The first time I was in Paris after the war, I took Madeleine to the theater along with Gustl and one of the other girls. Madeleine was in such a marvelously gay and carefree mood that night that it was hard to believe, as the people who knew her best had been telling me, that she had come out of the convent more disturbed than ever.

In the ensuing years, she ran true to form. Socialists aren't really concerned enough about religion to care what anybody is. Still, once she was back in a predominantly Jewish setting she converted back to Judaism. She also went to medical school, worked very hard and became a doctor. Just like Lene.

At the age of thirty-seven, after her work as a doctor had been made impossible by many serious difficulties and illnesses, and after a brief, unhappy marriage, she turned on the gas and committed suicide.

There are times when the easy answers are not the best ones. Madeleine was split so many ways all her life that it is easy to say the religious split was the one split too many. Too easy. Her problems, it must be remembered, went all the way back to Vienna. She was always going to be a dependent person. She was never going to be able to stand rejection. She needed acceptance so badly that the Mother Superior would have had to be a positive genius to have presented the arguments against conversion without making her feel rejected.

It wasn't a fourteen-year-old girl who responded to that final rejection by turning on the gas jets. It was a thirty-seven-year-old woman.

The guilt of the survivor is one thing; the problems of life quite another. I can think of two of our more brilliant boys. One of them, a Cuban, had a bittersweet romance which had begun on the *St. Louis.* The girl was killed in a concentration camp. He came to the United States. In the course of time, through sheer accident, he ran into the best friend of his dead sweetheart, a warm and gentle girl but in no way the beautiful, vivacious girl he had been in love with. They are now happily married and have three wonderful children. He is a successful and highly respected member of his profession. And still I know that there are times when he remembers his first love and wonders how it would have been if . . .

And still, she knows she was his second choice; that he had been attracted to her in all probability only because she was so intimately associated with what he took to be the happiest time of his life. But that happens. Young girls die of many causes, and their sweethearts live on to wonder what might have been. Other girls catch the man they have always wanted on the rebound and wonder when his eyes grow sad and meditative whether he is thinking of . . .

It happens. We are not speaking of the accidents of wartime now, we are speaking of the human condition.

The other boy, who belonged to no particular group, also fell in love with a girl in the Home. He came over here with the second transport; she ended up in Argentina and married someone else. They stayed in touch. When she and her husband wanted to come to the United States, he wrote to ask me to sign an affidavit since he did not have enough money to satisfy the immigration authorities. They live in cities not too far apart and see each other from time to time. He is a highly skilled professional man but he has never been particularly interested in making money, nor has he ever married. At one time when he was feeling depressed he consulted a psychiatrist, an absolute idiot who really sent him into depression by putting his history together and coming up with the Oedipal Conflict. He was filled with guilt, he was told, because he had secretly been glad when he heard that his father had been killed and was paying penance by arranging his life so that he could never become a husband or father himself. Sheer nonsense to begin with, and nothing any competent psychiatrist would have confronted him with even if it had been true. They give licenses to such people and let them go out and see how much damage they can do.

This happens to be a man who is absolutely at home in America; he couldn't live anywhere else. One of the reasons he doesn't make as much money as he could is that he devotes a great deal of his time to voluntary work for the Quakers. Why shouldn't he? He is grateful to the Quakers for bringing him over. If he hasn't married because he never found a woman who meant more to him than the girl he lost, so what? That happens too. Men who have lost their first love, for one reason or another, and remain faithful to them foreverafter.

4. The Wrong One—Emil Geisler—III

Although I used a fictitious name for Emil in that *Saturday Evening Post* piece, all the children knew who I was writing about and the letters came flooding in with offers to help. Either to contribute money to ease his situation in Israel or to open their homes to him if he wanted to come to the United States. An astonishing amount of mail also came from perfect strangers, including a wide variety of marriage proposals—two of which I took to be sincere.

In relaying the information to Emil, I added that I was sending him half of my fee and suggested that he might want to use it for a trip to the United States. Obviously, I felt it would be good for him to see how many friends he had, and I suspect that the purpose behind the invitation showed through.

I also suspect that I made a grave mistake in telling him about the marriage proposals.

At any rate, Emil made it clear that the prospect of a visit to the United States did not exactly thrill him. He asked whether I would permit him to use the money for a trip to Paris where—he said pointedly—he also had many friends, with perhaps a visit to Saarbrücken along the way. Well, it was his money. He could do anything he wanted with it. Since my sabbatical year was coming up, we settled on meeting in Israel as soon as he returned.

Fine. He was going to return in time to spend Passover in Israel and he invited me, quite pleased at turning the tables, to join him for the first Seder. When I arrived, we spent the first part of the day making the rounds in the kibbutz. Apparently, he wanted to show me how many friends he had made since I had last seen him. In particular, a very nice French couple with a lovely daughter toward whom Emil played the role of fond, indulgent uncle.

The communal Seder was held in the barn of the kibbutz, and since it had been a long day for me he suggested as soon as it was over that I probably wanted to go back to the room and get some sleep.

Through all the day, the magazine article had never been mentioned. The first thing he said after he turned the lights out was: "Listen, Ernst. What you wrote is not completely true. I don't mind what you said but I want you to know I never was in Auschwitz."

Ridiculous. I had seen his name in the German records and more recently in Yad Va'Shem. He himself, I reminded him, had told me how he had been taken there. And what about those letters he had written to John Windmuller and Rudy Singer on the fifth anniversary of the raid on Montintin?

"Emil," I said, "I'm going to have to write another article now, you have opened up a whole new line of thought on this for me."

He said: "You can write what you want. I was never in Auschwitz and so I couldn't have escaped from there."

Where had he been all that time, then?

Well, it had been somewhere *near* Auschwitz. "In a little village. It was no trick at all to escape from there. Anyone could have done it."

Nothing I said could get him to change his story or to discuss it further. "Write what you want," he kept repeating. "You don't have to show it to me. But I tell you I have never been in Auschwitz and did not survive in that way."

What made it so bewildering wasn't so much that I knew he was lying. What made it so bewildering was that *he* knew I knew he was lying. I'm supposed to be a psychologist, and the question a psychologist asks himself in such a situation is: *What is he really*

saying to me? On the surface, he seemed to be saying that since he
was not a survivor of the concentration camp I had been wrong in
ascribing the *guilt* of the survivor to him.

Not very satisfying. If that had been his purpose he should
have been discouraging me from writing anything more about it.
Instead, he was encouraging me In fact, the more I thought
about it the more it seemed to me that the whole purpose of
telling me so transparent a lie had been to encourage me to go on
with it. "I wasn't in Auschwitz," he had been saying. "I was
someplace else." Taking Auschwitz out of the equation, *what had
he really been saying?* "You are looking in the wrong place,
Ernst"; that's what he was telling me.

I spent four more days in Stod Jam and the only time the
magazine article came up again was when he told me I had also
been wrong in saying he had looked upon Horst with contempt. (I
had also said it didn't matter because Horst didn't pay any
attention to him.) "We were very good friends, Horst and I," he
insisted. "Oskar and I were good friends too."

I'd be more willing to accept it about Horst, I said rather wryly,
than about Oskar. Oskar had separated himself completely from
all the other kids after the war, refusing to answer their letters and
insulting John Windmuller when he tried to help. And then,
remembering the letter in which Ernst had asked for Oskar's
address, I asked whether he had seen Oskar in Israel. No, he
hadn't. No, he didn't know whether Oskar had still been in Israel
when he came. No, he said with an abruptness that showed he did
not want me to pursue the matter further, he had made no
attempt to get in touch with him.

Oskar Stammler was the only one of our children who returned to Germany, and I wonder whether that shouldn't have
given me pause right there. But no. That it would be Oskar who
would return to Germany was not so surprising. His father had
been a successful lawyer in Frankfurt and one of the members of
the Passengers Committee aboard the *St. Louis.* Oskar himself
was light-haired, very erect and second only to John Windmuller
in the eyes of the other children. For sheer intellectual brilliance
he was at least John's equal, and if he did not have John's ready

acceptance of leadership it was because he had a mind which rejected any kind of consensus.

Oskar is a very difficult boy to describe because there were always those opposite strains running in him. While you wouldn't have called him artistic in those days he was our official photographer and very proud of his skill with the camera. (It was only in later years that he became a poet, and a drunken poet at that.) He wasn't moody like Horst, and he certainly wasn't antisocial. He was, in fact, one of our better soccer players; he may very well have had the greatest natural ability there too, except that he had torn a cartilage in his knee when he was younger and had to wear a rubber bandage while he played.

All in all, he was the kind of a boy who could be an important member of a group and still remain his own man. A majority of one. To Oskar, the political discussions that were beginning to engross so many of his friends from the *St. Louis* were no more than a way of evading the main issue. "My problem isn't that I'm economically downtrodden," he would say. "My problem is that I'm Jewish." That's why they had been persecuted in Germany, he would remind them. Because they were Jews. "Now, maybe there were others who were persecuted because they were Socialists but that doesn't mean I have to automatically line up with them."

And yet, as much as Oskar might scoff at politics as a way to salvation, he had a sensitivity to the unequal distribution of wealth that made him keenly aware of the advantages that his father's money had been able to buy him. Nobody was more aware than Oskar that it had been his father's "full pocket"—as the Germans say—that had got them on the *St. Louis*. And while that voyage hadn't exactly turned out the way it was supposed to he was also aware that "the man with the full pocket" had been able to buy his sons and daughters the kind of education that had left them far better equipped to deal with the situation than most of the other kids in the Home.

Those were the opposing tensions at war in him, and they manifested themselves in a tone of self-mockery that was never able to quite lose sight of his own, not necessarily welcome, superiority.

How it came about that the only one of our boys who returned to Germany had also been among the first to go to Palestine has always been a bit unclear. Sometime before the end of the war he had managed to meet up with the rest of his family to make a run for Switzerland. Turned back at the Swiss border, they tried to get to Italy across the Alps in the middle of a snowstorm. The best evidence, from his letters to John Windmuller and one of his own poems, is that his father froze to death in the Alps. Or perhaps his father was shot and it was the corpse that froze. The only thing that seems reasonably certain is that Oskar's father and sister perished somewhere up there in the storm, and that Oskar somehow staggered down the mountain into Italy.

From here, the story grows even hazier and more ambiguous. He hangs around the streets of Italy for an indeterminate time, a wild, despairing drunk. At some stage he goes to Palestine. There is no question that he is there when Israel became an independent country and through the subsequent war of liberation. When he is ready to leave, he writes John Windmuller that he is broke and wants to go back to Germany. Immediately, John sends food parcels to him. So do we. John sets out to collect enough money so that Oskar will be able to return to Germany with some kind of a stake. For his troubles, he gets back a ranting, abusive letter: "I do not need your help. I did not ask for your pity. I will take care of myself."

"This is a case for you, not me," John tells Lene, who is by this time a practicing psychiatrist. He sends the money anyway. Oskar accepts it without a word of thanks and returns to Germany.

Why back to Germany? I knew how Oskar's mind worked well enough so that I could almost hear his rationale. The United States hadn't allowed his family to land; France had done nothing to help them escape, Switzerland had refused to let them in. In Israel, the German refugees were being constantly attacked for immigrating out of necessity rather than because of a real desire to build a Jewish country. Who were they, Oskar would ask, to point an accusing finger at Germany?

Germany had persecuted the Jews terribly, yes. But, he would say, there had been Germans who had stood up against the Nazis at the risk of their own lives, and there were now the new

Germans, the young Germans, who were filled with regrets over what had happened. It was toward these Germans he felt the greatest kinship, and it was with these Germans—I could hear Oskar say—that he would choose to stand.

The next news I heard of him, at least five years later, was more encouraging. Margot Cohn, who was now running a children's home in Germany, wrote that he was making a reputation for himself as the editor of a small but quite good Beatnik-type magazine in Stuttgart.

After the party which the children in the United States threw to celebrate my sixty-fifth birthday, I wrote up a newsy thank-you letter and sent it out to everybody whose address I had. Those who hadn't been there as well as to those who had. After all those years an answer came from Oskar Stammler.

> Your very kind letter surprised and touched me. For years I have been suppressing every memory of my childhood—probably because my own way of seeing it is painful to me. But with time we become more modest in our demands and are glad to have something like a past.
>
> You ask about my life. Since 1950 I have been in Germany with two rather long sojourns in Rome—and since '55 in Stuttgart. Not only am I a model married man, but something more—I am the father of two daughters and when you consider past confusions and my aversion to everything that resembled a family, it is rather surprising. I earn my living as a librarian, or as I am flatteringly termed, "scientific assistant" (since I never studied) in the Schiller National Museum in Marbach. I work three days a week. Perhaps you saw the Expressionist Exhibition in 1961 or 1962 at the Goethe House in N.Y.; I collaborated on that. In addition, I sit home and try to write well. This began many years ago with nothing but a full heart; I thought that was enough. But I soon realized how pitiful was the stuff that came out; since then it has become a real work, even a handicraft; I know of no finer. I do not publish much, since I work slowly. I enclose a sample. Of course I shall be happy to have a visit from you in Stuttgart. Many thanks for your long report, for the interest it shows, which still does not seem to be flagging. Many of the names came to life for me again—like "Jumbo" and, of course, John Windmuller, of whom I

think with a bad conscience. I should like to do my part to make life easier for Emil Geisler. Please let me know where I can send him something.

Because of a sudden change in plans which necessitated a professional trip to Japan, our prospective trip to Germany that summer had to be canceled. I wrote Oskar to tell him we would try to make it the following year. His answer came months later:

> When the war ended, I think I began to long for the haven not of my parents' house—that had become problematic—but the haven of the children's Home. At that time I also dreamt of being able to write about a period that seemed to me so significant. For that very reason, nothing came of it. Perhaps later on I shall try to undertake such a story, a sentimental journey but it surely will not be the story you are thinking of. By the way, a great number of books, reports, memoirs, pamphlets about this period have appeared. Yes, for quite a few years it was a good business here if a book had Jewish characters and the like. But it's my opinion that this sort of book is no longer in demand. Or worse; it is no longer the fashion.

Just before we were about to leave, the following summer, Lene broke her leg. I went to Germany to meet Oskar and his family alone. I found him eager to talk about what had happened to everybody else and very reluctant—not at all to my surprise—to talk about anything that had happened to him. A few months after my return, I wrote to him. I had definitely decided by then to write my own book, and so I told him in a postscript that I would appreciate anything he could tell me about what happened to him between Montintin and Stuttgart. This time, his answer came promptly. The letter has a somewhat different tone from the start. It is the old Oskar, full of self-mockery and yet somehow superior to whatever it is he is mocking. And then, in the last paragraph, from nowhere, comes the story:

> Your letter moved me very much; accept my thanks. For a long time I have wanted to tell you what a holiday your visit was for me. It made up for the many loose ends I see my past as; it has

long been hard for me to tie them up again into a kind of meaningful memory. A person like you—permit me, you are really a great big kid—you come bearing your naiveté like a gift; it makes possible a truly innocent enjoyment. I was as delighted as a child with you.

But now you want some hard facts. Dear Ernst—let us look each other squarely in the eye. You yourself found it was not easy to ask your questions—otherwise you would not have waited with them until your postscript. I should be glad to answer every one of your questions with precision: there would be the book that I shall still write, perhaps. You must know that for many years I had nothing, no profession, no home—though I did have friends, for the most part—and so I turned into something of a teller of tales about my adventures. That's enough of that. I live in the real world. Goethe was an old man when he wrote *Dichtung und Wahrheit* [Poetry and Truth].

Unshaped material is boring. Actually, when we went back to Stuttgart I took a poorly paid job in a travel bureau only because nobody there asked any questions. The older I get, the more I want not to be a "case" but to live out my life in my own way, on my own terms. Maybe the poem "Friends" (herein enclosed) which is dedicated to you, after all, tells you a bit more about it than I do.

One story at least I can write down for you, so that you won't call me an ingrate. On August 26, 1942, the gendarmes came to Montintin. The eighteen-year-olds had been warned and had spent the night in the woods; we who were a bit younger stayed in bed. Two fat gendarmes—like in Schweik!—accompanied me solemnly to the Klo [toilet] which was outside the house. I saw no way out. Just before we were taken away, our new *educateur*—Fišer—a Hungarian who spoke only French so that we little chauvinists didn't like him—rushed into the room. He was a thin, energetic man, said to be a student of Bergson. "Oskar, *jette-toi sous le lit!*" he ordered ["Oskar, get under the bed!"]. I obeyed his wild look. He pulled down the cover. The gendarmes tore open the door and then disappeared. I heard them thudding down the stairs. After a long while the door opened, Fišer silently handed me my rucksack, all packed, and took me to the fire escape leading out back into the woods. "*Allez!*"—and I was already jumping. So they took away poor Emil Geisler, who was lying in the sickroom. I didn't hear that until later on. Weeks after that a couple of us who had come from there met Fišer in Limoges. He handed us forged papers. Not one unnecessary word, but some kind of courage was communicated to us. I was to be called Louis Cabier. "*Ça te va?*" ["Is that all right?"] he asked. I was delighted both by the strange new turn of events, and by the shy tenderness of his voice. He was later shot in Lyon. . . . Such people I have met in many places. No, no, I am not running away from them. But sometimes you are nearer to them at a distance. And I am beginning to repeat myself—which I should like to avoid. I raise my glass and drink a toast to your health, and to you all. We should be in a sad way, dear Ernst, if there were no people like you.

Thanks for not getting bored, and till next year—

I remain your Oskar
with Heidi and the children

Epilogue

Just before I left Montmorency that last night to catch the train for Limoges, Mandel and I went out into the garden at Les Tourelles and buried all my diaries, pictures and records. During my trips to Paris as an official of the Unitarian Service Committee, I was unable to bring myself to go back and dig them up. Too many memories, too many ghosts. I suppose that in the back of my mind I was making a bargain with fate. I would go back for them when I could go back with Mandel. To go without him would be to admit that he was dead.

It was not until fifteen years after we had left that Lene and I rented a car and drove out from Paris, the same drive I had made a hundred times before and now seemed so different. The little village of Soisy at the edge of Montmorency had changed so much that we actually passed the old grounds by. And no wonder. Where the Villa Les Tourelles had once stood, there was now a huge modern housing development. We still weren't sure we had the right place until we saw the name that was carved into the pillar at the entrance: LES TOURELLES, it said. THE HOUSE OF THE CHILDREN.

Well, anyway, we had to admit, they couldn't have chosen a more fitting name for it.

This new Tourelles was even larger, on the whole, than ours had been. The tall apartment houses took up only about half of the grounds; the other half had been set aside for a children's park. We had arrived around noon on a warm summer day, and the place was teeming with children; young children not much different in age than ours had been. It was total disorientation; so much that was the same and so much that was totally different. *Déjà vu* combined with you-can't-go-home-again.

And then Lene pointed. There, just beyond the wall that divided the apartment houses from the park, stood our old infirmary, the same infirmary where Lene had spent so many of her hours and which now looked old and shabby and somehow . . . well, inappropriate. A shack was what it obviously was being used for; a tool shed.

At the entrance to the park, she suddenly stopped. "Ernst! Come over here! Read this!" Set into the wall was a gleaming plaque. The inscription that had so startled her read:

DEDICATED TO THE CHILDREN OF SOISY—HEROES OF THE RESISTANCE
BY THE GRATEFUL POPULATION

In honor of Maurice RICHARD, captain F.F.L.
Ardent Socialist militant—Accomplished Outdoorsman
Hero of the Underground
Shot at MAUTHAUSEN—1944 at the age of 32

Maurice Richard had been a deputy mayor, one of our greatest supporters and later, it appeared, one of Garel's Underground fighters.

Lene turned to the children who were playing all around us. "Do you know what this inscription means?" she asked them. "Do you know why this development is called the House of the Children?"

"But of course," said a little girl who was skipping rope. "It is because of the brave children of Tourelles who lived here through the bombs."

How in the world, Lene asked, could she know about that? It had been fifteen years since we were there. She hadn't been born yet.

They were all babbling then, only too eager to share their knowledge with a pair of passing strangers. "Why wouldn't we know about it? Our teacher told us all about it at school." And while we stood there they gave us the full history of the children of Montmorency. We had become a part of their curriculum. They taught about us in school.

From our children to their children. What better monument could we have asked than that?